HELL AND BACK

Also by Tim Parks

HELL
AND BACK

*Reflections on Writers and Writing
from Dante to Rushdie*

TIM PARKS

ARCADE PUBLISHING • NEW YORK

FIRST NORTH AMERICAN EDITION 2002

Originally published in England by Secker and Warburg, a division of
Random House, U.K.

Library of Congress Cataloging-in-Publication Data

 Parks, Tim.
  Hell and back : reflections on writers and writing from Dante to
 Rushdie / Tim Parks. —1st North American ed.
   p. cm.
  Includes bibliographical references.
  ISBN 1-55970-610-4
   1. Literature, Modern—History and criticism. I. Title.
 PN511 .P18 2002
 809—dc21   2001045787

Published in the United States by Arcade Publishing, Inc., New York
Distributed by Time Warner Trade Publishing

Visit our Web site at www.arcadepub.com

10 9 8 7 6 5 4 3 2 1

Designed by Susan Thomas / Digital Zone

EB

PRINTED IN THE UNITED STATES OF AMERICA

Many thanks to Robert Silvers and all the crew at the *New York Review of Books* for their generous help and encouragement.

Contents

Acknowledgements

The essays in this volume have appeared or are scheduled to appear, some in slightly different form, in the following publications:

'Hell and Back' was published in *The New Yorker*.
'The Universal Gentleman' was published in the *New York Review of Books*.
'Here Comes Salman' was published in the *New York Review of Books*.
'Surviving Giacomo' was published in the *New York Review of Books*.
'The Hunter' was published in the *New York Review of Books*.
'Different Worlds' was published in the proceedings of the Nobel Symposium on 'Translation of Poetry and Poetic Prose', and later, in shorter form, in the *New York Review of Books*.
'Sentimental Education' was published in the *New York Review of Books*.
'A Chorus of Cruelty' was published in the *New York Review of Books*.
'Voltaire's Coconuts' was published in the *Literary Review of Books*.
'Literary Trieste' was published in the *New York Review of Books*.
'Party Going' was published as the introduction to the new

Vintage Edition of *Party Going* and also in the *New York Review of Books*.

'The Enchanted Fort' was published as the introduction to the new Penguin edition of *The Tartar Steppe* and also in the *Threepenny Review*.

'In the Locked Ward' was published in *The Lancet* and later in the *New York Review of Books*.

'Fascist Work' was published in the *New York Review of Books*.

'Sightgeist' was published in the *New York Review of Books*.

'A Prisoner's Dream' was published in the *New York Review of Books*.

'Unlocking the Mind's Manacles' was published in the *New York Review of Books*.

'Christina Stead, Our Luck' was published as the introduction to the *New York Review Books* edition of *Letty Fox: Her Luck* and will be published in the *New York Review of Books*.

'Writerly Rancour' was published in *Pretext*, the magazine of the University of East Anglia.

HELL AND BACK

Hell and Back

[Dante Alighieri]

'Good Master, what shall I do to inherit eternal life?' the rich man asks Jesus. 'Sell all that thou hast, and distribute unto the poor,' is the reply, 'and thou shalt have treasure in heaven.' At which the rich man is sorrowful and turns away. 'It is easier,' Jesus remarks to his disciples, 'for a camel to go through the eye of a needle, than for a rich man to enter into the kingdom of God.'

Some 1,300 years later, banished from his native Florence and thus largely bereft of this world's goods, Dante Alighieri, politician, poet and philosopher, was nevertheless still having trouble threading the eye of that needle. It seems there are other attachments aside from wealth that make it difficult for us to turn our backs on this world. Passion for one: Dante had loved a woman who rejected him, married someone else, then compounded the affront by dying young and thus remaining for ever desirable. Ambition was another: aside from a cycle of secular love poems, Dante had written a provocative work of political philosophy suggesting the kind of state in which man would be free to pursue perfection. It was not a scenario in which divine grace appeared to be very important. Now, quite suddenly, he found himself confused, disoriented:

> Midway in the journey of our life
> I came to myself in a dark wood,
> for the straight way was lost.

1

So begins the *Inferno*. It's a feeling that many approaching forty, as Dante was when he wrote the lines, will recognise. How to proceed? As daylight breaks in the dark wood, the poet sees a mountain before him. It is Purgatory, it is the way to Paradise. All is well. But suddenly three ferocious beasts are blocking his path. The needle's eye is defended by a wolf, a leopard, a lion. They are lust, pride and avarice, say some commentators. They are incontinence, malice and mad brutishness say others. They are Dante's Florentine enemies, the French monarchy and the papacy, say yet others. Whatever or whoever, they are insuperable.

Just as the poet despairs, a figure emerges from the gloom and offers an unusual alternative. By special intercession of his dear departed Beatrice, now in Paradise, Dante is to be given the opportunity to approach the blessed place through Hell. A vision of the damned will surely teach him to turn away from the things of this world. After some hesitation, he agrees. It was a fatal decision. Hell would never be the same again.

'For all of us,' Borges wrote, 'allegory is an aesthetic mistake.' Schopenhauer, Benedetto Croce and D.H. Lawrence all concur. 'I hated, even as a child, allegory,' writes Lawrence. Reduced to a series of equivalences, he complained – white horse equals faithfulness and truth – a work of literature is explained away. It does no more than state a position. We read it once and we never need read it again.

The *Divina Commedia*, most celebrated of all poems, is almost always presented to us as an allegory. Certainly this is the case with the huge and heavily annotated edition my son is poring over in high school in Verona. Who is the figure who appears to Dante in the wood? He is Virgil, the great Roman poet of the *Aeneid*, emblematic in the Middle Ages of the best that can be achieved by reason and conscience. He will take Dante as far as mere earthly knowledge can take a man. Who is Beatrice? The personal embodiment of heavenly truth, say the commentaries.

She will take over where Virgil, with his human limitations, is obliged to leave off. And the pilgrim poet? Obviously he is Everyman, or Christian as Bunyan was to call him. Would Bert Lawrence, we wonder, have read a poem thus described even once?

Yet long after the fires of Hell have burned themselves out, the debate about the *Divina Commedia* rages on. Leafing through the commentary that Robert Hollander has prepared to accompany his new translation, one is immediately aware of a fierce rift between different schools of opinion on the poem: the Romantics, who were convinced that Dante sympathised with the sufferers in Hell, thus subverting the Christian tradition, and the traditionalists equally convinced that, while the pilgrim in the poem sometimes wavers, the poet behind the work wholeheartedly endorsed every last lacerating pang of a misbegotten, unrepentant humanity. The academic Hollander is decidedly among the anti-Romantics and enters the fray with gusto. Meanwhile, his poetess wife, who was responsible for establishing the versification of the new translation, has recently written a poem of her own, 'A Mix Up in Dante', that has two unrelated characters from the *Inferno*, the Tuscan Francesca and the Greek Odysseus, enjoying a casual affair in a mishmash of contemporary settings; it's a piece that implicitly supports her husband's position that these two figures, adored by so many, are nothing more than incorrigible sinners. Until one has read the *Inferno* itself, it is hard to understand why the debate is so heated.

The poet turns away from this world. He is going to descend the nine circles of subterranean hell, shin down Satan's hairy legs to a hole (that needle's eye?) at the very core of the planet, squeeze through, then climb out of the globe at the antipodes, scale the mountain of Purgatory and achieve Paradise. That is the overall trajectory of our allegory: man in contact with sin, man rejecting sin, man purifying himself, man returning to his maker.

But by virtue of this holy pilgrimage, Dante also intends to

3

become one of the most famous poets of all time, human, historical time. That is an integral part of his project, and he doesn't disguise the fact. What's more, the journey will offer him a chance to stage one last poignant meeting with the ever beloved Beatrice. He will see and talk to her again.

So has he really turned away from this world? Well, yes and no. The poem teems with contradictions and antithetical energies. Virgil, we soon suspect, despite the commentaries, is not merely the abstract apex of human piety and reason. More interestingly, he is indeed the great poet whom Dante most sought to emulate, a charming individual who is not to be admitted to Paradise for the simple reason that he lived too early to accept Christ's offer of salvation. It's an outrage.

Beatrice, meanwhile, is Beatrice Portinari whom Dante has worshipped, despite rebuffs, since he was nine years old. And the pilgrim poet, as it turns out, is not Everyman at all, but Dante Alighieri in person. The same goes for the damned when we meet them. Never merely murderers, thieves or pederasts, they are magnificently, abjectly themselves, still sinning and suffering in a place that, far from abstract or notional, is scorchingly, stinkingly real.

But how can a living man go unscathed through Hell? And how can a reader follow him? Will the poem be *bearable*? 'Abandon all hope you who enter here,' announce the words above the gate. Hopefully, we go through. First, Dante sees the wretched souls of those 'who lived without disgrace yet without praise'. Rushing aimlessly back and forth, they suffer because they would rather be anyone but themselves. Well, we're used to people like that. Six hundred years later T.S. Eliot would watch them flowing every day over London Bridge. 'I could not believe death had undone so many,' Dante says. Nothing new here.

Then, across the River Acheron, in the limbo of the first circle of hell, are other noble souls who, like Virgil, perished before Christ got round to saving us. Homer and Plato are here, though sadly they don't appear to be producing anything new. With them are the souls of the tiny children who die unbaptised. It's a strange mix. Their only torment is that 'without hope we live in longing'. Again it's not something the average reader will be entirely unfamiliar with. Thus far we can handle it.

But these opening scenes are only a foretaste of what's to come, or perhaps a response to the exigencies of the encyclopaedic vocation of the poem (all the famous dead will have to be put somewhere). Nevertheless, Dante is immeasurably sad as he reflects that 'beings of great worth were here suspended'. Already we sense how difficult it is for the human mind to be in tune with the divine will. Is it possible Homer isn't in Heaven? The reader notes with disquiet that having encountered all the greatest poets before we're barely inside the porch of Hell, Paradise is going to have little to offer in that department.

Then the real horror begins, the souls tossed this way and that on stormy winds, torn apart by a three-headed dog under endless rain, sunk in bogs, sunk in boiling pitch, sunk in shit, sunk in blistering tombs, sunk in solid ice. Dante sees sinners forever unconsumed in consuming fire, forever scratching the scabs from their flesh, forever metamorphosing into snakes and lizards, forever upside down in filthy holes, forever brushing off burning embers that sift constantly down onto scorching sand.

There is no change, no rest, no night nor day, no meal breaks. And even more disturbing, when the damned are not being whipped or clawed by demons, they are punishing each other, shoving each other about, gnawing at each other's necks, insulting each other. *L'enfer, c'est les autres.* In short, if Hollywood wishes to avoid legislation against excessive violence on the big screen, the *Inferno* is not a picture to make during an election period. How can Dante pass through it all unscathed? And how can Robert Hollander conclude the introduction to his and his wife's new translation with the remark that 'this is not a bad place once you get used to it'?

'So as not to be hurt,' says the *Taittiriya Samhita* 'before coming near the fire, he wraps himself in the metres.' It's a formula often repeated in the Vedic texts. Whether 'he' be god, priest or mere mortal man, in order to approach the sacrificial fire, through which alone the heavens can be conquered, he must 'wrap himself in the metres'. Such advice is more practical than it may at first seem. The real punishment of Dante's damned is not this or that torture – many in Purgatory will face similar sufferings – but the fact that the torture can know no solution. Neither release nor oblivion are available. And while the body – in so far as the damned have a body – is forever in pain, the mind revolves unceasingly around a particular image or experience. An adulteress is trapped for ever in her moment of passion, a suicide is irretrievably marooned in the circumstances that led him to dash his brains out against a prison wall. In this sense, Dante's damned are not unlike those ghosts who always appear in the same place in the same clothes, conservative creatures shackled for eternity to some experience they can never go beyond.

It is thus understandable that while the trials of Purgatory will take place on a breezy mountainside open to the sky, the tortures of the inferno must be closed inside an inverted subterranean cone that funnels down in narrowing circles to the pit of ultimate despair. It is a place of obsession, a place where time has stopped and thought has become its own prison. To get through such horror, we must wrap ourselves in the metres, for metre obliges us to keep moving on.

Now perhaps we see why Dante chooses a poet as a guide, a poet renowned for the perfection of his verse. What is Virgil's role throughout the *Inferno*? As he leads Dante from circle to circle, he first directs his attention, inviting him to engage with the damned – after all, he must learn from his experience – but then, and this is crucial, he decides exactly how long he is to be allowed to stay and talk in any one place. 'We must not linger here,' he says. 'Let your talk be brief.' The constant danger is that the poet will find himself paralysed, blocked as the damned are blocked, and as he himself was at the beginning of the poem.

> The many people and their ghastly wounds
> did so intoxicate my eyes
> that I was moved to linger there and weep.

So says the pilgrim poet at the opening to Canto 29. It's an understandable response when you've just spoken to a decapitated nobleman holding his head by the hair. But Virgil is having none of it. 'What are you staring at . . . the time we are allotted soon expires and there is more to see.'

In short, Virgil sets the pace. It is not that we now need to start thinking of him as a personification of metre. Just that he understands as no one else does the mutually tensing, only apparently contradictory vocations of poetry: to take us, yes, to the core of things, through evocation, but then to get us out on the other side unscathed, with the reassuring, even anaesthetising, progress of verse.

The metre Dante chose to wrap himself in involved the arrangement of hendecasyllables, lines of eleven syllables, in a verse pattern known as *terza rima*. That is: the poem progresses three lines at a time, the first and the third rhyming and the second setting up the rhyme for the opening line of the next threesome, each stanza, if they can be called that, standing alone, pausing a moment, but in that very pause passing the baton to what quickly follows. Once we have a sense of the role this structure is to play in the story – how it thrusts us before what is too awful to contemplate, then snatches us away from it – we can begin to appreciate how difficult the *Inferno* is to translate, and how all-determining the initial decision: What form am I going to use?

A dozen and more modern translations are strewn on the desk before me, too many to analyse in detail, each with its merits and

its drawbacks, each the fruit of enormous labours. The choice of
staying with Dante's *terza rima* is, of course, only for the boldest,
or perhaps one might say the most reckless. Here is Dorothy L.
Sayers, Christian, scholar and detective writer, giving us the
speech in which that epitome of recklessness, Ulysses, confesses
that he was not a family man and remembers his fatal, hubristic
voyage through the pillars of Hercules:

> No tenderness for my son, nor piety
> To my old father, nor the wedded love
> That should have comforted Penelope
>
> Could conquer in me the restless itch to rove
> And rummage through the world exploring it,
> All human worth and wickedness to prove.
>
> So on the deep and open sea I set
> Forth, with a single ship and that small band
> Of comrades that had never left me yet.

How the timbers strain here. One suspects the hero's oarsmen
of being selected from among the worthy authors of *Hymns
Ancient and Modern*. Rove and rummage as the translator might
through the resources of Victorian verse, all too often the rhyme
clangs like a buoy in fog, rather than quietly chiming the passage
from one moment to the next.

No stranger himself to rhymed narrative, Longfellow saw the
danger and plumped for blank verse. Yet though this enables him
to shadow the original more closely, he too often seems to offer
little more than a review of nineteenth-century poetic diction.
Here he is among the miseries of Canto 5:

> And as the cranes go chanting forth their lays,
> Making in air a long line of themselves,
> So saw I coming, uttering lamentations,

Shadows borne onward by the aforesaid stress.
Whereupon said I: 'Master, who are those
People, whom the black air so castigates?'

Over the thirty-four cantos and nearly five thousand lines of
the *Inferno*, the 'aforesaid stress' can only mount up.

More recently, Robert Pinsky, remarking on how much more
easily Italian can be rhymed than English and at the same time
appreciating the importance of the *terza rima* in the poem,
decided to go for a '*terza* half *rima*', as it were; this together with
a versification so full of enjambment that the division into three-
line stanzas often appears quite arbitrarily imposed on the sense.
It seems appropriate to quote Pinsky as he deals with the subject
of mangling. Here we are in Canto 28 presenting Mohammed at
a time when there was no need to fear an ayatollah's response.

No barrel staved-in
And missing its end-piece ever gaped as wide
As the man I saw split open from his chin

Down to the farting-place, and from the splayed
Trunk the spilled entrails dangled between his thighs.
I saw his organs, and the sack that makes the bread

We swallow turn to shit.

Despite Pinsky's facility – and often the translation is fun – one
is everywhere aware of the effort required to achieve even these
half-rhymes, while in the process the focus of the verse is often
obliged to fall on the most unlikely of words. 'Bread', for
example, is not in the original and readers may be forgiven for
having the absurd impression, if only for a moment, that the
bread is made by 'the sack', the intestine. Then of course
everything becomes clear as the word 'shit' pulls us up brutally

mid line. But this is something Dante never does, for of course such effects break up the all-important flow.

In 1993, a book mistitled *Dante's Inferno* presented the translations of twenty contemporary poets, each tackling two or three cantos. James Merrill's introduction gives us a clue to the uneasiness one feels with so many contemporary translations, and not just of Dante. 'The problem,' he announces, 'with most translators is their limited command of the language – their own I mean; they can always get help with the other. Hence the bright idea of asking some of our finest poets to weave this garland.'

Leaving aside the self-congratulation and the inappropriate-ness, surely, of referring to any edition of the *Inferno* as a 'garland', the notion that one can get somebody else to tell you what the original means and how it feels, so that you can then rewrite it, is suspect to say the least. Why read poetry at all if someone else can tell you what it's like? There is no substitute for an intimate experience of the original and long immersion in the culture that surrounds it. Invariably, the star poets work hard at evocation and drama in their various individual styles, almost always to the detriment of the overall rapidity and homogeneity of the narrative. Here is Mark Strand leaving us in limbo:

> There was no howling that I could hear,
> nothing but sighs that rose
> to shake the everlasting air
> sighs of painless woe
> from milling crowds of men and women
> and children who would never know
> relief.

The subordinate clause, 'who would never know relief', has been added to the original and creates a most dramatic and mannered stop right at the beginning of the next terzina. Meantime, the crucial information that the children are very young – *infanti* –

(they are the unbaptised) is omitted and instead we have a banal standard formula, 'men and women and children', as if merely to say, everybody. The danger of 'poetic' translations is that they risk losing both an accurate account of the scene and a rapid movement through it. When things go wrong we are up to our ears in poetic effect and misery.

'Prosa rimata', Boccaccio called it, 'rhymed prose'. One of the poem's first and greatest admirers, the author of the *Decameron* praised Dante's decision to write in the vernacular rather than in Latin, and likewise to avoid the temptation of lavish poetic effect. Hell is impressive enough without. It's not surprising, then, to find Pinsky making the observation that some of the most effective translations of the *Divina Commedia* have been in prose. Certainly the 1939 prose translation by the scholar John Sinclair is still a very safe bet if you want to sit down, read the *Inferno* right through and then get up again. But doesn't this contradict what I said earlier about the effect of the *terza rima*? 'There are verses, in the genre called prose,' said Mallarmé, 'sometimes wonderful verses and in every rhythm.' Here is Sinclair introducing us to the second circle:

I came to a place where all light was mute and where was bellowing as of a sea in tempest that is beaten by conflicting winds. The hellish storm, never resting, seizes and drives the spirits before it; smiting and whirling them about, it torments them. When they come before its fury there are shrieks, weeping and lamentation, and they blaspheme the power of God, and I learned that to such torment are condemned the carnal sinners who subject reason to desire.

A little later one of those sinners speaks: it is the charming adulteress, Francesca.

O living creature gracious and friendly, who goest through the murky air visiting us who stained the world with blood, if the King of the universe were our friend we would pray to Him for thy peace, since thou hast pity of our evil plight. Of that which thou art pleased to hear and speak we will hear and speak with you while the wind is quiet, as here it is.

These sentences have an austere rhythm of their own, while the archaic diction and phrasing seems more acceptable without the alarm bell of forced rhyme. Sinclair's version is rapid, to the point, almost always close to the original, and yet . . . if only visually, there is something lacking. We miss the sense of constant even division, of opening and of closure, the reassurance of manifest artifice.

The new translation by Robert and Jean Hollander is, as an introductory note tells us, a reworking in free verse of Sinclair's prose, reinforcing its rhythms, removing archaisms and awkwardness, often altering the interpretation where Sinclair is not convincing. Here are their versions of the passages quoted above.

> I reached a place mute of all light,
> Which bellows as the sea in tempest
> Tossed by conflicting winds.
>
> The hellish squall, which never rests,
> Sweeps the spirits in its headlong rush,
> Tormenting, whirls and strikes them.
>
> Caught in that path of violence,
> They shriek, weep, and lament.
> Then how they curse the power of God.

And again:

Oh living creature, gracious and kind,
That comes through sombre air to visit us
Who stained the world with blood,

If the King of the universe were our friend
We would pray that He might give you peace,
Since you show pity for our grievous plight.

With any translation of the *Inferno*, one can quibble ad
infinitum, if only because the original just will not stay still; it
won't be pinned down to any formula. That said, the Hollanders'
translation is definitely a welcome addition, and to my uncertain
ear, coming to all these versions fresh from a rereading of the
original, it certainly seemed the most accessible and the closest.
Unfortunately, as we shall see, the commentary Robert Hollander
offers to accompany the text is not so well pitched.

Whenever Indiana Jones enters an ancient temple or burial
ground, we know what is about happen. However much our hero
respects and venerates an antique past, this sacred place, frozen in
time, stacked with precious horrors and holy artefacts, is,
nevertheless, going to be utterly destroyed. As the edifice comes
crashing down, Jones, in the nick of time, will rush out of the
crumbling portals into the fresh air of a world where nothing is
sacred, except perhaps lucre and serial romance.

Although it would be facetious, even blasphemous, to suggest
that the same thing happens in the *Inferno*, still it has to be said
that over the centuries the effect of Dante's passage through Hell
has been no less devastating. If the poet survives his journey
unscathed, the same cannot be said of the infernal abode. Its
ecology is too fragile for even this minimal tourism. While the
souls of the dead float weightlessly over this most artificial
environment, every step taken by the gravity-bound poet sets off
a little landslide. And if the first scholarly commentaries on the
Divina Commedia began to appear almost as soon as it was in

circulation, that is partly because there was an immediate apprehension that the place of punishment was in urgent need of shoring up. Robert Hollander takes his turn at this ghoulish maintenance duty with remarkable vigour.

Dante is sent through Hell in order to gain 'greater knowledge', as Virgil says. Thus much of the poem is made up of question and answer. As each new horror unfolds, we must 'understand' it. So we learn that on crossing the Acheron each soul is assessed by the monster Minos who indicates which circle he or she must go to by arranging his tail in the appropriate number of coils. How Minos distinguishes, in the case, for example, of the eighth circle, between the ten very different ditches that await the dismayed sinner on arrival, we don't know. Does he uncoil and re-coil? It is a peculiarity of explanations that they tend to invite further questions.

Meanwhile, other information is coming in thick and fast. We learn that milder sins are punished in the upper circles and more heinous crimes below, in the city of Dis whose gates in the fifth circle mark the descent into 'nether hell'. We learn that sins of incontinence are less wicked than sins of will; that the sins of sodomy, blasphemy and usury are punished together because they all involve violence against God or His natural order. Who would have thought? We learn that the dead are granted knowledge of future events on earth, but not of the present situation. Such a state of affairs involves the drawing of some difficult lines, does it not? Presumably as time progresses and the future becomes the present the dead must now forget what shortly before they knew. Is this really an imaginable world?

But all these are minor points. Most importantly, and exhaustively, we learn that each and every sinner is punished by being subjected to a sort of intensification or symbolic inversion of his dominant crime. Being eternally boiled in pitch, for example, John Sinclair's notes explain, is an appropriate punishment for those who have accepted bribes in public office, because pitch is sticky, prevents clarity of vision and rarely allows the sinner to surface. Diviners, on the other hand, who usurped God's power by looking into the future, are properly served by having their heads reversed on their shoulders so that they are constantly looking backwards. On three or four occasions the poet wonders at this appropriateness:

> O Supreme Wisdom, what great art you show
> in heaven, on earth, and in the evil world,
> and what true justice does your power dispense!

How reassuring, or at least distracting, such symmetry is. Then, in so far as each crime can be presented as a breaking of bonds, within family or society, or more seriously between creature and creator, our exploration of hell's bureaucracy leads quite naturally to a discussion of the state of Italy, and in particular Florence, where all these crimes, the poet assures us, are daily being committed. Indeed Dante's Florence and Dante's *Inferno* often seem contiguous in the poem, as if Hell were nothing more than one more busy Tuscan metropolis.

So it is that among the underworld's gay community, Dante can profit from a long discussion on Florentine politics, past and future. Since such matters, together with all the other Italian gossip, are a key subject of the poem, the inclusion of informative notes at the end of each canto is useful and welcome. In this regard Hollander is impeccable. The text is presented generously spaced – Italian on the left, English on the right – and with ample commentary easily and unobtrusively available at the end of each canto. As neatly organised as Hell itself.

Still, we should not lose sight of the fact that the attention to current affairs, like the enchantment of the verse and the intriguing topography of infernal justice, are part of a series of strategies for preventing us from being overwhelmed by the suffering of the damned. With similarly anaesthetic intent, Dante likes to toss in the odd conundrum from time to time to tease the lively intellect. Sinclair, for example, becomes concerned because he can't quite see the appropriateness of the punishments of the tenth ditch of the eighth circle. Hollander shares with us his perplexity that a character in the fifth ditch seems to have come straight to Hell, bypassing Minos's sorting procedure. How can this be? Screams of torture fade away behind the clamour of such intriguing questions.

In Canto 29, when Dante mischievously tells us that the inner part of the eighth circle is twenty-two miles in circumference, Hollander manfully resists the temptation to engage in the agitated algebra that has produced so many scale maps of the poet's Hell. But a few cantos on, an obscure reference to the physical stature of Satan has our commentator rising beautifully to the bait. Dante writes: 'I in size am closer to a giant than giants are when measured to his arms.' Hollander informs:

> That is 'I am, proportionally, closer in size to a giant than a giant is to Lucifer'. For the size of the giants, ca. Seventy feet, see the note to *Inferno* XXX 58–66. Let us, merely for the purposes of calculation, agree that Dante was six feet tall. The equation is simple: $6/70=70/x; x = 817$. Thus Lucifer is at the very minimum 817 feet tall. Since both the giants and Satan are only halfway out of the ice that leaves him towering from the waist up, over the ice by at least 409 feet.

Fascinating, isn't it, how mathematics can contribute to matters metaphysical! But if we don't want to concentrate on mutilations and misery, we needn't limit ourselves to elaborating internal textual references. Dante knows he has set in motion a system here that will amuse ad infinitum. This morning, for example, my newspaper offers the announcement:

ASTROCARTOMANTE Alessandra riceve pomeriggi serate

distintissimi. (Fortune teller – tarot and astrology – receives real gents only afternoons and evenings.)

I ask myself: assuming Alessandra doesn't repent, where is she going to lodge in hell? If she is indeed a diviner, the fourth ditch of the eighth circle and an eternally twisted neck await her. But in the argot of Italy's classified ads, *'astrocartomante'* is code for prostitute. This would put her in the sins of the flesh, perhaps, somewhere in the milder upper rooms of Hell.

On the other hand, there is hypocrisy here, is there not? Alessandra is a whore passing herself off as a fortune teller. Hypocrisy would plunge her way back to the eighth circle, but the sixth ditch this time, where she will drag her heels eternally under the weight of a leaded mask with gilded surface. Dante, as I recall, includes but one prostitute in the *Inferno*, inserting her, rather surprisingly, into the ditch where the flatterers wallow in shit. Why? Because when a lover would ask her, 'Have I found favour with you?', the lady would reply: 'Beyond all measure.' Our poet is nothing if not witty.

'Beyond all measure.' It is measure and measurement that make Hell 'not a bad place once you get used to it'. The many pleasing symmetries, between crime and punishment, between landscape and spiritual reality, between life and afterlife, give us a sense that all, even in Hell, is well.

Well, it isn't. Suddenly, and dosing out the encounters with great cunning, Dante brings us up against an individual. A figure detaches itself from the crowd and tells a story of intense personal experience. It is Francesca recalling her passion for Paolo, or it is the noble Farinata rising erect from a scorching tomb. Pier delle Vigne gives an account of his tragically blighted career and suicide. His damnation seems incidental. Ulysses wonderfully recreates the folly of his last and most glorious exploit. Who cares what circle he is in?

At these and other moments, as pity, sympathy or even

admiration swell in the poet's breast, we know that for all the satisfactions of moral pigeon-holing, nothing has been explained. The individual, for better or worse, treacherous, Promethean or merely unreasonable, is so much more than a single sin. There is a fierce tension here. Hell's ramparts tremble. Sensibly, Virgil hurries us on.

Not so Hollander. Ominously, in his introduction, he has already told us that: 'Dante, not without risk, decided to entrust to us, his readers, the responsibility for seizing upon the details in the narratives told by the sinners, no matter how appealing their words might be, in order to condemn them on the evidence that issues from their own mouths.'

But if, after reading this, you are concerned you might get it wrong, not to worry. Hollander, unlike Dante, won't let you. He uses his commentary not just to give us valuable information but to make sure that we do indeed add our weighty condemnation to God's. Again and again he tells us what the poem means and how we should feel about it. In his view of things this inevitably means feeling rather less than we felt when we read the poem. Ulysses, for example, Hollander tells us, despite being admired for his Promethean spirit by so many poets and thinkers (Tennyson, Benedetto Croce and Primo Levi are briefly listed) is 'in common parlance, a con artist, and a good one too. He has surely fooled a lot of people.' But not our commentator. Of Francesca, he warns us that, however poignant her words, she is in fact entirely calculating; she just wants to win our pity while in fact 'it is pity itself that is here at fault'.

This challenging assertion looks forward to a key line in the *Inferno* where, when Dante shows pity for the diviners, Virgil protests: 'Qui vive la pietà quand' è ben morta.' Literally: 'Here pity – or piety (*pietà* can mean either or both) – lives when it is good and dead.' The Hollanders, determined to spare us misunderstandings, translate, 'Here piety lives when pity is quite dead.' Sinclair more faithfully and enigmatically offers, 'Here pity lives when it is quite dead.'

But let us not quibble over the translation, since the Hollanders' version seems in fact the only contextually comprehensible reading of the line. Let us also leave aside the ungenerous reflection that Virgil, who himself shows pity elsewhere, has a particular axe to grind with the diviners since his *Aeneid* was frequently read, not as a poem, but as an instrument of divination. Pity for them was not justice for him! Let us even assume, as Hollander would wish us to, I think, that the comment refers to the whole of Hell and not just to this particular ditch. All the same, and however we phrase it, we cannot escape the fact that Dante is drawing our attention here to a scission within the very notion of what piety, or godliness, is.

The two qualities, pity/piety, stem from the same etymological root; we had hoped they were inseparable. Instinctively, we seek to keep them together. But a contemplation of Hell, where God's terrible vendetta is visited on the damned for all eternity, obliges us to see that if we want an ordered cosmos with Paradise on top and Hell at the bottom, then pity will have to go. Hell, a pitiless place, is the price one pays for Paradise and more in general for the delirium of believing that human actions can reverberate for all eternity.

Looked at this way, Sayers' translation of the thorny line is intriguing. 'Here pity, or here piety, must die,' she writes, acknowledging the interesting alternative that it might be pity that lives, as it certainly does in Dante's poem, while orthodox piety and its grim fortifications collapse.

Another difficult and provocative remark makes it clear that Dante appreciates the revolutionary potential of the tensions that galvanise his tale. In Canto 12 the poet finds himself slithering down a landslide that 'shifted under my feet'. In the now familiar tone of reassuring explanation, Virgil tells Dante that when Christ came briefly down to Hell after his crucifixion, carrying off a

select few in the process, the infernal place was severely shaken.
He goes on:

> so that I thought the universe felt love,
> by which, as some believe,
>
> the world has many times been turned to chaos.
> And at that moment this ancient rock,
> Here and elsewhere, fell broken into pieces.

This is a very dangerous idea. The entrance to Hell bore the claim that the place was founded by 'primal love', but here we have a suggestion that love is alien to order. Love leads to chaos because it tends to forgive, it isn't interested in coiling tails and carefully divided ditches.

Whether he originally intended it or not, Dante has found that to bring pity into Hell makes for the most powerful poetry, as qualities that stir our souls are infinitely punished by a system we nevertheless feel we must accept as divine. Having happened upon that formula, he cannot resist pursuing it. What could be more seductive to an artist than the serendipitous discovery? But each time he does so he exposes an essential tension at the core of Christianity, a quarrel between rival visions of justice and of love that has kept Western society uneasily on the move for centuries, so much so that today it has become very hard for us to contemplate inflicting pain of any kind. To read the *Inferno* is to savour at its most elemental and intense one of the profound moral conflicts that has shaped the contemporary psyche. If twenty-first-century man went to Heaven he would soon be demonstrating to have Hell abolished.

Point the infernal brickwork as he will, even Robert Hollander is not immune from some chaotic sentiment. When Dante is moved at the sight of his old homosexual friends and wishes to greet them with an embrace, our commentator forgets to remind us that such affection for people God has eternally condemned is out of place. Rather than castigating the fraudulent intentions of a sinner who puts the blame for his sodomy on his 'bestial wife', Hollander applauds the poet for 'a remarkable lack of the typical Christian heterosexual scorn for homosexuals'. It is a rare lapse, but telling.

Whenever a magical world crumbles and its demons are put to flight, you can be sure they will turn up again elsewhere, and without the reassuring distance old boundaries guaranteed. So, on reading Dante, one is powerfully struck by how present he is in our modern literature. Hell is gone, but, like New York's mental patients, the damned have been let loose among us. They are there in Eliot, in Kafka, in Borges, and above all in Beckett, where they loom from the trash cans of *Endgame*, from the heap of sand in *Happy Days*. And if, having read the Hollanders' excellent translation, you are yearning for a more sophisticated commentary on the *Divina Commedia*, you might do worse than to turn to Beckett's novel *Watt*, where he recreates for the modern reader the *Inferno*'s strange force field of symmetry and suffering, of a language that evokes and anaesthetises. Here is Watt exploring a Hell in need of renovation:

This garden was surrounded by a high barbed wire fence, greatly in need of repair, of new wire, of fresh barbs. Through this fence, where it was not overgrown by briars and giant nettles, similar gardens, similarly enclosed, each with its pavilion, were on all sides distinctly to be seen. Now converging, now diverging, these fences presented a striking irregularity of contour. No fence was party, nor any part of any fence. But their adjacence was such, at certain places, that a broad-shouldered or broad-basined man, threading these narrow straits, would have done so with greater ease and with less jeopardy to his coat, and perhaps to his trousers, sideways than frontways. For a big-bottomed man, on the contrary, or a

21

big-bellied man, frontal motion would be an absolute necessity, if he did not wish his stomach to be perforated, or his arse,
or perhaps both, by a rusty barb, or by rusty barbs. A big-
bottomed big-bosomed woman, an obese wet-nurse, for
example, would be under a similar necessity. While persons at
once broad-shouldered and big-bellied, or broad-basined and
big-bottomed, or broad-basined and big-bellied, or broad-
shouldered and big-bottomed, or big-bosomed and broad-
shouldered, or big-bosomed and broad-basined, would on no
account, if they were in their right senses, commit themselves
to this treacherous channel . . .

Both the horror and the humour of such a passage owe
everything to Dante, while the distance between the anguished
tension of the *Inferno* and the despairing hilarity of *Watt* can in
part be traced back to the corrosive powers that animate the
earlier work.

The damned, then, show no signs of making themselves scarce.
Like the poor, they are ever with us. But can the same be said of
Beatrice and the blessed? Alas, no. Clinging to the wreckage,
Ulysses and his sinful crew survive for a thousand reincarnations,
but the good ship Paradise, it seems, was lost with all hands.
Fortunately Dante was not aboard. Having threaded the world's
most treacherous passage and dreamed up, for the other side, a
Purgatorio and *Paradiso* of great beauty and complexity but little
excitement, he then awoke to find himself once again under the
stars, where he remains with us to this day. It is a poor and
shadowy sort of immortality for a man who no doubt believed he
would be in the blazing light of Paradise with the saints and the
angels; but at least the *commedia* of literary fame, unlike that of
Heaven and Hell, is not one that need be underwritten by the
sufferings of the damned.

The Universal Gentleman

[Jorge Luis Borges]

'Romantic ego worship and loudmouthed individualism are . . . wreaking a havoc on the arts,' announces a twenty-three-year-old Borges in the first essay of *Selected Non-Fictions*. The date is 1922. The piece is entitled 'The Nothingness of the Personality'. In bold, polemical spirit, he declares: 'The self does not exist.'

Fifty-six years later, old, adored and blind, Borges finds himself lecturing on the subject of immortality. He remarks: 'I don't want to continue being Jorge Luis Borges; I want to be someone else. I hope that my death will be total; I hope to die in body and soul.'

In the first statement the self doesn't exist; in the second it is sufficiently real to be a burden, indeed *the* burden. It will not be difficult to read all of Borges's work as driven by the tension generated between these two positions: self the merest invention, easily dissolved and denied; self the most disturbing imposition, frightening in its implications, appalling in its tenacity and limitations. All the same, the curious thing in the later statement is the confession: 'I want to be someone else.' Is that an option? It is something we shall have to come back to.

Born a shy boy in 1899 in the macho town of Buenos Aires, the young Borges must soon have had occasion to feel different from others. His parents contrived to exacerbate his self-awareness in all kinds of ways. Half-English, his father, Jorge Guillermo Borges, had his children brought up bilingual. Here was distinction. There was an English grandmother, an English nanny, above all a well-stocked English library where Jorge Luis and his younger sister Norah did their first reading. Coddled at home till the age of nine, Jorge Luis was then plunged, as if in some perverse behavioural experiment, into a tough local school. A bespectacled stammerer, eccentrically dressed in Eton blazer and tie, he had five years here to learn about bullying before the family was obliged to move to Switzerland to find a cure for Jorge Guillermo's incipient blindness.

Now Borges was the boy who didn't know French and German. He learned them. Living in Geneva, he spent his teens reading voraciously in four languages, so that by the age of twenty he had already discovered most of the writers who would be important to him throughout his long career. The impressive list that all accounts of his life must necessarily repeat (for Borges always kept his sources to the fore) includes, among many others, Berkeley, Hume, William James, Cervantes, Chesterton, Schopenhauer, Baudelaire, Carlyle, Wells, Nietzsche, Stevenson, Poe, Whitman (in German) and the author of *The Thousand and One Nights*.

The Thousand and One Nights was his declared favourite. But having read and reread this Arab exotica in Burton's lavishly lubricious version, it must have been clear to the young Borges that there was now another thing he didn't know about, another thing that threatened to set him apart: sex. Certainly his timidity and innocence were evident to the other members of the family. Jorge Guillermo, a compulsive philanderer, ever dependent on and ever betraying his domineering wife, decided that the boy's education was not complete. Before returning to Argentina, Jorge Luis must visit a European brothel. The matter was arranged, but alas, this lesson was not so easily mastered. Wide and adventurous reading would not be matched by wild adventures and women. Unsettled, Jorge Luis settled at home and, unlike Father, remained ever faithful to Leonor, his remarkable mother.

*

'Intention', begins the first essay. The word is given a paragraph all to itself. It is a flourish, a cannon shot. We are about to read a manifesto. The author wants 'to tear down the exceptional pre-eminence now generally awarded to the self' and in its place to 'erect . . . an aesthetic hostile to the psychologism inherited from the last century'.

The tone is understandable. The 1920s were, after all, the decade of manifestos. Borges had been in Spain, he considered himself an Ultraist, a committed man. But it is marvellously ironic and an indication of some wit on the editor's part that this new collection of his non-fiction should begin thus. For very soon Borges would appreciate that a successful attack on the cults of selfhood and personality would necessarily have to play down the role of intention, since intention is one of the most obvious and powerful manifestations of the self: 'in art nothing is more secondary than an author's intentions', he will be telling us in a later essay. When speaking of achievements, literary or otherwise, he loves to introduce such formulas as, 'almost unwittingly', or 'without wanting to or suspecting he had done so'. 'A great book like the *Divina Commedia*,' he typically concludes one piece 'is not the isolated or random caprice of an individual; many men and many generations built towards it.'

Yet, ironically, the intention so succinctly stated on the opening page of *Selected Non-Fictions* remains a fair description of Borges's own remarkable achievement in the years to come, an achievement which is anything but unwitting. Intentionally, he played down intention. He accomplished what he set out to do. Even the man's exemplary modesty, everywhere evident in these essays and unfailingly celebrated by those who knew him, was, if we can use the expression, an 'engaged' modesty, a pondered modesty, and very much part of this determined and lifelong project of 'self-effacement. Whether or not we choose to see that project as linked to Borges's feelings of social and sexual inadequacy, or the fact that he remained emotionally and economically dependent on his mother right into middle age is irrelevant.

Borges's career begins when he returns to Argentina in 1921 after seven formative years in Europe. His parents tell him it's OK to stay home and write. He doesn't need to go to university, he doesn't need to find a job. So he reads and writes, makes literary friendships, and courts well-to-do young women who have no intention of marrying him or making love to him. The more they have no intention of loving him, the more he reads and writes. When his father falls ill and eventually dies, Borges is obliged, in his late thirties, to find work. He writes as a columnist for a women's magazine, appropriately entitled *El Hogar*, Home. Eventually he is forced to accept a minor clerical job in an overstaffed suburban library. Most of his nine years there will be spent in the basement reading and writing and trying to avoid his colleagues. Finally, in his early forties, he believes he has met the woman of his life. He walks Estela Canto through the warm Buenos Aires evenings, phoning Mother from call boxes at regular intervals to reassure her he will be home soon. When Estela rejects his offer of marriage, Borges steps up his reading and writing.

So the output is considerable. Each of Viking's recent compendiums of the three major strands of Borges's work – poetry, short stories and essays – runs out at just above or just below five hundred pages, and of the essays we are told that this new collection contains only 161 out of a possible twelve hundred. At the same time it's worth noting that only a very few of the pieces in any of the books exceed six or seven pages. The long work was as alien to Borges as work in general was compulsive. A rehearsal of one or two plots from the most celebrated story collections, *Fictions* and *The Aleph*, may help us to understand why this was so and what was that 'aesthetic hostile to psychologism' that Borges eventually hit upon.

A certain Pierre Menard, author of a miscellany of minor philosophical, critical and poetical works (his 'visible *oeuvre*'), dedicates the greater part of his life to reproducing Cervantes' *Don Quixote* word for word. This he does not by copying, nor by immersing himself in Cervantes' world, but by coming to the story 'through the experience of Pierre Menard'. 'If I could just be immortal, I could do it,' he says. As it is, we are given but one fragmentary example of his success in reproducing the original (though how he himself can know this, if he won't reread *Don Quixote* for fear of copying, remains a mystery), as follows:

> . . . truth, whose mother is history, rival of time, depository of deeds, witness of the past, exemplar and adviser to the present, and the future's counsellor.

Our admiring narrator comments that while the words are banal period rhetoric in the mouth of Cervantes, coming from Menard, they are remarkable. 'History, the mother of truth! – the idea is staggering. Menard, a contemporary of William James, defines history not as a delving into reality, but as the very fount of reality.'

The implications of the story are as evident as its unravelling is hilarious. If Menard can reproduce Cervantes then individuality is quite superficial. 'Every man should be capable of all ideas and I believe in the future he shall be.' History, far from being 'the mother of truth' is mere clutter. We could all write everything that has been written. And how fascinating if I can now see a snippet of *Don Quixote* in praise of the military life as being influenced by Pierre Menard's reading of Friedrich Nietzsche! Too intelligent to waste time arguing a position, Borges dazzles by conflation. The most improbable writers are wondrously superimposed. Humanity is one. Or maybe not. Pierre Menard is

27

a typical example of Borges's tendency to be ironic about a position he finds congenial.

It is standard orthodoxy to praise Borges for bringing all kinds of innovations to fiction, but in a way it may be easier to think of him as working out the consequences of removing from it all the innovations of the previous six or seven hundred years. Along with our modern nominalism and our ingenuous belief in history and individual character, the perplexing notion of personal responsibility will likewise have to go. In 'The Lottery in Babylon', we discover that everything that happens to people, good or bad, is not the result of their psychology or relationships, but rather the immensely complex working out of a state lottery into which each citizen is automatically and periodically entered and which, rather than dealing in money, dispenses happiness, unhappiness and tedium in every imaginable form. The random nature of their lives allows the Babylonians to enjoy all aspects of experience and become, as it were, everybody. 'Like all men of Babylon, I have been proconsul; like all, I have been a slave. I have known omnipotence, ignominy, imprisonment.' Again the accident of individuality is eliminated, there are no decisions, no responsibility, no success, no failure, no self.

The same occurs in 'The Immortal'. A group of men gain immortality and as a result lose all interest in life, since over an infinite period of time everything must happen to them, good and bad. Any action becomes unimportant, no more than 'the echo of others that preceded it with no visible beginning, and the faithful presage of others that will repeat it in the future, *ad vertiginem*'. So there can be 'no spiritual or intellectual merits'. Homer has forgotten his Greek. What is the point of remembering anything?

Typically, Borges revels in the elimination of what are normally considered the inescapable conditions of our existence, but at the same time never fails to underline the ludicrous or terrifying consequences. As with any ghost story, 'The Immortal' gains its disturbing power from the unspoken message that it is better to be either alive and engaged or dead and gone rather than, as Cioran would put it, to 'fall out of time' altogether. Thus the narrator of 'The Immortal', who has sought and gained eternal life, now seeks to return to mortality, and is overjoyed when, some sixteen hundred years later, he succeeds. The pain that promises eventual death now becomes pleasure:

> Incredulous, speechless, and in joy, I contemplated the precious formation of a slow drop of blood. I am once more mortal, I told myself over and over, again I am like all other men. That night, I slept until daybreak.

The pattern in 'The Aleph' is the same. Overwhelmed by the vision of a place in which all places simultaneously intersect, the narrator urgently needs to forget in order to return to normality. Again and again, the self seeks, or is granted, infinite extension, is terrified, returns to the 'ordinary' world.

Ordinariness itself, on the other hand, is not a condition Borges wishes to write about, except by exploring the implications of its opposite. Perhaps this is because the 'ordinary' situation he finds himself in is so unattractive. An ugly fascism has conquered Europe. Officially neutral, Argentina is spiritually pro-Nazi. This is ugly. Peronism is rampant. Estela no longer goes out for walks with him. Mother continues to buy his clothes but Borges doesn't care for the maid she has hired. The library job is unbearable, but, even more unbearable, in 1946 Borges finds himself fired for having expressed his anti-Peronist views. He has no income. The learnedly facetious detective stories he has written with close friend Adolfo Bioy are not a solution. They have generated more perplexity than royalties. Forced to take up lecturing to make ends meet, Borges must visit, of all people, a psychologist in an attempt to overcome his chronic shyness. He cannot speak in public. The psychologist, needless to say, has a useful smattering of Freud, a man Borges has charmingly dismissed in a single line of a story entitled 'A Survey of the Works of Herbert Quain'.

Taken one by one each of the short stories, at least of *Fictions* and *The Aleph*, is striking, dazzling. Nevertheless, to read them all one after another is to grow a little weary. Where the self is not perilously extended by a brush with infinity, we have satires of people whose individuality is exposed as a vain boast. The first time we hear that two rivals die only to discover they are the same person, we are fascinated. There is great insight here. The second time something of the kind occurs, we admire again the brilliance, the extraordinary wit, the admirable range of philosophical reference with which this idea is worked out. The two are theologians of the early Christian world. Or they are Argentine painters, or they are gaucho knife fighters. Then they are gaucho knife fighters again. By the time, in the later stories, we reach the fifth or sixth presentation of two or more central 'characters' obliged to recognise a mysterious oneness, we have realised that Borges has effectively eliminated the idea of a diversified community (so useful when it comes to protracted storytelling). There are now only two conditions: the single self here and now, and all humanity throughout all time. Of course these two conditions are actually the same: any antagonism is cancelled out in the oneness of all human experience.

Putting it another way, we might say that Borges reaches out to a transcendental oneness, the community of all men, but finds himself constantly returned to Borges. There is nothing, or nothing we would wish to contemplate, in the middle. Gradually, he begins to tire of establishing the elaborate and multiform disguises behind which oneness lurks. There are so many hats a rabbit can be pulled from. Or rather: we begin to see the rabbit before Borges pulls it out. We even begin to wish he would leave it in there. And in fact this is what he eventually starts doing in the supposedly 'more realistic stories' of the collection *Brodie's Report*. But we see that rabbit all the same. It is time to turn to the essays.

'That crowded day,' Borges writes in a piece entitled 'A Comment on August 23, 1944' 'gave me three distinct surprises: the physical degree of joy I felt when they told me that Paris had been liberated; the discovery that a collective emotion can be noble; the puzzling and flagrant enthusiasm of many who were supporters of Hitler.'

This is Borges writing inside history. He has not chosen the subject matter, it is forced upon him; he is obliged to recognise surprises. In particular, finding himself at one with public enthusiasm must have come as a big surprise indeed, for Borges. Immediately, his brilliant mind sets to work to understand, to place this experience, and particularly the inexplicable happiness of these Nazi sympathisers, within the reference points of his considerable erudition. Needless to say, he has no intention of talking to those sympathisers. They are incoherent, they enjoy only a low level of consciousness, any 'uncertainty was preferable to the uncertainty of a dialogue with these siblings of chaos'. For Borges, the moral, intellectual and aesthetic are always inseparable.

After some reflection, the first conclusion he reaches is that these people are merely succumbing to the reality of what has happened, somewhat dazzled in the meanwhile by the power of the symbols 'Paris' and 'liberation'. But such a banal explanation could not long satisfy a man like Borges, for whom it was always important that an explanation be both profound and beautiful. Happily, some nights later, he recalls that in Shaw's *Man and Superman* a character has a dream 'where he affirms that the horror of hell is its unreality'. Borges then has no difficulty relating this idea to the doctrine, a thousand and more years before, of 'John Scotus Erigena, who denied the substantive existence of sin and evil'.

The writer then compares these textual references to his memory of the day Paris was occupied. A Germanophile had come to give Borges the news, announcing in stentorian tones the imminent fall of London and the pointlessness of any opposition. Behind the apparent enthusiasm, Borges had sensed, with great psychological acumen, that the Nazi sympathiser was himself terrified by the completeness of Hitler's victory. Nazism, he concludes, like Erigena's hell, (or indeed, if it comes to that, the worlds of 'The Immortal' and of 'The Lottery of Babylon') 'suffers from unreality'. One can die for it and lie for it, but in the end it is 'uninhabitable', one cannot actually want it. 'Hitler is blindly collaborating with the inevitable armies that will annihilate him, as the metal vultures and the dragon (which must have known that they were monsters) collaborated, mysteriously, with Hercules.'

In just a page and a half, then, Borges has brought a historical experience, private and public, into line with his reading and with his tendency to see antagonists as obeying a larger and ahistorical design beyond their immediate intentions. Most of all, he has redeemed reality, however unpromising his own personal situation may have been at the time. Whether we agree with what he says or not (something largely irrelevant when reading Borges), we find ourselves with a feast of ideas to consider and, above all, the example of how a remarkable mind comes to grips with the world in a constant back and forth between personal experience and the ideas of others.

Borges is a great orchestrator. There is his name on the front cover of the book and then, in the index at the back, the three hundred or so names of his close collaborators, the authors he constantly quotes and examines and uses to examine others: sixteen entries for Walt Whitman, thirty-eight for Schopenhauer, twenty-eight for De Quincey. This is the community Borges moves in, the orchestra he conducts and seeks at once to lose himself in and to make his own. Twenty entries for Plato and Platonism, twenty-four for Chesterton, thirteen for Benedetto Croce. 'The History of literature' – this remark from Paul Valéry appears on more than one occasion – 'should not be the history of authors and the course of their careers or of the career of their works, but rather the history of the Spirit as the producer or consumer of literature'. Borges's essays attempt to invoke that spirit by bringing the most disparate voices together. And what better way to start than by showing that every quotation can be corroborated by another? He follows Valéry with this remark from Emerson:

> I am very much struck in literature by the appearance that one person wrote all the books ... there is such equality and identity both of judgement and point of view in the narrative that it is plainly the work of one all-seeing all-hearing gentleman.

How wonderful the word 'gentleman' is there. Perhaps this 'one person' is the 'someone else' Borges claimed he wanted to be.

Over the sixty-four years of the production covered in *Selected Non-Fictions*, Borges comes at a huge range of subjects – the tango, suicide, the apocryphal Gospels, Argentinian literature, translation, the paradoxes of Zeno, German literature in the Age of Bach – plus dozens of biographical sketches of the most disparate figures, and he never tires, never sinks into mannerism. Again and again he takes on a new subject, marshals his reading, his faithful friends of old, gives us fresh ways of seeing things, suggests lucid, often conflicting, frequently bizarre ways of understanding the world. It is astonishing. And though the yearnings are ever the same – the desire to annihilate time, to approach a transcendental perception of life, to grasp an ungraspable truth – Borges never stoops to wishful thinking. Here he is speaking of Emerson's monism and assuming a position which seems an implicit criticism of much of his own endeavour:

> Our destiny is tragic because we are, irreparably, individuals, restricted by time and by space; there is nothing, consequently, more favourable than a faith that eliminates circumstances and declares that every man is all men and that there is no one who is not the universe. Those who profess such a doctrine are generally unfortunate or mediocre, avid to annul themselves in the cosmos . . .

Is this an ironic triumph of self-effacement? Or is it that Borges feels he comes closest to that 'all-seeing all-hearing gentleman' when able to hold two conflicting views, if not simultaneously, then almost? Here he is only two years on from the Emerson piece leaning quite the other way over the question of Argentine provincialism, its tendency to believe the country is cut off from European tradition and must thus establish its own separate world:

> This opinion strikes me as unfounded. I understand why many people accept it: such a declaration of our solitude, our perdition, and our primitive character has, like existentialism, the charms of poignancy. Many people may accept this opinion because, having done so, they will feel themselves to be alone, disconsolate and, in some way, interesting.

I am trying to suggest that while much of the work in the five hundred-plus pages of Viking's *Collected Fictions* actually detracts from the marvellous achievement of the best stories, the opposite is true of the essays. Here, accretion is of the essence as we watch Borges twisting and turning to deal with new contingencies, to write for different kinds of publications, to accommodate contradictory intuitions, to strike an impossible balance, to align a film he has seen, a book he has read, a historical figure, a political event, to an essential core of reading and its related force field of ideas. Taken as a whole, *Selected Non-Fictions* is the more interesting, more seductive book. Joyce is the twentieth century's great genius, but both *Ulysses* and *Finnegans Wake*, in so far as they express the exasperation of a highly personal style, are 'unreadable' and parts of the latter actually 'incompetent'. 'Psychologism' is anathema, but we have an entirely convincing psychological reading of the *Divina Commedia* that prompts Borges to field the provocation that the whole work was undertaken to allow Dante to stage an imagined encounter with the dead woman who had rejected him. All literature is the work of the same spirit, but on rereading Shakespeare and his contemporaries Borges has no difficulty in resolving that most celebrated of authorship arguments: only Shakespeare could have written Shakespeare. Pierre Menard take heed.

It is this process of Borges's coming to terms with things, his seeking, for example, to be outside Argentinian politics but then finding himself involved in a visceral antagonism with Peron, that makes the essays so engaging. As if, at last, and precisely because they were not written to be collected, we had the sustained, chronologically fascinating narrative that Borges never wrote, the tale of his own self constantly seeking to shake off that self. In fact, it occurs to me now that perhaps I was wrong at the beginning of this essay to imagine that Borges achieved his intended goal; perhaps he is right to go on claiming (in his sixties) that 'the true essence of a writer's work is usually unknown by that writer'. For as piece after piece in the collection brings together dozens of quotations from all ages to suggest the oneness of human experience, so we grow ever more aware of a deep divide that separates him, and indeed us, from most of those he cites.

The phenomenon is most evident in a strand that runs throughout the book and is, one suspects, the author's favourite. It involves the rapid consideration of this or that metaphysical view of the world. So we have 'A Defence of Basilides the False', who, in the second century believed human beings to be the deficient improvisation of a lesser God. Borges justifies the idea thus: 'What better gift can we hope for than to be insignificant? What greater glory for a God than to be absolved of the world?'

And Borges considers J.W. Dunne's bizarre book *Nothing Dies*, published in 1940, which claims that we already possess eternity since the future is pre-existent. Our dreams are proof of this. 'In death we shall recover all the moments of our lives and combine them as we please. God and our friends and Shakespeare will collaborate with us.' In a complex discussion Borges dismisses Dunne's reasoning, but concludes: 'So splendid a thesis makes any fallacy committed by the author insignificant.'

In short, and this occurs again and again, we are offered an aesthetic appreciation of a metaphysical position, or a whole philosophy, regardless, but never unaware of its probable truth. So angels are attractive ('I always imagine them at nightfall, in the dusk of a slum or a vacant lot . . . with their backs to the sunset') while the Trinity is 'an intellectual horror, a strangled specious infinity, like facing mirrors'.

Borges is prodigiously generous with these savourings. The doctrine, from Pythagoras to Nietzsche, of repeating cycles of existence is shown to be ugly, but Phillip Henry Gosse's theory that at the moment of creation God created not only an infinite future but an infinite past too, which explains why although the world begins with Adam nevertheless that first man could have come across the fossils of animals that had never been, is very beautiful. What separates Borges from Gosse of course, and indeed almost all the others he quotes, is that for Gosse what mattered was whether his theory was true or not. These people were fundamentalists, or at least believers, and always earnest scholars. Borges is not only incapable of fundamentalism and traditional religious belief, but even incapable of attacking it per se. He is as far removed from scholasticism as it is possible to be. In this he declares his modernity. Butterfly-like, he sucks nectar here and there, and finds it to be largely the same nectar. It is difficult to imagine such an attitude being struck pre-Nietzsche.

The same underlying irony, though this is not unwitting, emerges from Borges's constant assault on history. Frequently a date, the fifth century for example, is introduced with the qualification 'of our era' ('the fifth century of our era') to remind us of all the other fifth centuries. Frequently, a writer generally celebrated for epitomising the avant-garde of his time is presented by Borges as, on the contrary, akin to some quite different period. Apollinaire is close to the twelfth-century author of *Chanson de Roland*: 'He was so unmodern that modernity seemed picturesque, and perhaps even moving, to him.' Oscar Wilde, far from being *fin-de-siècle* man par excellence, is actually a creature of the eighteenth century, akin to Gibbon, Johnson and Voltaire. But such claims, which pitch the beauty of imaginative parallel against the ugly sloth of received ideas, largely serve to illuminate the target they cannot destroy. Borges is kicking against the pricks. His secret task, perhaps, was to remind us of the limits of even the most powerful imagination.

Meanwhile, many beautiful and ugly things were happening in the writer's life. Having survived the first period of Peronism, he was, to his astonishment, made Director of the Argentine National Library by the generals who had ousted the dictator. It was 1955. Borges had often thought of paradise as a library. But exactly as the Pearly Gates were opened to him, his declining sight, a consequence of a congenital condition, finally gave out. 'No one,' he wrote in 'Poem of Gifts', 'should read self-pity or reproach/into this statement of the majesty/of God, who with such splendid irony/granted me books and blindness at one touch.'

Blindness and its attendant dependency, writes Borges's bland biographer, James Woodall, 'was not a problem for Leonor'. Mother accompanied the writer on his now frequent lecture tours. Mother walked the streets with him, to hear his rehearsal of performances that shyness still made a torture. But oddly, now that he couldn't see them, being with women was rather easier. Often very young women. They were invited to intimate seminars in pleasant cafés to learn Old English with him. Evidently the writer's imagination hadn't deserted him. They collaborated on anthologies and textbooks. Did Borges consider them his intellectual equals? Was the all-seeing gentleman also a gentle-woman? With its scores of literary biographies and book reviews only a page and a half of *Selected Non-Fictions* is dedicated to a woman: Virginia Woolf, a writer whose transcendental yearnings are very close to Borges's own. He had translated *Orlando*.

Famous now, finally secure economically, Borges was seized by a longing for the domestic happiness that had always eluded him. In 1967, he married an old friend and widow with whom he had lost touch for twenty years. How long was it before he appreciated that this was not the beautiful thing he had wanted? The energetic and ambitious Norman Di Giovanni, Borges's translator and uncomfortably close collaborator over the next few years, claimed that the writer was already unhappy when he, Di Giovanni, first met him only months after his marriage. Crass statements of the variety, 'he had a lousy marriage – and I was getting divorced from my first wife,' give us a measure of the distance between Di Giovanni and Borges.

Still, it is truly difficult to leave somebody in a beautiful and gentleman-like fashion. Three years after their wedding, the unsuspecting Elsa Borges went to the door to find, not her husband back for lunch, as he had promised, but a lawyer and a group of men from a removals company with instructions to remove his books. *The Thousand and One Nights* was going back to Mum. 'A New Refutation of Time', the essay in which Borges most energetically sets out to deny the reality of substance and time, ends with a brutal, indeed breathtaking volte-face: 'The world unfortunately is real; I unfortunately am Borges.' Here is drama.

But what does Borges ultimately understand by the aesthetic? What makes something beautiful? An essay entitled 'The Wall and the Books' begins: 'I read, a few days ago, that the man who ordered the building of the almost infinite Chinese Wall was the first Emperor, Shih Huang Ti, who also decreed the burning of all the books that had been written before his time.' Borges ponders the relation between these two extraordinary gestures of construction and destruction; are they complementary, or do they cancel each other out? After much ingenious hypothesising, he is obliged to concede that the enigma remains intact. But this is never a problem for Borges, who enjoys 'those things that can enrich ignorance'. He concludes:

> Music, states of happiness, mythology, faces worn by time, certain twilights and certain places, all want to tell us something, or have told us something we shouldn't have lost, or are about to tell us something; that imminence of revelation as yet unproduced is, perhaps, the aesthetic fact.

The 'imminence of revelation'. When do we most frequently sense it? When reading. On three or four occasions in this collection Borges fields the idea that 'each time we repeat a line by Dante or Shakespeare, we are, in some way, that instant when Dante or Shakespeare created that line'. Reading is a transmigration of souls, the sacred act by which Borges can become, if only for the period of the reading, somebody else. In its yearning for and respect of another's otherness, and likewise our shared oneness, reading has a profound moral content. It is beautiful *and* good. 'A book is a thing among things . . . until it meets its reader . . . What then occurs is that singular emotion called beauty, that lovely mystery which neither psychology nor criticism can describe . . .'

Beauty is the superimposition of separate minds in the experience of art. It is in this sense that we must understand Borges modest boast, often repeated, that he was first and foremost a reader not a writer. As the most immediate fruit of that reading, bringing together the writer's consumption and creation of literature in the paradise of his personal library, the essays are his greatest gift to us.

These reflections may help us to understand the relation between Borges's wonderfully lucid prose and his underlying vision. In the early days he had been more baroque, he had sought to amaze in each sentence. One or two of the early essays in the collection give us a taste of this. He was excited by the invention of compound words (imagining, for example, a word that might mean at once sunset and the sound of cattle bells). But later, and under the influence of his friend Bioy, he moved to a prose at once simpler and more assured, and above all to a style that erases, so far as is possible, everything personal. His quarrel with *Finnegans Wake*, for example, is precisely its creation of a personal language, largely through the invention of compound words.

The result of this switch from the personal to the urbane, the romantic to the classical, is that the complex and dazzling connections that his mind was ever generating now come to the fore with greater clarity, unencumbered with 'literary' ornament or that tiresome 'look-at-me' cleverness that characterised so much of the avant-garde writing of the period. In particular, in the essays the style becomes, as it were, the pure transparent air through which the echoes of all the writers he is exploring can be heard. A medium in which many minds can meet.

Garrulous as he had once been shy, blessedly famous as he had been obscure, Borges toured the globe, accepting countless literary honours, cheerfully chattering to hangers-on, determined to redeem his early sin, as he described it, of having been unhappy. Mother was dead at last. Well aware that his best work was behind him, he dictated poetry and lectures to nice young women. Were the girls more important to him than the pieces he was composing? Certainly a great deal of the poetry would have been better left out of the large and largely dull selection Viking have put together, while only a process akin to sanctification could account for the Harvard University Press's decision to publish in full the transcripts of his bumbling Norton Lectures. In editing the selected non-fiction, however, Eliot Weinberger has been sharper and kinder, offering us only such late material as is as exciting as anything else in the collection. He also adds sufficient biographical notes to spare most readers from looking at James Woodall's uninspired biography. It is amusing, however, to discover from Woodall that Borges's politics were such that he was glad to accept the Grand Cross of the Order of Bernardo O'Higgins from the hands of General Pinochet. This in 1976. Ten years later, terminally ill, Borges made a final attempt to extract himself from Argentine history, by going to Geneva to die. At last he was back in the place of his early reading, the town where he first met Schopenhauer and Berkeley and Cervantes. Shortly before the music stopped, he married the young companion then in the chair beside him, Maria Kodama.

But now that he is in paradise, with whom does Borges find he shares his identity? To say his mother would be banal. Everybody knew they were one throughout. To say his arch-antagonist General Peron would be a mockery, though I suspect of the kind that Borges himself, after a little time for adjustment, might have proposed. Let me close with an act of conflation that I hope will be understood as a tribute to the fascinating thought processes which animate this wonderful writer's work.

In 1961, Borges shared the first International Publishers Prize with Samuel Beckett. He never mentions Beckett in the *Selected Non-Fictions*, nor from what I have been able to gather, did he ever read him. Let us count the ways in which the two writers are similar. Both men came from countries considered peripheral to the cultural centre, countries undergoing periods of intense nationalism, from which these writers largely dissociated themselves. Both suffered from chronic inhibitions. Both spoke the same four languages: Spanish, French, English, German. Both translated. Both had domineering mothers. Both were obsessed with Dante. Both were theologians and atheists. Both were writers whose adventurous fiction was largely fed by their readings of philosophy (in many cases the same philosophy). Both opposed Nazism in courageous ways. Both mocked modern scholasticism and have been appropriated by it. Both were fascinated by the extent to which language has an inertia of its own, which speaks itself regardless of individual intentions. Both were childless. Both concentrated on those experiences essential to all men, rather than the dramas generated by different characters and contingent circumstance. Both became fascinated by the multiplicity of the self and the inability to escape the self. Both wondered at the border between finite and infinite, mathematics and metaphysics. Both lived more or less contemporaneously into highly praised old age. Both longed for extinction.

'Racine and Mallarmé,' Borges claimed, 'are the same writer.' Now that they are 'quite dead at last', as Beckett's Malone put it, can we say as much of Borges and Beckett? 'If people vary at all,' writes Henry Green in *Party Going*, 'it can only be in the impressions they leave on others' minds.' To read Borges is an entirely different experience, a different encounter, a different transmigration, than to read Beckett. Whatever their status in a bibliophile's paradise, we can only wonder that two men who insisted on the oneness of human experience and who themselves had so much in common, should also have such sharply distinct, but equally enchanting voices. The all-seeing gentleman is a genius of impersonation.

Here Comes Salman

[Salman Rushdie]

'The art [of the novel],' wrote Schopenhauer, 'lies in setting the inner life into the most violent motion with the smallest possible expenditure of outer life.' Salman Rushdie would not agree. It is not that there is no inner life in his novel *The Ground Beneath Her Feet*. Nor indeed does one feel that Rushdie would require any external occurrences at all to set his fertile mind in motion. It is just that the sheer quantity of events that crowd these 575 pages is such as to overwhelm any depiction of inner life or any mind's attempt to grasp the half of them. For brevity's sake, more elaborate syntax will have to give way to the list – as so often it does in Rushdie's prose – if we are to offer the slightest idea of what is between these covers.

We have, in the first third of the book: Bombay in the forties and fifties, with the immensely complex shenanigans of various extended families, scams, superstitions, Zoroastrianism, arson, cricket, politics, suicides, murders, love at first sight, cinema interiors, mythology, rock music and goat farming (the inner life is present most strikingly in the form of bizarre psychic experiences).

Then: London in the sixties with more of most of the above, plus drugs, sex, pirate radio stations, music business entrepreneurs, a delightfully erotic young lady who can pass through walls, Chelsea boutiques, record contracts, a car accident, deep coma and intimations of a variety of catastrophes. In the Bombay section I omitted to mention an earthquake and some lessons in photography. We discover that Lou Reed is a woman and that

Kennedy survived both Lee Harvey Oswald and the second gunman on the grassy knoll, only to be murdered later by the same bullet that slew his brother (and incumbent president) Bobbie.

Finally we have New York and the US in general through the seventies, eighties and nineties, with more selections of the above (especially the mythology), plus some rock concerts (though still fewer than the murders and earthquakes). There is stardom and its penthouses, the discovery that 'alternative worlds' are in 'tectonic collision', a recording-contract dispute with global ramifications, more extremely weird psychic experiences and even Orphic expeditions to bring back the dead (though this may just be a morbid form of voyeurism), and – to close – earthquake, death, murder and, at the last – why not? – happy love.

In his novel *Haroun and the Sea of Stories*, Rushdie has his charming young protagonist say: 'I always thought storytelling was like juggling . . . You keep a lot of different tales in the air, and juggle them up and down, and if you're good you don't drop any.' In *The Ground Beneath Her Feet* Rushdie tosses up a great many balls, most of them very large and decidedly colourful. Certainly he is determined to dazzle. Whether he manages to keep them usefully in the air or not is something it is hard at first for the reader to judge, since the pages are very soon, with respect, so full of balls that the mind can only boggle. Rushdie's dazzle is not of the variety that illuminates or clarifies. He seems nervous of letting more than a page or two go by without some melodramatic event to distract our attention. In the London section, I see I forgot to mention a potion-brewing, fashion-queen witch-murderer. I also forgot to say that the whole story is told by one who declares himself one of the world's great sceptics and rationalists.

Along with a considerable school of critical thought, Rushdie is among those who have sought over recent years to turn the energy of the 'multicultural' and the hybrid into an elaborate aesthetic with a serious moral and political slant. Most readers will be familiar with the way his books mix different narrative traditions, confuse the historical and fantastical, East and West, gods and men and, not least, characters and author. So when something over halfway through *The Ground Beneath Her Feet*, its Indian rock-star hero, now resident in England, finally records the song that will make him famous, it is evident from the novel's discussion of this turning point that Rushdie is inviting analogies with his own work. Shortly before the recording we read: 'He hasn't fully grasped how to make of multiplicity an accumulating strength rather than a frittery weakness.'

But when the breakthrough comes, with the psychic hero boldly firing his support musicians and recording instrument after instrument one over the other all on his own, the new star is able to announce:

> What I want the music to say is that I don't have to choose . . . I need it to show that I don't have to be this guy or that guy, the fellow from over there or the fellow from here, the person within me that I call my twin, or whoever's out there in whatever it is I get flashes of beyond the sky; or just the man standing in front of you right now. I'll be all of them, I can do that. Here comes everybody, right? That's where it came from the idea of playing all the instruments. It was to prove that point.

The energy of the Rushdie aesthetic is thus to come from a rejection of the pathos of choice, of that need, with which most of us will be all too familiar, to become one thing or another, 'this guy or that guy', taking decisions from day to day. Instead, everything is to be maintained in a fizz of promise, potential, multiplicity and openness. It will be noted at once that such an attitude, repeatedly expressed throughout Rushdie's work, falls easily into line with that area of contemporary culture which likes to associate its desire to remain for ever young with the political ideals of tolerance and peaceful cohabitation. And indeed for Rushdie, the hybrid, or simply the multiform, comes to be seen as an antidote to that fundamentalism which has treated him so scandalously. Of the Moor in *The Moor's Last Sigh*, he remarked in an interview, 'he was a poetic type, which means, I suppose, that he was someone in whom all the cultures flowed and therefore was unable to take absolutist views'. Albeit with the uncertain glue of that 'I suppose', the aesthetic and the political are wedded together. Being 'poetic' has to do with entertaining various cultures and remaining, as it were, suspended between them and their various implications. In the confrontation between 'the pure and the impure, the sacred and the profane', Rushdie is, he tells us, 'on the side of the profane', the melting pot.

The more one considers this line of argument, the more one suspects that certain of its assumptions are flawed. In *Haroun*, Rushdie posits a world where all the stories there are flow together in beautiful harmony in one great ocean. An evil 'cultmaster' wishes to destroy this ocean. Novelist and critic Hilary Mantel glossed the idea appreciatively thus: 'This tyrant hates stories because he aims to rule the world, and fiction creates an alternative world, a multiplicity of worlds he can never command.' In this view of things – almost a critical orthodoxy these days – storytelling is seen as inherently liberal in so far as it offers alternatives to some outside-the-story reality. The story is thus understood as of its nature a hybrid on the factual world we know, its alternatives affording imaginative escape from that world's political powers.

But is this the case? Do stories flow together in tolerant harmony distinct from our 'factual' world? Aren't they rather, with their rival visions, in urgent conflict with each other to establish what the nature of our world is, what the 'facts' really are? Aren't evil 'cultmasters' themselves supported by elaborate stories within the terms of which they do not consider themselves evil at all? Far from objecting to stories in general (usually they will be well content to have people read innocuous tales that have nothing to do with anything), don't they rather object to those particular stories that undermine their own? Good storytelling is always seductive and potentially coercive (*Midnight's Children* was a most seductive tale). It draws us, powerfully, to its own position, which, however complex and open to interpretation, may be very far from compatible with other positions. Its enchantments, like Prospero's, are enchantments that bind as much as they please, insisting that reality is this way or that. It is in this sense that Shelley thought of poets, not as charmingly sensitive people unwilling, as Rushdie's Moor, to choose between rival systems, but as 'the unacknowledged legislators of the World'.

'The only leaps of faith I'm capable of,' we read in *The Ground Beneath Her Feet*, 'are those required by the creative imagination, by fictions that don't pretend to be fact, and so end up telling the truth.' Perhaps when one begins to feel that it is enough to write fiction to be engaged on the right side of some global moral battle and indeed to 'end up telling the truth', then there is a risk of growing careless. For just as it is notoriously difficult to do anything without making choices and becoming this guy or that (Rushdie's musician, after all, becomes the guy who dismissed his support musicians), so, and this is particularly true of writing, the things one merely 'ends up' saying will rarely bear examination.

The Ground Beneath Her Feet is narrated in the first person by the self-styled rationalist and war photographer Rai Merchant, the secret third in a love triangle whose other members, Ormus Cama and Vina Apsara, are the book's larger-than-life rock-star heroes. Vina dies in an earthquake at the beginning of the book and Rai explains his decision to tell his tale thus:

We all looked to her [Vina] for peace, yet she herself was not at peace. And so I've chosen to write here, publicly, what I can no longer whisper into her private ear: that is, everything. I have chosen to tell our story, hers and mine and Ormus Cama's, all of it, every last detail, and then maybe she can find a sort of peace here, on the page, in this underworld of ink and lies, that respite which was denied her by life. So I stand at the gate of the inferno of language, there's a barking dog and a ferryman waiting and a coin under my tongue for the fare.

Rushdie loves the grand narrative gesture and there is a sprint for the portentous in his writing which often comes at the expense of sense. Rai chooses to tell the story so that Vina can find 'peace on the page'. Presumably, as a man who insistently pronounces himself a rationalist, he means so that *he* can find peace (the dead, after all, for a rationalist, are beyond our reach). As we approach the end of the book, however, we discover that Rai is now blissfully happy with a new girlfriend. Why then is he writing? Whose peace is at stake? And why, if the book is inspired by a need to get a grip on their love triangle, will it have to include so much extraneous material? Again, if the page is, as he so melodramatically claims, an 'underworld of ink and lies', is it reasonably a place where one would expect to find peace anyway?

Then what are we to make of the word 'lies' after Rai's confessional solemnity in the opening lines of the paragraph? And why does he use the word 'respite', a temporary cessation of the painful, if what we are talking about here is a final laying to rest? The more one progresses with Rushdie's novel the more one feels that its most formidable enemy will not be any evil fundamentalism, but simply a moment's attention on the part of the wakeful reader.

There are further questions to ask about this passage. Since the story of Orpheus has been amply introduced only a few pages earlier with Vina singing Eurydice's part from Gluck's opera shortly before disappearing, presumably swallowed up by the shaky ground beneath her feet, must we then understand the narrator's entry to the underworld as an Orphic expedition to *recover* the lost lover rather than, as he claims, to lay her to rest? What would Rai's new girlfriend think about such a project? The idea of a narrative as a doomed expedition of retrieval is one I find fascinating, but this particular ball is quickly dropped, the analogy is not repeated, and in any event we will shortly discover that Rai is tone-deaf and hence hardly an Orpheus candidate. It is rather his friend and rival, Ormus the musician, who will assume the roll of Orpheus obsessively seeking the dead Vina (by casting about for lookalikes) in the final chapters of the book. Why then was the parallel so dramatically invited?

The love triangle is fairly static and its story is quickly told. Growing up in Bombay, the awesomely handsome and musically talented Ormus Cama fritters away his teens seducing the local girls. After spending her early childhood in the USA, the slightly younger Vina Apsara, of mixed Asian-Indian and Greek-American parentage, comes to Bombay where she will eventually find herself living with the family of the, again slightly younger, Rai Merchant. Vina is awesomely beautiful and has an extra-ordinary voice. The nine-year-old Rai falls immediately and irretrievably in love with her. Shortly afterwards the twelve-year-old Vina and the nineteen-year-old Ormus fall immediately and irretrievably in love with each other.

From this point on, a series of delays stretches out developments over a lifetime (thus allowing Rushdie to fill the spaces with all kinds of digressions and sub-plots). With surprising chivalry, Ormus agrees to wait until Vina is sixteen before so much as kissing her. Four years. They enjoy a night's delirious pleasure (which Rai is able to describe in detail), but then Ormus's hasty offer of marriage causes Vina to run off and the following morning complicated coincidences lead the couple to lose sight of each other for ten years, during which time Vina will, if only fleetingly, become Rai's lover. Having moved to America,

Vina rediscovers Ormus when his first successful record is released, but at this point, following a car accident that was actually a murder attempt, the hero is in a coma in a house by the Thames. At the sound of Vina's voice Ormus immediately reawakens and over the next year she nurses him back to health.

The two now team up as a super-successful rock band, but again Ormus's request of marriage (in this at least he knows who he wants to be) is rejected. Despite her love, the sassy Vina has no intention of renouncing her promiscuous nature. At this point Ormus forces a pact on her: they will not touch each other for ten years, during which time he will remain celibate, but at the end of that period they will marry. Throughout these ten years Vina continues to sleep with Rai, though Ormus, who is aware of her more casual lovers, never knows this.

Finally, the now amazingly famous rock stars marry. All continues as before without revelations, confrontations or any particular development, until Ormus's intensifying psychic obsessions eventually become too much for his wife. Ormus is convinced that two worlds (apparently that of the book and our own world outside the book) are involved in a progressive collision that is causing socio-political upheaval and indeed earthquakes. Vina walks out on him and Rai is encouraged to believe he can at last break up the official couple and win his woman. To this end he follows Vina on her first solo tour, but at precisely the point where a decision must be made she disappears in an earthquake in Mexico, thus somewhat validating her husband's nightmare prophecies.

The dynamic of the triangle has potential. All three characters are presented as in search of the solid ground of identity. Of himself the narrator says: 'at my worst I have been a cacophony, a mass of human noises that did not add up to the symphony of an integrated self'. The racially mixed Vina with her miserable infancy is 'a rag bag of selves, torn fragments of people she might have become'. Ormus has serious identity crises resulting from his belief that he is in some way inhabited by the personality of his stillborn twin, Gayomart. These are less positive presentations of the multiple self. All three protagonists sense that the dramatic gesture of choice and (above all) exclusiveness in love will confer a longed-for identity. But Vina in particular is also aware that exclusive love can be coercive and limiting, and it is she who allows the triangle to form and deliberately perpetuates it over thirty years, thus keeping all three characters in a state of tension, on the brink of an identity that is never quite established.

The scenario, as I said, is promising and from time to time Rushdie launches into some penetrating reflections on the conflicting claims of identity, love and trust, in life and in art. He has read widely and thought a great deal. But he seems unable or unwilling to dramatise these relationships in a way that would allow us to savour their emotions and dilemmas. In the end almost none of the book's action or energy springs from them. His twin vocations for multiplicity and hyperbole work against the prolonged and concentrated meditation needed to bring the inner life of a love triangle onto the page. Just as Ormus Cama is reluctant to choose between conflicting personalities, so Rushdie is determined not to settle on one form or another of the novel. His choice of the first person, for example, with all its scope for transmitting the pathos of a frustratingly limited knowledge, offers an excellent approach to his story. But its conviction soon dwindles when Rushdie allows his narrator inside other characters' heads and starts using him, and them, as the merest of mouthpieces for his own many ideas and areas of interest. A section where the largely uneducated and very adolescent Vina is allowed to be an authority on Bombay cinema interiors is particularly unconvincing, and dull to boot. One moment we are being given a lecture on Neoplatonism, then the narrative suddenly slips into cartoon flippancy full of pun and rhyme, only to clang out at the end of a paragraph with some portentous eschatological warning. Rather than a convincing voice, or the continuation (for the claim is frequently made) of a satisfying oral tradition, this only reminds us of certain prevailing and largely literary notions of the modern. In short, and again like his rock star Ormus, Rushdie makes no secrets of playing all the instruments. 'Here comes everybody' – an improbable quotation from *Finnegans Wake*, afforded through a first-person narrator (not present when the words were spoken) to a young Indian rock musician – thus tends to mean, here comes Salman.

While the mixed and hybrid is justified both by its liberal openness and its reflection of a contemporary global situation, Rushdie's insistent use of hyperbole is to take us to those extremes where nature may betray what lies beyond the 'curtain of *maya*'. The two vocations come together in the book's use of mythology. Inflated by frequent comparison to mythological figures taken from both Western and Eastern traditions, Ormus and Vina, Eastern practitioners of what we have always thought of as a Western musical form, are to be held up as potential archetypes, suggesting a deep pattern of truth beneath the superficial clutter of daily reality. Typical passages read thus: 'Glistening serpents of hair lay across the wooden veranda. Medusa. It crossed my mind [Rai is referring to a time when he was nine years old] that we should look at her [Vina's] face only in a burnished shield lest we be turned to stone.' Or again: 'Many different versions of the first encounter between Vina Apsara and Ormus Cama are presently in circulation . . . depending on which journal you read you might have heard that he transformed himself into a white bull and carried her away on his back . . .'

These mythological allusions are then set off against the narrator's declared scepticism to generate a dialectic between two opposed interpretations of life, the one usually, though not exclusively, associated with the mystical East, the other with the rationalist tradition of the West. The two views come into most immediate conflict in Rai's relationship with the mythical and myth-hungry Vina. Of her interest in the sacred music of India, the narrator announces: 'I must conclude – and this is hard for a lifelong sceptic like me to write – that what Vina wanted was a glimpse of the unknowable.'

However interesting Rushdie's intentions – and there can be little doubt that he means this to be the intellectual core of the book – the dialectic never convinces. The project is dogged by two extravagant decisions, or perhaps they might best be described, within the terms of Rushdie's poetics, as protracted 'indecisions'. The first involves the sheer weight of mythical reference that is foisted upon the central characters (all of whom are themselves remarkably well versed in both Western and Eastern mythologies). Vina, for example, a girl whose father turned gay and abandoned her mother who later hanged herself after slaughtering her second husband and his family (Rushdie is anything but ungenerous with background), a girl, then, whose early life is presented along the lines of the most gruesome and sensationalist 'realism', will be compared with (among others): Medusa, Cinderella, Eurydice, the Egyptian Queen Hatshepsut, Europa, Rati (wife of the Indian god of love), Helen of Troy, an apsara (semi-divine nymph in Indian mythology), Pallas Athena, Psyche, Dionysus, Galatea *and* Pygmalion.

The same wearisome profligacy of interconnection is afforded both to other characters and to the book's many events. (Of one girl who predicts an earthquake we read: 'If she was our Cassandra, then maybe – just maybe – Bombay was about to fall like Troy.') Instead of finding a suggestive and potentially convincing structure in myth, the reader begins to suspect only fuzzy thinking and overkill. It may be that the problem of establishing the characters' identities is more Rushdie's than theirs.

The other obstacle set before our engagement with this presentation of rival interpretations of reality is the decision to have our sceptical narrator give credence to events that, if accepted as factual, eliminate a priori the very possibility of scepticism. Of Ormus Cama we read that 'within moments of his birth (he) began making the strange, rapid finger movements with both hands which any guitarist could have identified as chord progressions'. These movements, Rai tells us, were filmed and are now available on video. Later we learn that Ormus (his name is a Latin hybridisation of the Zoroastrian god Ormazd or Ahura Mazda), in contact with his dead twin Gayomart (another Zoroastrian figure), is being given the words and music to many of the greatest rock songs exactly two years, eight months and twenty-eight days before they are released in the West. He actually plays 'Yesterday' as his own song in a Bombay club before it appears as the work of the Beatles. Rai remarks: 'I am the least supernaturally inclined of men, but this tall story I have no option but to believe.' While the inspiration here is presumably comic, the result in terms of the book's larger debate is that the position of the sceptic is untenable and the proposed dialectic spurious. It is rather as if Browning's Karshish were to declare his familiarity with well-documented miracles before being presented with the enigma of the resurrected Lazarus.

Critics championing Rushdie will often suggest that we have difficulty understanding him because we are unfamiliar with the tradition he is working in (though they rarely remark that he is most successful precisely where that tradition is least understood). It would seem appropriate then to consider how he uses some of his Indian material.

Alienated from family affections 'like an astronaut floating away from a space capsule', Ormus Cama is saved by Vina Apsara's love. Rai remarks in a long parenthesis:

(It is said that when Kama, the love god, committed the crime of trying to shoot mighty Shiva with a dart of love, the great god burned him to ashes with a thunderbolt. Kama's wife, the goddess Rati, pleaded for his life, and softened Shiva's heart. In an inversion of the Orpheus myth, it was the woman who interceded with the deity and brought Love – Love itself – back from the dead . . . So also Ormus Cama, exiled from love by the parents whom he had failed to transfix with love's arrow, shrivelled by their lack of affection, is restored to the world of love by Vina.)

Even those unfamiliar with Indian myth will have grounds for suspecting that the analogy cannot hold. Kama's attempt to shoot a love dart at Shiva is presented as a crime, while it could hardly be considered a crime for Ormus to seek affection from his parents. The reference to darts should also alert us to the fact that Kama is akin to the Greek Eros and has nothing at all to do with filial love. One does not fire off Eros's arrows at one's folks (there has been no suggestion of a desire for incest!). The parallel thus becomes doubly inappropriate, indeed triply so if one further considers that while Rati can only appeal to Shiva's clemency, Vina saves Ormus directly herself. Nor could it be claimed that this distortion is a deliberate attempt on Rushdie's part to develop the character of his narrator Rai, whose erudition, on the contrary, appears to be coextensive with his author's and whose point of view generally coincides with Rushdie's as presented in interviews. Some two hundred pages later Rushdie remembers that his narrator is sceptical of these mythological interpretations and gives us this: 'When Vina starts with her fanciful mysteries, all you can do is lie back and wait for her to lose interest, which never takes too long. Here she is, back again at the story of Kama and Rati.' But previously it was Rai/Rushdie using this particular analogy, not Vina/Rushdie.

The story of Kama and Rati is worth considering in a little more detail. Warned by Brahma that they would be destroyed by the anti-god Taraka unless Shiva bore a son to destroy him, the gods begged Kama to shoot one of his darts at Shiva so that he would fall in love with the girl Parvati who could then bear the great creator and destroyer a son. The idea of crime doesn't enter into it. Unimpressed, Shiva shrivelled Kama with a blaze from his famous third eye (not with a thunderbolt). At this point versions diverge, some suggesting Kama was brought back to life and others saying not. But the two can be reconciled in the version that tells us how Kama was brought back only to a dispersed and invisible life. In his recent work on Indian mythology, *Ka*, Roberto Calasso comments on the story thus: 'Flowers, bees, mangoes, cuckoos: it was into you that Desire [Kama] dispersed when Shiva's blaze consumed him. Henceforth a humming or a birdcall, a flavour or a scent, would open a wound in those far from their loved ones.' Calasso concludes with a quotation from the fifth-century poet Kalidasa. 'And many were wounded if it is true that "upon seeing things of great beauty or hearing sweet sounds even a happy man may be seized by a fierce nostalgia."'

The myth will perhaps help us to shift the debate on our reaction to Rushdie's work to more pertinent ground than that of the sterile back and forth of whether or not we can appreciate Indian tradition. Fantastical as it is, Kama's story illuminates a landscape we recognise all too well. There is an attempt, an erotic attempt, to coerce the great power that drives the universe. It fails miserably. Erotic love is helpless in the face of necessity. However far from realism, myth, unlike some contemporary fiction, always has a very strong sense of what is possible and what is not – hence the irony of Rushdie's using this story to suggest the power of love, rather than its weakness. Yet something is gained from that attempt and its defeat. The natural world takes on a splendid, if painful sweetness. This too we recognise, and our recognition is the token both of the myth's conviction and its seduction. We feel we inhabit the world it describes.

Do we expect our fiction, in whatever form it comes, to have powers of clarification and evocation, to thrill us by getting close to the grain of our inner life, our most intimate and enigmatic experiences; or do we wish it merely to end up proclaiming that famous one-word 'prophesy' Sal Paradise in *On the Road* imagines himself as bringing to his friends in a bar in downtown Denver: 'Wow!'? Again and again in *The Ground Beneath Her Feet*, Rushdie deploys the rhetoric of clear-sightedness. Relentlessly and accurately he satirises, 'the swallowing of various forms of gibberish that has replaced the exercise of intelligence'. But having satisfied readers, he hopes, that they are in the hands of the world's least credulous person, he then proceeds, equally relentlessly, to offer nothing more than the most muddled and spuriously mystical of melodramas, the very thing he had appeared to be satirising.

Admirably energetic as he is alarmingly approximate, here is our author towards the end of the book drawing on the work of one of the sharpest minds the world ever produced: Plato. Vina's father Shetty has just remarked that if Ormus really wants to be with his dead wife, the noble thing to do would be 'to shoot himself in the mouth'. Ever ready to instruct, narrator Rai remarks:

> Shetty doesn't know it, but he's echoing Plato. This is what the great philosopher has Phaedrus say in the *Symposium*'s first speech about love: *The gods honour zeal and heroic excellence towards love. But Orpheus . . . they sent back unfulfilled from Hades, showing him a phantom of the woman . . . because he seemed to them a coward . . . [who] didn't venture to die for the sake of love, as did Alcestis, but rather devised a means of entering Hades while still alive.* Orpheus, the despised citharode – the singer with the lyre or, let's say guitarist – the trickster who uses music and wiles to cross boundaries, between Apollo and Dionysus, man and nature, truth and illusion, reality and the imagination, even between life and death, was evidently not to austere Plato's taste. Plato, who preferred martyrdom to mourning, Plato the ayatollah of love.'

We shall pass over the bullying techniques of agglomeration

and inflation everywhere evident in this prose. Here it is the sheer rashness of Rushdie's writing that takes the breath away. I shall not presume to come to Plato's defence; the most cursory reading of the *Symposium*, witty, fluent, ever as precise as it is profound, will show how inappropriate these remarks are. In contrast, the imprecision of Rushdie's work – Alcestis is *not* a martyr – is, at this point, no more than we expected. Yet one would have thought that he would have hesitated a moment before the word 'ayatollah'. There at least, one would have expected a moment's attention, a truly pertinent comment. Not so. The temptation of the flourish is too much for him. Plato is the 'ayatollah of love'. At one point in *The Ground Beneath Her Feet*, a minor character speaks of myth as 'the software of universal consciousness'. Are we then to refer to Rushdie as 'the Bill Gates of mythology'? Or, since a good parallel should be reversible, can we from now on think of the ayatollah as the Plato of Islam?

We live in an age where initiation into the mysteries of a religion or cult has very largely been replaced by initiation into the notion that there is no such mystery into which to be initiated. As it turns out this may prove to be the hardest initiation of all into the most trying of mysteries. By making the double gesture of appearing clear-sighted and then filling his pages with supernatural incident and metaphysical muddle that could mean anything or nothing, Rushdie appeals to those who, while understandably unwilling to subscribe to any belief so well defined as to be easily knocked down, nevertheless yearn to have all the mystical balls kept perpetually spinning in the air before them. Closet New Agers will be thrilled. The potential readership is huge.

Surviving Giacomo

[Giacomo Leopardi]

His mother rejoiced when her children died in infancy. They would go straight to heaven and would not weigh upon the family budget. Faith and thrift would always be problems for Giacomo. His father, Count Monaldo Leopardi, had squandered the family fortune through 'generosity, pride, or folly' and was deprived by papal order of the right to handle money. Pious and penny-pinching, his wife, Marchesa Adelaide, took over the management of their estates. This was in 1803, on the dusty hills above the southern Adriatic, scorching in summer, freezing in winter. The noble couple were in their mid-twenties and their first-born son just five.

To assert offended manhood, Monaldo cultivated literary ambitions – an interminable production of bigoted and reaction-ary tracts – which it was felt could not lead to the same economic catastrophe as his previous sallies into politics and trade. Never-theless, he lavished considerable sums on building up what, for the very small town of Recanati, was a vast library of 25,000 volumes. Through this library he entered into a relationship with young Giacomo that was at once one of complicity, against Adelaide, and competition, with each other. For the next thirty years, when Giacomo the poet asked Monaldo the pamphleteer for money, Monaldo could make a point of surreptitiously conceding it to a fellow sufferer behind his wife's stiff back, or of informing his young rival that he would have to confront the formidable matriarch in person.

The story of Giacomo's youth spent entirely in his father's

library has assumed legendary status in the history of Italian literature. Rarely emerging to play with brothers and sister, the boy had no companions at all outside the family and no interests outside of books. By the age of ten he had mastered Latin, Greek, German and French. Hebrew and English would soon follow. Presumably destined for the priesthood, he received the tonsure at twelve and donned a monkish habit. His tutors were outstripped and admitted as much. Left to his own diligent if random devices, he produced philological commentaries, sonnets, tragedies, epigrams, philosophical dissertations, *A History of Astronomy*, a *Life of Plotinus*, and any number of translations from the classics. Adolescent self-consciousness was developed to the point that 'thinking about breathing', as Monaldo later wrote, 'he would have difficulty getting his breath, reflecting on the subtleties of urination he would be unable to pass water'. Much pacing to and fro was required before he could steal from himself 'a moment's inattention'.

All the same, when beautiful cousin Gertrude made a three-day visit with her much older husband, the boy did manage to fall in love. In a pattern that would repeat itself throughout his life, the lady paid him no attention and left without saying goodbye. Giacomo reacted with *A Diary of First Love* and a number of Petrarchan sonnets. When the effect wore off, he embarked on a translation of Hesiod's *Theogony*.

It was grotesque and in his late teens Giacomo at last awoke to find the outward sign of that grotesqueness. Under the priest's habit was a hunch, result of a long-untreated scoliosis. How could he not have seen what was happening? The study that had seemed the passport to his father's respect and the scholastic glory that must ensue had become his curse and set him apart for ever. Beset by asthma and constipation, insulted by street urchins, already aware that no woman would ever find him attractive, Giacomo was more and more often afflicted by a death wish he had felt since earliest infancy. From the age of eighteen on, his overriding obsession was escape.

Concomitant with this anguished awareness of lost youth came what Giacomo would refer to as his three 'conversions': literary, political and philosophical. From the arid erudition of his father he moved almost overnight to an appreciation of the value of beauty in poetry. Immediately, he set out on translations of the first book of *The Odyssey*, the second of the *Aeneid*. This at seventeen. A year later, he jettisoned Monaldo's blind defence of papal dictatorship and declared himself in favour of a united Italy. Immediately, he wrote a number of long, patriotic hymns.

Finally, at twenty-one, he abandoned his parents' and above all his mother's Christianity. Having once walked in superstitious dread of treading on the crosses formed by paving stones, he now discovered a world, as he put it, of 'solid nothingness'. In the cold light of reason, both religion and youthful illusion evaporated and happiness became 'forever unavailable'. Thus in 1819, in one of the most backward towns of the most backward state in a decidedly backward and obscurantist Italy, Giacomo Leopardi stepped tentatively into the world of the absurd, a mechanistic universe going nowhere and to no end.

Despite severe ophthalmia, another lifelong plague, the young man's busy pen was now occupied on three fronts: lyric poems, invariably as sad as they were beautiful; brief philosophical dialogues of bizarre whimsy and unparalleled pessimism; and finally the pages of his *Zibaldone*, or day book, a diary of his intellectual and emotional development that would ultimately run to almost three thousand pages. In more and more open conflict with his parents, he was now desperate to leave. But how could Monaldo let this boy with his weak health, great talents and dangerous views out into a world where liberalism and revolution were everywhere in the air? How could Adelaide even contemplate the unnecessary expense of lodging him anywhere but home? Giacomo attempted to acquire a passport and escape north with money stolen from the family safe but was foiled and humiliated. His dream of a 'land full of marvels' away from the 'living burial' of Recanati would have to wait until he was twenty-four when Monaldo finally relented and allowed his son to visit Adelaide's brother, Marchese Antici, in Rome.

Thus far the story of Giacomo Leopardi presents little problem for biographers. The family palazzo and above all the library where he grew up are still there to be visited. They present a small and sharply defined world in which the poet's youth and the dynamic of those relationships that shaped it are well documented in an abundance of letters and memoirs. Most of all the economy and direction of the story are obvious and our sympathies undivided. The frail, sensitive if, alas, ugly genius will finally escape his monstrous parents to spread his wings in the wider and more generous society of those splendid Italian cities that so inspired his English, French and German contemporaries.

It was not to be. Leopardi hated Rome, as later he would never be on anything but the most uneasy terms with Milan, Bologna, Florence and Naples. 'All the greatness of Rome,' he wrote to his sister Paolina, 'has no other purpose than to multiply the distances and numbers of steps you have to climb to see anyone at all.' The place was dirty and noisy, the people stupid. On his first day he met the elegant and erudite Abbot Cancellieri, a man not only well placed to introduce Giacomo into Roman society, but kind enough to have praised the young prodigy's philological studies in his own publications. 'A prick,' Giacomo wrote to his brother Carlo, 'an endless stream of gossip, the dullest and most despair-inducing man on earth'. But surely, the envious Carlo replied, in a big city 'there's always a pretty whore to look at'. This was true, but would the whores look at a sickly hunchback? 'The ugliest, crassest Recanati tart was better than all the streetwalkers of Rome,' came the poet's improbable retort. Despite winning the unqualified admiration of a number of scholars, and in particular the Prussian ambassador Niebuhr, Leopardi was soon longing to be home. Monaldo was delighted to have him back. Another week or two and the young man was desperate to leave again.

It is at this point that most biographers, and critics, begin to establish, as if in self-defence, a distance that will ultimately amount to a gulf between Leopardi's sublime poetry on the one hand and his profound pessimism and capricious behaviour on the other. Thus in *Leopardi, A Study in Solitude*, the only substantial biography in English, now reprinted after many years, Iris Origo remarks:

> There are two Leopardis: the poet and the man. The man, as he revealed himself in many of his letters and his diaries, was a querulous, tortured invalid, mistrustful of his fellow men, with a mind sometimes scornful and cantankerous and a heart intolerably sad and lonely. But to this unhappy man was granted a poet's gift: a capacity for feeling so intense and an imagination so sensitive and lively that he could perceive, in the most common sights of daily life, the 'heavenly originals' of which, according to Plato, all earthly objects are but copies.

In an essay that appeared in the *New York Review of Books* the scholar D.S. Carne-Ross wrote: 'much as one must often pity Leopardi, it is hard sometimes not to feel, with a certain exasperation, that he deliberately made bad worse, as though to prove a point about the inevitable wretchedness of existence'.

One of the consequences of taking this line is that Leopardi's poetry, and in particular the thirty-six lyric poems of the *Canti*, is to be elevated to the highest of pedestals ('English with all its riches has nothing to set beside the best of these poems,' says Carne-Ross), while the reflections of the prose dialogues collected as the *Operette morali*, or indeed of the quite extraordinary *Zibaldone*, are to be dismissed, or damned with faint praise.

65

Basing her remarks on an essay by Benedetto Croce, Origo writes: 'On the problems of life he [Leopardi] bestowed much thought, and he clothed that thought in fine language, but the conclusions which he reached cannot be said to possess any great novelty.' She then simplifies his vision thus: 'The universe, he says, is an enigma and an insoluble one; human life, when weighed in the balance, is an unhappy affair, and the more highly developed a man is in feeling and in intelligence, the less fitted he is to live happily. Such happiness as men do enjoy is founded upon "illusion".'

Albeit with some bet-hedging, Carne-Ross reaches the same conclusion. 'I doubt . . . if too much independent value should be claimed for his "philosophy". In an entirely honorable sense, it was rigged, as a poet's thinking often is, to serve his art.'

How vigorously Leopardi would have disagreed! Indeed he *did* disagree, for he frequently faced the same criticism during his lifetime. Praising the style of *Operette morali* as 'the finest prose in Italian this century', his arch-enemy, the supremely Catholic Niccolò Tommaseo nevertheless referred to Leopardi as 'a frog endlessly croaking "There is no God because I'm a hunchback, there is no God because I'm a hunchback"'. Dutifully, Origo documents Leopardi's standard response to such attacks: that critics should seek to confute his ideas (which actually are far from simple) rather than blame his deformity. But one has to turn to a very different kind of biography, Rolando Damiani's *All' apparir del vero*, (sadly unavailable in translation) to find the poet's most spirited rebuttal: on hearing, in 1834, that an article in a German review had once again ascribed his negative thinking to his desperate state of health, Leopardi wrote: 'it seems people have the same attitude to life that an Italian husband has to his wife: he needs to go on believing she is faithful even when all the evidence is to the contrary'.

The tension and ambiguity that everywhere galvanise Origo's fascinating biography spring from her attempt to reconcile an honest account of Leopardi's unhappy existence and corrosive thought with this same, as the poet saw it, banal but absolutely necessary desire to believe that 'life is a beautiful thing'. The irony she never quite grasps is that both the philosophy she largely ignores and the poetry she loves are inspired by Leopardi's prolonged meditation on the same contradictory impulses that are driving her pen as she seeks at once to tell her story truthfully and escape its implications unscathed. In short, as Giacomo saw it, Nature has endowed us with a reasoning faculty which inevitably pushes us towards an awareness of the utter insignificance of our existence, yet at the same time, and paradoxically, Nature also offers us considerable resources for putting that reasoning faculty to sleep, and in particular for inventing all kinds of grand ideas – national, religious, romantic and social – to keep the brutal truth at bay. Such ideas and the adventures that sprang from them were to be cultivated at all costs – hadn't Leopardi himself espoused the national cause, didn't he fall in love on three occasions, wasn't his very writing driven by a ludicrous ambition for literary glory? – yet he insisted to the end that such aspirations, and indeed all the fruits of the imagination, whether individual or collective, were 'illusions'. The bottom line would always be sickness and death. It is as if, sitting beside Coleridge as he wrote his '*Dejection*: an Ode', Leopardi had, yes, encouraged him to rediscover 'the beauty-making power of imagination', but then pointed out that whether he succeeded or not, he would all too soon be back with 'the inanimate cold world' again, and hence dejection. For 'nothing is more reasonable than boredom'. And after years of disillusionment and dejection, death could only be welcome.

Interestingly, it was a death that prompted Iris Origo to write her biography of Leopardi. As she emerges in her engaging autobiography, *Images and Shadows*, this rich and beautiful daughter of Berenson's Chiantishire is almost the last person you would expect to take a serious interest in Leopardi. True, her father dies young and her mother is neurotic and narcissistic to a degree – not the perfect childhood – but loving grandparents give a sense of solidity, the palatial family villa (originally built for Cosimo Medici) is full of famous friends and lively conversation. To top all, first love, when it comes, is wonderfully and romantically requited: Antonio has an Italian title, Iris has American cash. Who could ask for more? Together they buy an entire Tuscan valley and set about turning it into productive arable land with a system of farms run on the old *mezzadria* system where the peasants give half their produce to the *padrone*. Fascism offered subsidies for such developments. It was still possible at this point to imagine the regime was benevolent. Within the year, a son, Gianni was born. Inspired by a genuine spirit of philanthropy, underpinned by a successful marriage, the Origos' project progressed to the benefit of everyone and the pages of her account of those years turn to that scent of warm earth and crushed olives that has sold so many books to the idle dreamers of colder climes. Above all, Iris herself was overwhelmingly busy, resourceful, powerful, *happy*. 'I have never in my life found a day too long,' she tells us.

What on earth, you wonder, has such a woman to do with a man reputedly determined to be wretched, a man who never got further in love than holding a beloved's hand, or collecting autographs for her (how humiliating!), or playing go-between for a rival (even worse!), a man who changed his shirt only once a month, dribbled his food, smelt, ate on his own at ungodly hours, ogled courting couples from his bedroom window, accepted money for jobs he never meant to finish, ridiculed both the liberal vision of progress and the consolations of religion?

Giacomo refused to read the newspapers, but briefly in the summer of 1832, exactly 101 years before Origo began research on his biography, the poet did toy with the idea of launching a paper himself. It was to be called 'Le flaneur' – the time-waster.

Its selling point would be its complete lack of any 'positive ideas', 'non-political, non-philosophical, non-historical, non-fashionable, non-artistic, non-scientific . . .' Its imagined readership? Those 'tolerant of all that is futile'. But at the first hint of problems with the Florentine censors, Giacomo characteristically dropped his project. An entertaining daydream, it had served its purpose. What has the busy likes of Iris Origo to do with a man like this?

The terrible answer comes without warning in a chapter of *Images and Shadows* harmlessly entitled, 'Writing'. After explaining that the big Tuscan farm left little opportunity to pursue adolescent ambitions, Origo tells us, 'Then, in 1933, after Gianni's death, in an effort to find some impersonal work which would absorb at least part of my thoughts – I turned back to writing again.'

Her eight-year-old son has died. No narrative, no explanation. 'After Gianni's death . . . impersonal work'. But how impersonal? For what is Leopardi's great theme if not death, and in particular the death of young people, which is the cruellest unmasking of life's illusions.

> *nel fior degli anni estinta*
> *Quand'è il viver più dolce, e pria che il core*
> *Certo si renda come'è tutta indarno*
> *L'umana speme. A desiar colei,*
> *Che d'ogni affanno il tragge, ha poco andare*
> *L'egro mortal; ma sconsolata arriva*
> *La morte ai giovanetti . . .*

> (Cut off in the flower of my years
> When life is sweetest, and before the heart
> Can know how human hopes are all
> In vain. It isn't long before the afflicted
> Learn to call on she
> Who can save us from all affliction.
> But death comes inconsolable to the young . . .)

Cruelly, Origo has been dragged from her busy life to join Leopardi where he always was, or imagined himself to be, at death's door. Embarking for the first time in her life on a sustained project of scholarly research, she thus no doubt shared the experience that had been Giacomo's since adolescence, that of seeking distraction in reading or translation only to find that the content you were working on brought you inexorably back to the pain that led you to seek distraction in the first place. Of twelve children born to Giacomo's mother, Origo is bound to record in her opening chapter, only five survived, only one outlived her.

Impersonal or otherwise as her approach may be, Iris Origo certainly did sterling work. She sifted through a wealth of original sources and above all the vast *Zibaldone* to give us an account of Leopardi's life that still holds up today. What she loses to the overwhelmingly meticulous scholarship and acute psychological insight of a more recent biography like Damiani's, she makes up in the at-once eager but anxious nature of her engagement with the poet. Damiani, who edited and annotated the *Zibaldone*, is clearly at home with Leopardi's pessimism and entirely familiar with such minds as Schopenhauer and Nietzsche, Cioran and Beckett, to whom the Italian poet looks forward, familiar in short with that whole strand of negative Western thought that opposes to the enlightenment the simple reflection that 'knowledge has not helped us to live'. For Origo, in contrast, coming from a quite different tradition, Leopardi is a risk, indeed a peril, a dark sea she might never have plunged into had it not been for her son's death. She senses that Leopardi has more to say about that death than perhaps anyone else, but it is not something she is eager to focus on in her own writing. Recreating scenes of Recanati life from fragments in the poetry, she tends to the sentimental and picturesque; she also thrusts upon Leopardi's mature work a Platonism he entertained only briefly in his teens and attacked savagely in the *Operette*; and she is clearly relieved to record Giacomo's happier moments, notably sitting at café tables greedily tucking into ice creams as he watched the world go by. It is at these points that you feel Origo would be more at ease describing the colourful bustle of Italian street life than Leopardi's torturous lucubration. Yet faithfully she gives us the facts, she quotes the very darkest passages from *Zibaldone* and even steels herself for the story of Leopardi's unshriven death, aged thirty-eight.

> Five years before, on almost the last page of the *Zibaldone*, Leopardi had written: 'there are two truths which most men will never believe: one, that they know nothing, and the other, that they are nothing. And there's a third which proceeds from the second – that there is nothing to hope for after death.' This conviction, and with it a pride in rejecting 'all the vain hopes with which men comfort children and themselves, all foolish consolations', remained with him to the end.

The word 'pride' discreetly registers Origo's instinctive dissent.

Why is it that in a world long used to atheists and sceptics, Leopardi, more than any other writer I can think of, is still to be criticised for his negative vision? The answer, I suspect, will be the same as answers to such questions as: Why did the poet's contemporaries frequently seek to blame his atheism on evil influences, notably his early mentor, the revolutionary Pietro Giordani? Why were people constantly putting about the rumour that Giacomo had converted (to the extent at one point that some pro-papal tracts published by his father were widely assumed to be his own)? Why did a Jesuit priest publish a letter claiming to have led Giacomo to Christ? Or again, why were the *Operette morali* inscribed in the Vatican's Index of Prohibited Books and actually hunted down and destroyed after his death, while the *Canti*, which include the same ideas, were not? How can it be that *I libri dello spirito cristiano* (Books of Christian Spirit – a religious list within the Rizzoli group) published, as recently as 1996, a collection of the *Canti*, claiming that they are of Christian inspiration? Finally, how is it that in the still profoundly Catholic Italian education system, an apparent nihilist like Leopardi can be taught alongside Manzoni, the great pillar of Catholic achievement in modern Italian literature? Origo records Leopardi's meeting with Manzoni at the Gabinetto Vieusseux in 1827. *I promessi sposi* had just been published to ecstatic praise; an early edition of the *Operette morali* severely criticised. Manzoni, the handsome libertine turned fervent Christian, was surrounded by admirers; Leopardi, the erstwhile Christian turned atheist, sat alone. 'He had no good news to impart,' observes Origo.

The answer to all these questions lies, I believe, in the peculiar nature of Leopardi's achievement in the *Canti*. Towards the end of her autobiography, Origo apologises for having said nothing about her son Gianni's death. She 'cannot bear' to write about it, she tells us. Yet in a wealth of reflections on the inextricable psychological tangle between pain and pleasure, happiness and unhappiness, one of Leopardi's central intuitions was of the way suffering can be transformed, albeit briefly, precisely in the mental construct of language. In a note in the *Zibaldone*, he thus describes what was clearly his own aspiration as a poet:

> Works of [literary] genius have this intrinsic quality, that even when they capture exactly the nothingness of things, or vividly reveal and make us feel life's inevitable unhappiness, or express the most acute hopelessness . . . they are always a source of consolation and renewed enthusiasm.

Leopardi saw, that is, how it was possible to say two contradictory things, or rather to make two contradictory gestures simultaneously – despair, consolation – thus acting out a paradox he thought central to the core of human experience. But how was this done? Here is his single most famous poem, learned by heart by every Italian schoolboy.

A Silvia

Silvia, rimembri ancora
Quel tempo della tua vita mortale,
Quando beltà splendea
Negli occhi tuoi ridenti e fuggitivi
E tu, lieta e pensosa, il limitare
Di gioventù salivi?
Sonavan le quiete
Stanze, e le vie dintorno,
Al tuo perpetuo canto,
Allor che all'opre femminili intenta
Sedevi, assai contenta
Di quel vago avvenir che in mente avevi.
Era il maggio odoroso: e tu solevi
Così menare il giorno.
Io gli studi leggiadri
Talor lasciando e le sudate carte,
Ove il tempo mio primo
E di me si spendea la miglior parte,
D'in su i veroni del paterno ostello
Porgea gli orecchi al suon della tua voce,
Ed alla man veloce
Che percorrea la faticosa tela.
Mirava il ciel sereno,
Le vie dorate e gli orti,
E quinci il mar da lungi, e quindi il monte.
Lingua mortal non dice

Quel ch'io sentiva in seno.
    Che pensieri soavi,
Che speranze, che cori, o Silvia mia!
Quale allor ci apparia
La vita umana e il fato!
Quando sovviemmi di contanta speme,
Un affetto mi preme
Acerbo e sconsolato,
E tornami a doler di mia sventura.
O natura, o natura,
Perché non rendi poi
Quel che prometti allor? perché di tanto
Inganni i figli tuoi?

    Tu pria che l'erbe inaridisse il verno,
Da chiuso morbo combattuta e vinta,
Perivi, o tenerella. E non vedevi
Il fior degli anni tuoi;
Non ti molceva il core
La dolce lode or delle negre chiome,
Or degli sguardi innamorati e schivi;
Né teco le compagne ai dì festivi
Ragionavan d'amore.

    Anche peria fra poco
La speranza mia dolce: agli anni miei
Anche negaro i fati
La giovanezza. Ahi come,
Come passata sei,
Cara compagna del'eta mia nova,
Mia lacrimata speme!
Questo è quel mondo? questi
I diletti, l'amor, l'opre, gli eventi
Onde cotanto ragionammo insieme?
Questa la sorte dell'umane genti?
All'apparir del vero

Tu misera, cadesti: e con la mano
La fredda morte ed una tomba ignuda
Mostravi di lontano.

To Silvia

Silvia, do you remember still
The time of your mortal life
When beauty shone
In your fleeting eyes and smile
While brightly pensive you stepped
Up to the brink of youth?
The hushed rooms and
Outside the streets hummed
With your endless singing
As you bent over girlish tasks
Quite content with the hazy future
In your head. It was May,
That fragrant month,
And so you spent the day.
I'd stand up from the books
I loved, the pages I slaved over
Where my early years and the
Best part of me were spent
And from my father's balcony
Listen for the sound of your voice
And your fingers' swift back
And forth across the heavy loom.
I looked up at the blue sky,
The golden streets and gardens,
There the sea far away, here the high hill,
What I felt in my heart then
Mortal tongue cannot tell.

What happy thoughts, what
Hopes, what hearts we had Silvia!
How human life and
Fate seemed to us then!
When all that hope floods back
Now, I'm overcome,
Bitter beyond consolation
And weep once more my own misfortune.
Oh nature, nature,
Why won't you honour
What you promised then? Why play
Such cruel tricks on your children?

Before winter had withered the grass,
Baffled and beaten by secret sickness
You were dying, dear soul, didn't see
Your best years blossom forth,
Didn't hear the praise that melts
The heart, of your jet dark hair
The soft shy passion in your eyes;
Didn't sit with friends on Sundays,
Brooding over love.

And soon my dear hopes
Had perished too: my youth too
The fates denied me. Oh
How utterly
Past you are now,
Best friend of better times,
My long-lamented hope!
Is this that world? These
The pleasures, love, adventures
We talked about so much?
Is this every man's inevitable lot?
When the truth dawned
You faded wretchedly; and raising

A hand showed me cold death
In the distance and a dark grave.

What a strange opening that is: 'Silvia, do you remember still/
The time of your mortal life . . . ?' The girl is dead ten years and
more. How can we address her? What would it mean for her to be
Silvia if she did not remember her mortal life? Does the word
'still' suggest there might have been a period when she did
remember, but now she has forgotten? In the *Zibaldone* Leopardi
remarked that the mind takes pleasure from situations where it
comes up against sensory limitations, intellectual enigmas or
merely sensory vagueness, because it is then free to fill in what is
empty or inexplicable. His simplest development of the theme
comes in the poem 'L'infinito' where, with his view of the
landscape blocked by a small hill, the poet is free to conjure
infinite spaces behind. Imagined immensity then allows for the
mind's 'sweet shipwreck', an effect Leopardi was always eager to
achieve and is certainly looking for in this poem. At the same
time, though, teased as we may be by conundrums, we are never
allowed to forget that Silvia is dead, she died young, and that
there is no reasonable consolation for such a death.

Another note in the *Zibaldone* dwells at length on the curious
pleasure generated by anniversaries, however unhappy, or by
revisiting places where some important experience, however
negative, was had. The fact that the mind rehearses the memory
allows the event to relive, albeit as no more than a 'shadow',
giving us the illusion that not all has been lost. Thus his poems
frequently present a complex weave of present, past and above all
might-have-been. We look back on Silvia looking forward to the
future. She did not grow up and enjoy her lovers' praises, but
here we have all the beauty of imagining her doing so, or, even
better, of imagining her imagining. Emblematic of man's
insignificance as a peasant girl's death may be, Silvia nevertheless
becomes, through the poem, one of the most celebrated figures

of her time. Likewise the poet achieves the blessing of celebrity, if only for having described his wretchedness so beautifully. It is as if, after all these years, past and might-have-been can almost be made to merge into each other.

A delicate play of antitheses underpins this mix of lament and celebration. 'Life' is 'mortal' (but what else could it be?). The eyes are 'smiling', but 'fugitive'. Silvia is 'happy', but 'pensive'. The word 'limitare' sits ominously beside 'gioventù', and so on throughout the poem. Meanwhile, lexically and syntactically, Leopardi matches his temporal back and forth with a language, at once disarmingly intimate in its speaking voice and at the same time unapproachably distant in its archaisms and Latinate focusing. These are not archaisms that take us back to any one time, and certainly not to any pre-existing style. Rather they fuse with the voice to create something that is as timeless and as beautiful a might-have-been as Silvia's prospected amours.

It is this linguistic aspect of Leopardi's poetry that has so far defeated, as he himself foresaw, all attempts at felicitous translation. Subjects of great immediate emotion and infinite sadness are allowed to take on a quiescent coolness, as if remembered from some extraordinary and disembodied distance. Not only is youth recovered in the musing limbo of the mind but the whole extension of the Italian language is given a second if shadowy life. After all, as this poem reminds us, where had Leopardi spent his youth if not over archaic texts? The subtle deployment of the archaic is a reminder of youth, of lost youth, for Leopardi.

It is for this achievement of looking unflinchingly at the very worst and briefly recuperating it in a beautiful and breathless calm – the calm, as it were, of someone who has survived his own decease – that people come to Leopardi, perhaps especially a young woman who has lost her child. Yet Giacomo never allows us to forget that these poems are carefully constructed mental pleasures, short-lived illusions. A spoilsport by vocation, he frequently finishes a poem with '*l'apparir del vero*' (the dawning of the truth), that is, a tomb.

In 'Ginestra, o il fiore del deserto' he offers as an image of his art the scented broom that grows on the lava slopes of Vesuvius above a ruined civilisation. The past passion of human life is immensely, reassuringly distant. The broom flourishes and perfumes the air. But it will be the first to go, Leopardi tells us, when the lava flows again. His claim for the paradoxical effect of 'works of genius' – quoted above – concludes thus: 'even if they have no other subject than death, they give their reader back – at least for a little while – the life he has lost'. After 'the little while' is over, we are returned, of course, to the present – 'the least poetic of times', Leopardi observed. Deprived of the enchantment of the verse, the grim vision of life we have encountered and the death wish that lurks beneath it is once again open to attack. But since the experience of the *Canti* is so cherished – after all, a poem can be read and reread – the guns are turned on the *Operette*.

Irretrievably insomniac, he enjoyed a long acquaintance with the moon. Beneath the cold silver light it spread over so many of his verses, Giacomo is the wakeful shepherd, while the rest of humanity wallows in the stupor of unconsciousness. Servants were infuriated when he demanded breakfast in the afternoon, lunch at midnight. Seeking some form of employment that would allow him to sever the umbilical cord with home, he wandered uneasily from Milan to Bologna, Florence to Rome. There was always a good reason for turning down what was offered. 'I haven't even the strength to die,' he joked. Rejected by women ('my dear, he stank'), he struck up a passionate friendship with Antonio Ranieri, a handsome young Neapolitan, risking accusations of homosexuality to enjoy a vicarious experience of the man's tormented love affairs. With astonishing kindness, Ranieri and his sister looked after Giacomo in the last years in Naples. The sister talked to him about deodorants and hung his shirt out in the sun so that the washerwoman's nose might not be offended. Ranieri fought off a jeering crowd as the small hunchback tucked into one of his extra large ice creams. In 1837, an asthmatic fit 'took his virginity' as Ranieri put it, 'intact unto the grave'. He thus didn't live to see the happy moment, in 1839, when his mother Marchesa Adelaide would finally declare that she had accomplished her dream and restored the Leopardi fortunes to their former glory. 'God forgive him,' she would say when her first-born was mentioned. He had lost both his faith and a great deal of money.

Some eight years after publishing her biography, Iris Origo's dreams were shattered once again, this time by the collapse of the Fascist regime and the allied bombings. She took in displaced children, helped escaping British airmen, wrote an exciting war diary. But even after the carnage was over, the dream couldn't be recaptured, for now the collective illusion of communism had replaced that of fascism and the farmers would no longer accept the *mezzadria* system. It was distressing that their aspirations didn't fit in with those of the Origos. In 1952, Iris returned to her biography of Leopardi to make extensive revisions. A considerable amount of new material had come to light, she tells us. But one cannot quite quell the suspicion that she returned to Giacomo to savour once again his miraculous expression of all that she found intolerable to say, but could not sometimes help feeling.

The Hunter

[G.W. Sebald]

In the closing pages of Cervantes' masterpiece, at last disabused and disillusioned, a decrepit Don Quixote finds that there is nothing for him beyond folly but death. When giants are only windmills and Dulcinea a stout peasant lass who has no time for knights errant, life, alas, is unlivable. 'Truly he is dying,' says the priest who takes his confession 'and truly he is sane.' Sancho Panza breaks down in tears: 'Oh don't die, dear master! . . . Take my advice and live many years. For the maddest thing a man can do in this life is to let himself die just like that, without anybody killing him, but just finished off by his own melancholy.'

Centuries later, observing the loss of all illusion that he felt characterised the modern world, the melancholic Giacomo Leopardi wrote: 'Everything is folly but folly itself.' And again a hundred and more years on arch-pessimist Emil Cioran rephrased the reflection thus: 'The true vertigo is the absence of folly.' What makes Don Quixote so much luckier than Leopardi and Cioran, and doubtless Cervantes himself, is that, as the epitaph on his tombstone puts it, 'he had the luck . . . to live a fool and yet die wise'. What on earth would have become of such a sentimental idealist had he returned to his senses, as it were, a decade or two earlier?

Vertigo – as indeed Sebald's other works, *The Emigrants* and the *Rings of Saturn* – tells the stories of those who reach disillusionment long before the flesh is ready to succumb, men – they are always men – engaged in a virtuoso struggle to generate that minimum of folly, or we could call it love of life, or even

81

engagement, that will prevent them from dying 'just like that', 'finished off by their own melancholy'.

But perhaps I have got that wrong. Perhaps on the contrary we should say that Sebald's characters are men who ruthlessly suppress folly the moment it does, insistently, raise its wild head. So wary are they of engagement in life that actually they are morbidly and masochistically in complicity with melancholy and all too ready to be overwhelmed by it. There is a back and forth in Sebald's work between the wildest whimsy and bleakest realism. One extreme calls to the other: the illusions of passion, in the past; a quiet suicide, all too often, in the future. Mediating between the two, image both of his art and of what fragile nostalgic equilibrium may be available to his heroes, are the grainy black-and-white photographs Sebald scatters throughout his books. Undeniably images of *something*, something real that is, they give documentary evidence of phenomena that, as we will discover in the text, sparked off in the narrator or hero a moment of mental excitement, of mystery, or folly, or alarm. They are the wherewithal of an enchantment, at once feared and desired, and above all necessary for staying alive. Not even in the grainiest of these photos, however, will it be possible to mistake a windmill for a giant.

There are four pieces in *Vertigo*. All of them involve a back and forth across the Alps between northern Europe and Italy. The first is entitled 'Beyle, or Love is a Madness Most Discreet' and it is the only one to offer something like the whole trajectory of a life through passion and engagement to disillusionment and depression. By using what was in fact Stendhal's baptismal name, Marie Henri Beyle, Sebald alerts us at once, and far more effectively than if he had used the writer's pseudonym, to the extent to which identity is invented as well as given and thus involves continuous effort. Beyle created Stendhal, as Señor Quesada dreamed up Don Quixote. The identity was one with the folly, its most positive achievement perhaps. But that is not to say that Beyle, whoever he was, did not live on, as even Quesada re-emerged for extreme unction.

In his opening sentences Sebald loves to give us a robust cocktail of date, place and purposeful action. Thus the Beyle piece begins: 'In mid-May of the year 1800, Napoleon and a force of 36,000 men crossed the St Bernhard Pass . . .' And the second piece starts: 'In October 1980 I travelled from England . . . to Vienna, hoping that a change of place would help me get over a particularly difficult period of my life.' And the third: 'On Saturday the 6th of September, 1913, Dr K., the deputy Secretary of the Prague Workers' Insurance Company, is on his way to Vienna to attend a congress on rescue services and hygiene.'

It is so concrete, so promising! All too soon, however, and this is one of the most effective elements of comedy in Sebald's work, the concrete will become elusive, the narrative thrust is dispersed in a delta as impenetrable as it is fertile. Thus Beyle, who at the age of seventeen was with Napoleon on that 'memorable' crossing, finds it impossible, aged fifty-three, to arrive at a satisfactory recollection of events. 'At times his view of the past consists of nothing but grey patches then at others images appear of such extraordinary clarity he feels he can scarcely credit them.' He is right not to. His vivid memory of General Marchmont beside the mountain track wearing the sky-blue robes of a councillor must surely be wrong, since Marchmont was a general at the time and would thus have been wearing his general's uniform. Italo Calvino reports making a similar error when looking back on a battle fought with the *partigiani* against the Fascists: 'I concentrate on the faces I know best: Gino is in the piazza: a thickset boy commanding our brigade, he looks into the square and crouches shooting from a balustrade, black tufts of beard round his tense jaw, small eyes shining under the peak of his Mexican hat. I know that Gino had taken to wearing a different hat at the time but . . . I keep seeing him with that big straw hat that belongs to a memory of the previous summer.' If crossing the St Bernhard with an army was, as Sebald concludes his opening sentence, 'an undertaking that had been regarded until that time as next to impossible', remembering that undertaking, even for a man with a mind as formidable as Stendhal's, turns out to be not only 'next to' but truly impossible.

This is hardly news. That the difficulty of every act of memory has a way of drawing our attention to the perversity of the mind and the complicity between its creative and corrosive powers is a commonplace. '*And the last remnants memory destroys,*' we read beneath the title of one of the pieces in *The Emigrants*. No, it is Sebald's sense of the role of this act of fickle memory in the overall trajectory of his characters' lives that makes the pieces in *Vertigo* so engaging and compelling.

Beyle/Stendhal's life as described by Sebald is as follows. Crossing the Alps the adolescent dragoon is appalled by the dead horses along the wayside, but later cannot remember why: 'his impressions had been erased by the very violence of their impact'. Arriving in Italy he sees a performance of Cimarosa's *Il matrimonio segreto*, falls wildly in love with a plain if not ugly prima donna, overspends on fashionable clothes, and finally 'disburdens' himself of his virginity with a prostitute. 'Afterwards,' we are told, 'he could no longer recall the name or face of the *donna cattiva* who had assisted him in this task.' The word 'task' appears frequently and comically in *Vertigo*, and most often in Thomas Bernhard's sense of an action that one is simply and irrationally compelled to do, not a social duty or act of gainful employment.

Despite contracting syphilis in the city's brothels, Beyle cultivates 'a passion of the most abstract nature' for the mistress of a fellow soldier. She ignores him, but eleven years on, deploying an 'insane loquacity', he convinces her to yield on the condition that he will then leave Milan at once. Exhilarated by his conquest, Beyle is overcome by melancholy. He sees *Il matrimo-nio segreto* again and is entirely unimpressed by a most beautiful and brilliant prima donna. Visiting the battlefield at Marengo, the discrepancy between his frequent imaginings of the heroic battle and the actual presence of the bleached bones of thousands of corpses, generates a frightening vertigo, after which the shabby monument to the fallen can only make a mean impression. Again he embarks on a romantic passion, this time for the wife of a Polish officer. His mad indiscretion leads her to reject him, but he retains a plaster cast of her hand (we see a photograph) that was to mean 'as much to him as Metilde herself could ever have done'.

Sebald now concentrates on Beyle's account of his romantic attachment to one Madame Gherardi, a 'mysterious not to say unearthly figure', who may in fact have been only (only!) a figment of his imagination. Usually sceptical of his romantic vision of love, one day this 'phantom' lady does at last speak 'of a divine happiness beyond comparison with anything else in life'. Overcome by 'dread' Beyle backs off. The last long paragraph of the piece begins: 'Beyle wrote his great novels between 1829 and 1842, plagued constantly by the symptoms of syphilis . . .'

The trajectory is clear enough. The effort of memory and of writing begins, it seems, where the intensities of romance and military glory end. It is the 'task' of the disillusioned, at once a consolation and a penance. In 1829 Beyle turned forty-seven. Sebald turned forty-seven in 1990, the year in which *Vertigo*, his first 'novel', was published. Coincidences are important in this writer's work. Why?

The Beyle piece is followed by an account of two journeys Sebald himself made in 1980 and 1987 to Venice, Verona and Lake Garda (all places visited by Stendhal). The third piece describes a similar journey apparently made by Franz Kafka in the autumn of 1913, exactly a hundred years after the French writer reports having visited the lake with the mysterious Madame

Gherardi. As Stendhal was referred to only by his baptismal name and not the name he invented, so Kafka, in what is the most fantastical and 'poetic' piece in the book, is referred to only as K., the name used for the protagonists of *The Trial* and *The Castle*. Or not quite. In fact Sebald refers to him as 'Dr K., deputy secretary of the Prague Workers' Insurance Company', thus bringing together Kafka's 'professional' existence as an insurance broker and his fictitious creation, begging the question of the 'identity' of the man who lies between the two.

Beginning in Verona, the last piece, 'Il ritorno in patria', shows the author interrupting 'my various tasks' to undertake a journey that will take him back to the village of his childhood in Alpine Bavaria and finally on to England where Sebald has his 'professional' existence as a university lecturer. In all three of these pieces the romantic and military adventures of the young Henri Beyle are very much behind our now decidedly melancholic characters, and yet they are ever present too. As if between Scylla and Charybdis, when Dr K. sits down to eat at the Sanatorium on Lake Garda, it is to find an ageing general on one side and an attractive young lady on the other. Returning to the building where he grew up, Sebald remembers his boyhood longing for the company of the pretty waitress in the bar on the ground floor, and the fact that he was forbidden to visit the top floor because of the mysterious presence of a 'grey *chasseur*', presumably a ghost, in the attic. Satisfying his curiosity forty years on, the narrator climbs to the attic to discover a tailor's dummy dressed in the military uniform of the Austrian *chasseurs*. It is hard to steer a course across the wild waters generated by these two somehow complicit follies. Was it not, after all, a combination of distressed damsels and military grandeur that did for Don Quixote? *Vertigo* offers a number of images of ships heading for shipwrecks.

But to the question of coincidences. In the second piece, entitled 'All'estero', we are introduced to a character who could not be further from Sebald's usually melancholic type, Giovanni

Casanova. So far we have heard how the writer, in deep depression, travels from England to Vienna, falls into a state of mental paralysis and is on the brink of becoming a down-and-out, when in desperation he sets out for Venice, a city so labyrinthine that 'you cannot tell what you will see next or indeed who will see you the very next moment'. One of the things he sees in Venice of course is the Doge's Palace, which causes him to think of Casanova.

With admirable reticence, Sebald has given us no reason for the cause of his depression, but if only because we have just read the Beyle piece – and there are various tiny hints scattered here and there – we suspect that romance is at least part of the problem, or, as Dr K. will think of it in the following piece: the impossibility of leading 'the only possible life, to live together with a woman, each one free and independent'. Just to see the name Casanova, then, to think of that great seducer and endlessly resourceful schemer, generates a fierce contrast. Yet even Casanova experienced a period of depression and mental paralysis. When? When, like some hero of Kafka's, he was imprisoned without explanation in the Doge's Palace. And how did he escape? With the help of a coincidence.

In order to decide on what day he would attempt to break out of his cell, Casanova used a complicated random system to consult the *Orlando Furioso*, thus, incredibly, happening on the words: 'Between the end of October and the beginning of November'. The escape was successful. Casanova fled to France, where he later invented for himself the identity Chevalier de Seingalt. But just as remarkable as this propitious consultation of the *Orlando Furioso* is the fact that 31 October turns out to be the very day upon which our author finds himself in Venice. Sebald is amazed, alarmed, fascinated.

Most evident outcropping of the underlying mysteriousness of our existence, coincidence, or uncanny repetition, seems to possess the power, at once comic and alarming, of galvanising the paralysed melancholic, jerking him out of his inertia. It is as if, disillusioned to the point where certain follies have become unthinkable (and contemporary Europe, as Sebald showed in *The Emigrants*, has good reason for being thus disillusioned), we can only be set in motion by a fascination with life's mysteries, the which are simply forced upon us in all sorts of ways. Between, or perhaps after, passion and glory lies the uncertain resource of curiosity, the recurring emotions of amazement and alarm. Any act of remembering will offer a feast.

Towards that midnight between October and November, Sebald rows out on the Venetian lagoon with an acquaintance who points out the city incinerator, the fires of which burn in perpetuity, and explains that he has been thinking a great deal about death and resurrection. 'He had no answers,' Sebald writes, 'but believed the questions were quite sufficient to him.' It is an echo, conscious or otherwise, of Rilke's advice to his 'young poet' to 'have patience with everything unresolved and try to love the questions themselves'. Rilke was another German writer who had considerable problems both with military academies and with love.

But it would be a mistake to imagine that Sebald presents coincidence in a positive light. Extraordinary parallels may, briefly, release the paralysed mind from its cell, get it sorting through old diaries, or tracking down books in libraries, or comically attempting on a bus, as in Sebald's case, to take photographs of twin boys who resemble exactly the adolescent Kafka, but they do this in the way an alarm or a siren might. There is a destructive side to coincidence. It has a smell of death about it. What was the night 'between the end of October and the beginning of November', if not the night before All Saints' Day, *I morti*, the Day of the Dead?

Why is this? To 'coincide' is 'to occupy the same place or time', says *Chambers Dictionary*, 'to correspond, to be identical'. The coincidence that Stendhal, Kafka and Sebald all take similar trips at similar times of year, the first two exactly a century apart, may set curiosity in motion. It also removes uniqueness from these events; the recurrence diminishes the original, replaces it, falsifies it, the way Beyle reports finding his memories of landscapes destroyed by their painterly representations, the way even an old photograph may be considered as stealing something of its original. Here we are approaching the core of Sebald's vision, the spring at once of his pessimism, comedy and lyricism. Engagement in the present inevitably involves devouring the past. Waking up in his Venice hotel on 1 November, remarking on the silence, Sebald contrasts it to the ceaseless surging of traffic he hears in the hotels of other cities, the endless oceanic roar of cars and trucks released wave upon wave from traffic lights. He concludes his description: 'For some time now I have been convinced that it is out of this din that the life is being born which will come after us and will spell our gradual destruction, just as we have been gradually destroying what was there long before us.' To be set, with Casanova, in motion, is to be returned to the business of destruction. The *chasseur*, or hunter, he who consumes his own sport (and what was Casanova if not a hunter?), is a recurring figure in this book. Occasionally Sebald hears an arrow whistle past an ear.

It is uncanny, on reading a work that makes so much of coincidences, to find it coinciding in unsettling ways with one's own life. Enviably adept at bringing together images and anecdotes that will deliver his vision, Sebald now tells us of his experiences in Verona, the town where I have lived for more than twenty years. Eating in a gloomy pizzeria, he is unsettled by the painting of a ship in peril on stormy seas. Trying to distract himself he reads an article in the paper about the so-called 'caso Ludwig'. For some years a string of local murders were accompanied by the claims of a group calling itself Ludwig. Some of the victims were prostitutes. There were also various incendiary attacks on discotheques, which the murderers felt to be dens of sin. Again the sexual and the military seem to have combined in the most disturbing fashion. How could Sebald not be appalled by the macabre German connection? And when the waiter brings his bill, he reads in the small print (again we have a reproduction) that the restaurant owner is one 'Carlo Cadavero', which is as much as to say, Charles Corpse. This is too much and the author flees on the night train to Innsbruck.

Aside from the fact that I was able to look up Carlo Cadavero's name in the Verona phone book, what struck me as uncanny was a comment from later in this piece when, returning to Verona seven years on, Sebald hears how the two adolescents, Wolfgang Abel and Marco Furlan, who created this terrible identity Ludwig, a sort of negative two-man Don Quixote, were tried and imprisoned. He remarks that although the evidence against them was 'irrefutable', 'the investigation produced nothing that might have made it possible to comprehend a series of crimes extending over almost seven years'.

Irrefutable? It would have been about the same time as Sebald's second trip that, while carrying out English oral exams at the University of Verona, I found myself looking at the ID of a young woman whose surname was Furlan. Seeing my eyebrows raise, she said, 'Yes, I am his sister. And he is innocent.' The exam was a test of conversational skills and Signorina Furlan went on to pass it in exemplary fashion explaining to me with the utmost conviction that the whole thing was absurd and her brother the sweetest most normal person on earth. Despite the irrefutable evidence, she believed this, as no doubt the sisters of those who later commit war crimes believe in all honesty that they are growing up in the most normal of families. They are. Not for nothing is Sebald's writing frequently set alight with images of terrible conflagrations that inexplicably consume everything, leaving the world to start again from under a veil of ash. Never mentioned, Shiva presides.

The time has come to say something about this writer's

extraordinary prose, without which his rambling plots and ruminations would be merely clever and disturbing. Like the coincidences he speaks of, it is a style that recovers, devours and displaces the past. He has Bernhard's love of the alarming superlative, the tendency to describe states of the most devastating confusion with great precision and control. But the touch is much lighter than Bernhard's, the instrument more flexible. Kafka is present here too, perhaps from time to time Walser, and no doubt others as well. But all these predecessors have been completely digested, destroyed and remade in Sebald and above all in the magnificent descriptions which mediate so effectively between casual incident and grand reflection. One suspects too that Michael Hulse's translation, which possesses a rare internal coherence of register and rhythm, is itself the product of a long process of digestion and recasting, a wonderful, as it were, coincidence. Some of the English is breathtaking. All the same, the most effective moments are often the more modest stylistically. Here is the author in a railway carriage with two beautiful women; knowing what we know of him, any approach to them is impossible, yet how attractive they are in their mystery!

Outside in the slanting sunlight of late afternoon, the poplars and fields of Lombardy went by. Opposite me sat a Franciscan nun of about thirty or thirty-five and a young girl with a colourful patchwork jacket over her shoulders. The girl had got on at Brescia, while the nun had already been on the train at Desenzano. The nun was reading her breviary, and the girl, no less immersed, was reading a photo story. Both were consummately beautiful, both very much present and yet altogether elsewhere. I admired the profound seriousness with which each of them turned the pages. Now the Franciscan nun would turn a page over, now the girl in the colourful jacket, then the girl again and then the Franciscan nun once more. Thus the time passed without my ever being able to exchange a glance with either the one or the other. I therefore tried to practise a like modesty, and took out *Der Beredte Italiener*, a handbook published in 1878 in Berne, for all who wish to make speedy and assured progress in colloquial Italian.

Only Sebald, one suspects, would study an out-of-date phrase book while missing the chance to speak to two attractive ladies. The determinedly old-fashioned aura that hangs about all his prose is part and parcel of his decidedly modern version of non-engagement. Yet, from the 'insane loquacity' of the romantic Beyle to the charming picture in the book's last piece of the schoolboy Sebald enamoured of his teacher and 'filling my exercise books with a web of lines and numbers in which I hoped to entangle Fraulein Rauch forever', few writers make us more aware of the seductive powers of language. Sebald's literary enticements seek to achieve an intimacy that will not be so destructive as other follies: the direct encounter, the hunter's knife. This truly is a 'madness most discreet'.

All of which leads us to the only possible objection that I can imagine being raised against this remarkable author. That to succumb to his seduction is to resign oneself to more of the same: the broken lives, the coincidences, these unhappy men and enigmatic women. Is it a problem? With his accustomed blend of slyness and grim comedy, Sebald tackles the issue himself in a section from the last piece of *Vertigo*. Sitting in the hotel in the village of his childhood, he observes a gloomy painting depicting woodcutters at work and recalls that the artist Hengge was famous for his pictures of woodcutters: 'His murals, always in dark shades of brown, were to be seen on the walls of buildings all around W. and the surrounding area and were always of his favoured motifs.'

The author sets out to tramp around the surrounding woods and villages to rediscover all these paintings, finding them 'most unsettling', which is to say, for Sebald, good, since only what is unsettling attracts his attention, heightens sensibility, warns of life's dangers, recuperates its horrors in pathos. He then gives us the following comment on Hengge's tendency always to paint the same subject, ending with a moment of alarming but also amusing vertigo, that dizzying empty space that Sebald finds at the core of every intensity.

Hengge the painter was perfectly capable of extending his repertoire. But whenever he was able to follow his own artistic inclination, he would paint only pictures of woodcutters. Even after the war, when for a variety of reasons his monumental works were no longer much in demand, he continued in the same vein. In the end, his house was said to have been so crammed with pictures of woodcutters that there was scarcely room for Hengge himself and death, so the obituary said, caught him in the midst of a work showing a woodcutter on a sledge hurtling down into the valley below.

As long as Sebald shows this kind of resourcefulness, then my only regret, when his task obliges him to repeat himself, will be the tendency of the new book to eclipse the old.

Different Worlds

A bilingual student of mine made the following observation. During a period of study in England, she had become an admirer of Milan Kundera, reading his work in English. Later, back in Italy, she had picked up an early novel of his, in Italian this time, that she didn't know. She remarked: 'It was only when I was three-quarters of the way through that I realised it was the same novel I had read first of all in England. I knew the plot was the same of course, but the book was so completely different that I was convinced it couldn't be the one I had already read.'

Checking recently through the Italian translation of an early novel of my own, a *noir* I suppose you would call it, scribbled in my second year in Italy, I was disturbed to find the following remark. The hero, a young Englishman in Italy who is about to turn to a life of crime, recognises that this has something to do with the change of language.

> . . . the only thing he had truly gained these last two years was the ability to speak a foreign language near perfectly and the curious freedom that ability now appeared to give him in the way he thought. As if he had shifted off rails. His mind seemed to roam free over any and every possibility. He must make a big effort always to think in Italian as well as to speak it (certainly he had been thinking in Italian when he stole the document case). It could be a way out of himself, he thought, and out of the trap they had all and always wanted him to fall into.

I wrote this – and promptly forgot it – in my late twenties, some years before I started translating anything with literary pretensions and many years before I began to read more seriously about language and linguistics. In the meantime, however, I have discovered the Italian proverb, '*Inglese italianizzato, inglese indiavolato*', which would have been such an appropriate quotation to have placed on the title page. Just as that proverb translates poorly into English, so my comment on the hero's sense of moral liberty in a foreign language, which seemed convincing enough in the original English, appears much less so in the Italian translation, where the reader is doubtless all too aware that his language is drenched in Catholic morality. The liberty Italian gave my hero had to do with its novelty, his unawareness of its implications, his being uninitiated in the culture it supports.

What I want to do here is to ask if there is any useful connection to be made between my bilingual student's surprise on reading Kundera in a different language, and my hero's perception that his appropriation of the Italian language would open the way to his appropriation of other people's property. And again whether there is a connection between these two events – one real, one fictional – and my own growing conviction that a very great deal of literature, poetry and prose can only be truly exciting and efficacious in its original language. It is a conviction that goes hand in hand with my decision not to write any more in Italian, never to translate into Italian, and never to translate poetry in any direction at all, except perhaps to put beside the original as a crib. This is a personal decision I should stress, not a prescription.

It is amusing, of course, that my student should have discovered the shock of the difference between the same text in different languages, with, of all people, Milan Kundera. For perhaps no other contemporary writer has been so ferociously attentive to the translations of his own work, nor dedicated himself to such scathing polemics at the expense of lazy and 'unfaithful' translation, polemics underwritten, it sometimes seems, by a belief in the possibility of a near identity between original and translation. Kundera speaks of having left a publisher because he changed semicolons into full stops. He speaks of a natural tendency of translators to reject repetition, to use richer and more literary vocabulary where the original text was lean and simple, and above all to return all 'stylistic transgression' to the most conventional prose.

Kundera is not alone, of course, in finding such shortcomings in translations, nor in identifying an author's stylistic transgression with his originality and indeed the *raison d'être* of his work. Explaining his own habitual use of repetition, D.H. Lawrence remarked: 'the only answer is that it is natural to the author'. Less defensively, Proust spoke of style as 'the transformation that the author's thought imposes on reality', suggesting an essential equivalence of style and vision. In this regard, I suspect we would all agree that the mark of a 'poetic prose' is its consistent and internally coherent distance both from what is recognisably conventional and indeed from the creative styles of other authors. It has its meaning, that is, within a matrix of texts from each of which it establishes its distance. We would thus tend to accept Kundera's claim that, 'For a translator, the supreme authority should be the author's personal style.' And presumably then his complaint, 'But most translators obey another authority, that of the conventional version of "good French"' (French being the specific case he is referring to). We might then go on to suspect, as Kundera clearly does, that if we find a work so radically different in different languages, it is because the translator has let us down.

But why are these translators so perversely obtuse? Is their conventionalising tic, as Kundera would have it, an occupational hazard, like the gravedigger's insensitivity, the politician's ambiguity? Or could it be that the recognition and reproduction of transgression is not, as it turns out, such a simple thing at all, not merely a question of accepting some unusual punctuation and repeating a word where the author does? Kundera does not discuss the fact that since the conventions – social, moral and linguistic – of any two cultures and languages may be, and usually are, profoundly different, any transgression of them is not absolute in nature, but has meaning only in relation to the particular expectations it disappoints. It needs the context of the conventions it subverts. Notoriously, it is in those places where poetic prose deviates from standard usage, establishing a personal style and creating meaning through its distance from something else, that translation becomes tormented if not impossible. For the 'something else' in French is not the same as the 'something else' in Czech.

Thus when Kundera writes: 'Partisans of flowing translation often object to my translators: "that's not the way to say it in German (in English, in Spanish, etc.)!" I reply: "It's not the way to say it in Czech either!"', he is being ingenuous. Translating poetic prose, and even more so poetry, means creating the miracle of the 'same difference' from different and sometimes potentially antithetical conventions: as if the transgression of a sixteenth-century Hindu widow in attempting to escape suttee could be made equivalent to that of a twentieth-century Scottish Moslem refusing to obey her husband's order not to go out to work.

The rare bilingual person, the person most thoroughly grounded in two distinct conventions, is the person most likely to be struck by the utter difference of the same text in their two languages. They are more keenly aware of the distinct value structures implied by the languages and the subversive force of whatever differences from convention are there established. Those who have merely learned another language, however well, are not so easily disorientated. They are more like my cheerfully criminal protagonist who shakes off the conventions and taboos implicit in his native tongue the better to enjoy the freedom of what is experienced, at least at first, as not much more than a delightful code, a mental playground. The only thing that can be subverted for this person is the morality he was brought up with and the language that is its vehicle.

Lawrence's novel *Women in Love* is an account of the felt necessity to escape a series of conventions which have outlived their usefulness. The pressures of convention are dramatised in relationships, but Lawrence immediately recognises language as the cement of convention. 'It depends what you mean,' remarks Ursula, on the first page, making a semantic problem of her sister's seemingly innocent question, 'don't you really want to get married?' I have long taught this book to Italian students by inviting them to compare passages of the original with the Italian translation, identifying the places where the two texts part company, and then trying to establish links between those departures. Since the translator is more than competent, these inevitably occur where the original prose is particularly transgressive: 'Birkin shut himself together,' Lawrence remarks. 'Gudrun shrank cruelly from this amorphous ugliness.' Or again: 'she was destroyed into perfect consciousness'. Or of Ursula: 'she was free, in complete ease'. Or: 'they could forget perfectly'. In each case, Lawrence distorts normal usages to suggest a complex psychology, and often to gesture to an underlying pattern of thought that is peculiarly his own. The Italian translation shrinks from the oxymoron of 'shrank' suggesting fear and withdrawal, followed by 'cruelly' suggesting aggression; it has no answer to Lawrence's subversion of 'pulled himself together' into 'shut himself together', it does not know what to do with the aberrant 'into' after the verb 'destroy', nor does it catch the oddness of 'in ease' instead of 'at ease', or the peculiarity of 'forgetting' – but what? – 'perfectly'. (The translations, in entirely standard Italian, are: '*Birkin si chiuse in se stesso*', '*Gudrun rabbrividì ferita dalla bruttezza informe*', '*dilaniata, in uno stato di lucidità perfetta*',

99

'*libera e totalmente a suo agio*', '*Erano immersi in un perfetto obblio*').

But those who know Italian, and many who do not, will appreciate how difficult it is to recreate such a style which gains its meanings from idioms and usages only hinted at in the original and unavailable in the translator's language. What's more, however unusual Lawrence's English, it should be noted that, in these examples at least, it flows wonderfully. It deviates from standard English, but is always attentive to the rhythms of English prosody. The unusual locution 'destroyed into perfect consciousness', for example, draws on the syntactical pattern of 'turned into', 'changed into', 'transformed into', introducing a semantic shock with the word 'destroyed' but keeping the same structure intact. Likewise, the preposition 'in' is separated from 'ease' by 'complete' to avoid the jarring of 'in ease' as opposed to 'at ease', thus creating the expectation of entirely standard usages such as 'in complete liberty', 'in complete harmony', only to surprise us with 'ease'.

Hence, to go back to Kundera, his suggestion that it is the 'partisans of flowing translation' who are hostile to creative and original writing is again ingenuous. Lawrence's prose flows well enough and presumably one would wish to be faithful to that fluency. It is part of his style. It is natural to the author. The problem is that the author is deviating from English in a manner, he has seen, that English allows, perhaps even suggests. In the same way, his characters find unconventional solutions which society, though not sanctioning, may well have hinted at. They are the solutions of people escaping from these particular conventions, not some notional idea of convention in general. Indeed, by living on its margins, Lawrence's characters define the society they wish to escape, as his own work defines the conventional novel he no longer wishes to write. To put it another way, when writing in English, there is no way of being entirely outside Englishness (or American-ness, or whatever the underlying linguistic context may be).

At the end of *Women in Love*, when one of the protagonists chooses the most drastic form of escape by walking out into the Alpine snows to die, Lawrence remarks on how close he was to a path that led over the Alps into Italy. 'Would that have been a way out?' he asks. 'No, it would only have been a way in again.' My contention is that translation itself is always 'a way in again': anything we write in a translation will always be understood in terms of the world, the conventions, the general literary context of the language we are working into, usually our native tongue. To imagine one can transport transgressions or deviations from other conventions and reproduce them in the same way and in the same place in the translation, thus generating the same meaning, is to be dangerously naive. So it happens that, rather than embarking on a transgression that in their own language would come across as no more than an oddity, many translators feel obliged to revert to the conventional. This hardly seems perverse. It does, however, have serious repercussions for our understanding of the status of a translated text.

I came to Italy at twenty-five, translated commercial and technical material for several years, then moved on to translating novels and I suppose we could say creative and transgressive prose in my early thirties. In those days, when choosing whether to accept a translation or not, I went very much on the question of what I call voice. If I felt I could mimic the voice of this prose in English, I would accept the book. If not, not. Since money was an important factor at that time, I should stress that these decisions did not always coincide with taste. I sometimes felt that, alas, I could not mimic a book I liked and would have to turn it down, or that I could manage a book I didn't like and, to make ends meet, would do well to translate it. Only years later, reading Goethe, and then Humboldt, did I come across the idea of 'elective affinity'. One can have an affinity with something one doesn't like, just as one can find areas of one's own personality less than desirable.

In my first translations, when it came to faithfulness, it seemed enough to me to shadow in my English, so far as I could understand it, the text's relationship with its own language. Later, however, as my knowledge of Italian and above all Italian literature broadened and deepened, I became aware that my understanding of texts I had translated in the past was being altered by my growing appreciation of the context in which they had been written. My translation, while attractive, could not, within an English context, transmit many of the book's gestures. On the contrary, the books would be understood in relation to an English literary matrix, perhaps suggesting meanings not apparent or even remotely intended in the original. This does not mean I would now translate these books very differently, only that I would be more aware of the various areas of loss. On the one hand, then, long immersion in another culture brings empowerment – we understand things better – on the other, it becomes a handicap – we begin to doubt whether some texts are translatable at all. Perhaps I am approaching my bilingual student's perception of absolute difference.

While I was working on my first literary translations and immediately before my first novel in English was accepted for publication, I wrote a novel in Italian with the odd title, *I nani di domani*, which, literally translated, means 'Tomorrow's Dwarves'. Unlike any of my other novels, this was a straightforwardly rumbustious comedy, an innocuous version of the evasion that characterises the English teacher turned criminal I mentioned earlier on. For both of us, the escape from English was an escape from moral seriousness. I was pleased with what I'd done, proud of having managed to write in Italian, albeit with a great deal of help from my wife, and began to send the typescript around, but although an agent took the book on, it wasn't published. I hazarded a translation into English, but with every sentence the book shed its charm. Indeed, it seemed infinitely more difficult to translate than the work of other writers. The reason, perhaps, was that the driving energy of the book had been the evasion of writing in Italian. I could not be interested in this material in English. Fifteen years on, a reputable house offered to publish the novel. They declared it charming, even hilarious. I went back and read it. What charm it had lay entirely in its naivety. Its frequent deviations from standard Italian were as innocuous and random as its satire of provincial life was superficial and caricatured. I felt it would be best not to publish it since it represented neither what I feel now nor even what I truly felt then. Its real meaning was its escape from something else, something the Italian reader wouldn't be able to understand because it wasn't available in the text: Englishness. Ironically, at about the same time, the early *noir* describing a character's move into crime sparked off by his transplantation into another culture was also accepted. This book, *Cara Massimina*, I am more or less happy with. It presents that evasion of a new language within the moral framework of the old.

I mention this episode because it offers the opportunity to make two reflections: first that, aside from economic reasons, a writer will change language successfully only when the particular aesthetic he has drives him to it. Not otherwise. One can see how, obsessed as he was by the compulsive nature of language, our lack of individual control over it and its distance from our experience of reality, a writer like Beckett would choose to work in a second language where any alienation he might feel, or lack of expertise he might fear, would play to his poetic. Joyce, on the contrary, whose project was exactly the opposite of Beckett's – an attempt to use all the resources of language to recover our experience of place and time, to make the text, as the young Beckett described it, 'not about something, but that something itself' – remained anchored, despite all his experiments and all his years abroad, to Dublin and to English.

The second reflection that arises out of the otherwise trivial episode of my Italian novel, is that the very notion of 'stylistic transgression' may have a very different value in different cultures. *I nani di domani* was accepted because its trangressions, even when intended and aimed at some particular target, could nevertheless be seen as the amusing shortcomings of the learner, of one seeking to become an initiate on the same level as the reader. In this sense, far from being subversive, the book was actually reinforcing convention. And Italian is a language where there has been very little seriously transgressive prose of the Lawrence or Beckett variety, and much extremely attractive writing within generally accepted, and in the end by no means despicable, conventions. This, after all, is a country where one of the leading satirical magazines will still reject an article because it too aggressively attacks Catholic sensibilities, a country where a famous writer and translator like Elio Vittorini could openly defend the radical cuts and changes he made to Lawrence's work on the grounds that not to make them would 'damage the beauty of the prose'. Certainly – for example – there is nothing transgressive that I can see in the Italian translations of Kundera's work.

Italy is thus a country with very different sensibilities from England, where these days a novel with even the most modest literary pretensions is obliged to be openly transgressive at the linguistic level, something that has led to the tedious multiplication of idiosyncrasies and the wholehearted, often uncomprehending, acceptance of different forms of English from all over the world. The quirky is at a premium. Thus, in a sense, to write in a rigidly 'conventional' prose becomes itself a form of transgression.

Shortly after winning the Booker Prize, Kazuo Ishiguro, the Anglo-Japanese writer, gave an interview to *Time* magazine in which he criticised his British contemporaries for writing in ways that made translation difficult. His rigidly austere prose, which so effectively expresses the emotional limitations of his protagonist in *The Remains of the Day*, was, he claimed, partly the result of his attentiveness to eventual translations. He pared his English down to what a translator in any language could easily handle. What Ishiguro could not have appreciated is that the underlying menace of that precise conventional voice disappears entirely in, say, Italian where such a controlled form of expression is common in prose fiction. The distance Ishiguro establishes from other writers in English has gone. What is disturbing, if one wishes to be disturbed by such things, is with what appetite the public laps up translated literary works whose essential cohesion has all too often been lost in translation. Might it be, I sometimes wonder, precisely that loss of depth that makes translations attractive?

And yet I translate and people tell me they enjoy my translations. So I would like to wind up by considering my relationship with one of the Italian authors I have translated and to look at a paragraph of his work in original and translation.

Roberto Calasso is about as different from myself as a writer could be. A meticulous scholar, admirably intellectual, he sternly avoids any autobiographical material. His creative reconstructions of Greek and Indian mythology have the advantage, from the translator's point of view, that they contain little that is culture-specific to Italy in terms of semantic content. They are attempts to enter and regenerate different mindframes, though of course they do so from an Italian starting point and in the Italian language. If my own writing has matured and changed radically over the last few years, it is largely due to my reflections on Calasso's work and on what it has meant to translate it. Sometimes, however, it occurs to me that I have come closer to putting him into English in the echoes of his writing in my own than in my translations. But here he is, introducing the god Apollo in *The Marriage of Cadmus and Harmony*:

Delo era un dorso di roccia deserta, navigava seguendo la

corrente come un gambo di asfodelo. Nacque lì Apollo, dove neppure le serve infelici vanno a nascondersi. Su quello scoglio perduto a partorire, prima di Leto, erano state le foche. C'era però una palma, a cui si aggrappò la madre, sola, puntando le ginocchia sulla magra erba. E Apollo apparve. Allora tutto divenne d'oro sin dalle fondamenta. D'oro anche l'acqua del fiume, anche le foglie dell'ulivo. Quell' oro doveva espandersi nel profondo del mare, perchè ancorò Delo. Non fu più, da allora, isola errante.

As I suggested, Calasso's book involves a daring recreation of Greek mythology and one is struck throughout both by the vatic authority of the tone and the presentation of myth as real event, or at least as something that requires no apology. The voice combines certain poetic or archaic elements, particularly of diction and focusing, with the short, even terse sentences that we tend to associate with modern prose. That is, while it draws on literary resources from previous periods, it does not appear to be a pastiche, but rather uses them to acquire a peremptory authority that is all its own. Since not everyone reading this will understand Italian, let me try, however unsatisfactory this approach may be, to give you a brutally literal translation so that you can grasp, in however crude a form, the content offered.

Delos was a spine of deserted rock, it sailed about following the current like a stalk of asphodel. Born here was Apollo, where not even the unhappy servant girls go to hide themselves. On that lost rock to give birth before Leda were the seals. There was, however, a palm tree to which the mother clutched, alone, bracing her knees on the sparse grass. And Apollo appeared. Then everything became gold right from the bottom. Of gold also the water of the river, also the leaves of the olive tree. That gold was to expand into the depth of the sea. Because it anchored Delos. It was no longer, from then on, a wandering island.

From the purely semantic point of view, this is a faithful translation. The Italian is not standard Italian and this likewise is very far from standard English. The focusing, particularly, is bizarre in both texts, most notably in the flourish, 'Born here was Apollo . . .' ('*Nacque lì Apollo . . .*') But one transgression is not equivalent to the other. Where the Italian elegantly and fluently – for there is rhythm and alliteration in plenty here – gestures back towards archaic forms to acquire its lofty tone, the English drifts aimlessly about the syntactical currents of the original; and if it is not incoherent semantically, it certainly is so in terms of register and thus risks drawing more attention to its own vagaries than to its content (in a way the Italian does not).

So the English will have to be changed. But how? A standard modern English would be banal and inappropriate. The only solution would seem to be to draw on the resources of an older English as Calasso has drawn on those of an older Italian. But notoriously these resources are not equivalent. In short, to be faithful to Calasso's strategy and the reading experience it generates, which I so enjoy, I shall have to appropriate – that awful word – the text into an English context. But any notion of translation without appropriation is nonsense. The only way not to appropriate a text is to leave it in its original language. Here is the published translation:

Delos was a hump of deserted rock, drifting about the sea like a stalk of asphodel. It was here that Apollo was born, in a place not even wretched slave girls would come to hide their shame. Before Leda, the only creatures to give birth on that godforsaken rock had been the seals. But there was a palm tree, and the mother clutched it, alone, bracing her knees in the thin grass. Then Apollo emerged, and everything turned to gold, from top to bottom. Even the water in the river turned to gold and the leaves on the olive tree likewise. And the gold must have stretched downward into the depths, because it anchored Delos to the seabed. From that day on, the island drifted no more.

There is neither time nor space here to go through this translation line by line: suffice it to say that when I have invited students to compare these passages they invariably remark on the very different syntactical structuring of the two texts, and the more generous lexicon of the English. Thus '*Nacque lì Apollo*' has become: 'It was here that Apollo was born . . .', the English retaining the focus on 'here' at the expense of a much longer and more regular locution. And the rhythmic, alliterative '*Su quello scoglio perduto a partorire, prima di Leto, erano state le foche*' (On that lost rock to give birth before Leda were the seals) has become: 'Before Leda, the only creatures to give birth on that godforsaken rock had been the seals.' Once more the fore-grounding of the place and, in this case, the focus on 'seals' at the end of the sentence, has been kept at the expense of a certain expansion. The Italian is powerfully elliptical, in a way that much poetic material in Italian gestures back to Latin ellipsis. While this is sometimes possible in English, it is rarely so when the content is determined by another language.

Meanwhile in lexical terms, one notes how '*serve infelici*' (unhappy servant girls) has become 'wretched slave girls' '*perduto*' (lost) has become 'godforsaken', '*nascondersi*' (hide them-selves), has become 'hide their shame', and the word 'seabed' has been introduced to offer an anchor to 'anchored' which in English seems to require an indirect object.

How long it would take to discuss each one of these and all the other decisions involved in the translation of this brief text! How complex it all is, not just syntactically, but in terms of the larger literary context. At first sight, it would appear that I offer the perfect example of Kundera's obtuse translator, substituting one sentence for two at one point, using more literary words, entirely reorganising almost all the sentences. But Italian is *not* English and the spirit guiding these decisions is clear enough. The English is groping for a rhetorical tone, a register, comparable to that of the Italian, drawing on an archaic, perhaps biblical language with which my vicarage youth makes me all too familiar. Given the larger and more layered lexicon of English, the move away from 'unhappy' to 'wretched' is dictated by the need to gesture to the classical world through the use of a slight archaism (*'infelice'* in Italian sits happily with either a modern or archaic register). In English a 'servant girl' would normally be a 'maid', which would tend to make us think of the British upper classes, hence the switch to 'slave girls'. 'Hide themselves' is as inelegant as third-person plural reflexives tend to be in English and, what's more, not immediately comprehensible here, hence the interpretative introduction of 'hide their shame'. The 'lost rock' would not easily give the Italian sense of 'far away from anywhere', nor would it, as does the word *'perduto'*, offer alliteration (*'perduto a partorire, prima . . .'*). The choice of 'godforsaken' does give that sense and offers a rhythmic alliteration with the earlier 'gives', albeit at the risk of introducing a concept not present in the Italian. The last sentence of the translation, 'From that day on, the island drifted no more', completely rearranges the Italian to discover a poetic register complete with alliteration that matches the original in gesture if not in exact semantics.

So the text is now in English. It is faithful in that it suggests a consistent, coherent relationship between this voice and a literary past, not unlike that of Calasso's text. It includes much of the same alliteration, rhythm and peremptory fluency. Am I happy with it? Yes and no. The main failing comes in the translation of *'E Apollo apparve. Allora tutto divenne d'oro sin dalle fondamenta.'* This is clearly the climax the text has been working towards. And here I lost my nerve. Having already used an 'and', rather than a relative, to link the previous sentence, I chose to begin this sentence with 'Then'. This would be all very well if the next Italian sentence didn't begin with 'Allora'. Unable in the translation to start a second sentence with 'then', I thus chose to run the two sentences together. Looking at the whole thing in Italian and English we have:

> *E Apollo apparve. Allora tutto divenne d'oro sin dalle fondamenta.*
> Then Apollo emerged, and everything turned to gold, from top to bottom.

Clearly the English loses drama by not introducing a fullstop after 'emerged'. Worse, it loses the now extravagant alliteration of 'Apollo apparve' (an alliteration then echoed, as it were, in 'Allora'). Why? I was worried about the semantics of 'appeared' as a description of birth, thinking that this word might be more acceptable in Italian than English. I also felt the alliteration was now overly heavy. I thus settled for 'emerged' which, on reflection, seems no more appropriate than 'appeared', since one does not, I don't think, speak of babies as 'emerging', though technically one might see that this is a more accurate choice. But my real mistake here was not to think in terms of the relation of style and content, not to understand what Calasso was up to. Apollo is the god of 'appearance', of beauty, of art. With him, appearance, as it were, appears, for the first time. And with this sentence the alliteration, the artifice of the paragraph, now comes to the surface in a way that no one can ignore. Had I been aware of all this, I would surely have had the courage to write: 'And Apollo appeared.'

But even assuming I made this correction, my difficulty here does little more than suggest a deeper loss that takes place in this translation. We have noted that almost all the changes I have made to adjust register and rhythm involve a slight loss of concision, a slight expansion. But perhaps the best way I can explain my misgivings is by quoting the next paragraph from the original.

L'Olimpo si distacca da ogni altra dimora celeste per la presenza di tre divinità innaturali: Apollo, Artemis, Atena. Irriducibili a una funzione, imperiose custodi dell'unico, hanno stracciato quella lieve cortina opaca che la natura tesse intorno alle sue potenze. Lo smalto e il vuoto, il profilo, la freccia. Questi i loro elementi, non acqua o terra.

Here Calasso begins his presentation of the Greek obsession with appearance and aesthetics, the sharp line, the fine profile, a love affair with clarity, the territory of Apollo. And clearly it is to this that his prose is aspiring. Indeed we could compare the sharpness of Calasso's focusing with the clarity of gesture on those black-on-white designs that characterise the pictorial vases of the early Hellenic period. A literal translation will be so ugly and clumsy as to give only a vague idea of this intention. But here it is:

Olympus detaches itself from every other celestial dwelling through the presence of three unnatural divinities: Apollo, Artemis, Athena. Irreducible to one function, imperious custodians of the unique, they tore away that flimsy, opaque screen that nature weaves around its forces. The enamel and the void, the profile, the arrow. These their elements, not water or earth.

Once again it is clear that this will not do. The intention is lost in the extravagant unusualness of the English which seems to have no point of contact with the rhythms of any known English prosody. Once again, as we shall see, the published translation seeks a rhetorical gesture similar to that of the original, but at the expense of that concision that welds the style of the Italian to its subject. Note in particular what heavy weather is made of that crucial and crucially brief sentence, '*Lo smalto e il vuoto, il profilo, la freccia.*'

> If Olympus differs from every other celestial home, it is thanks to the presence of three unnatural divinities: Apollo, Artemis, Athena. More than mere functions, these imperious custodians of the unique stripped away that thin, shrouding curtain which nature weaves about its forces. The bright enamelled surface and the void, the sharp outline, the arrow. These, and not water or earth, are their elements.

The problem in this case is that one simply cannot translate the semantic freight of '*smalto*' or '*profilo*' as used here in Italian with just one word. And then of course there are questions of rhythm and balance to consider, two aesthetic qualities as dear to Apollo as clarity. Yet precisely because one appreciates how much Calasso's text is doing, one fervently wishes one could have followed the Italian more closely. Perhaps the most dangerous moments for a translator are those when he so admires the original, so understands its surrounding context, that he wishes his own language were the same as the language he is working from, and then stubbornly tries to make it so. This is the territory of Nabokov's translation of Pushkin, which is all but unreadable; it is the experience of the bilingual person who is shocked by the idea that the same text can be so radically different in two different languages, as different indeed as those two languages are from each other. It is the starting point of all Kundera's criticism. It also explains, I hope, why I have decided never to translate into Italian. And never to translate poetry. The more poetic, or transgressive, a text is, the more it departs from familiar usage, so the more it comes to be about the language it is written in, not in a narrow linguistic sense, but in the sense of all that language stands for and supports. While I feel I can manage this conundrum with prose, where content still plays its very large part, I find poetry, not being a poet, quite beyond me.

Sentimental Education

[Vikram Seth]

Salman Rushdie's novel *The Ground Beneath Her Feet* is to be 'supported', we hear, by a new release from the rock band U2. As if in coy echo, the promotional blurb to Vikram Seth's *An Equal Music* tells us that 'bookstores have invited string quartets to perform during his readings'. Simultaneously? While the phenomenon of celebrity publishing has accustomed us to the idea that the book itself may be the least exciting part of an overall package, it is disturbing to find two authors with such literary ambitions allowing our eyes, or indeed ears, to be distracted from the pleasures of the text. The multimedia experience may be fashionable, but in literature distinction and discrimination are of the essence. One reads, for preference, in a quiet place.

There are uncanny parallels between Rushdie's and Seth's latest efforts. Like chalk and cheese it seems impossible not to mention them together. Both books are by hugely successful, male, anglophone, Indian-born authors now in early middle age. Both feature musicians as protagonists. In each case those protagonists are involved in a love triangle. In each case the musician-lovers lose sight of each other for ten years allowing a third to slip in. Both first-person narrators seem driven to tell their story out of a sense of loss, the need to overcome pain and disillusionment. Much, very much, is made of the intimacy generated by creating music together and in both cases the music played comes to be seen as a manifestation of a transcendental realm of feeling. But while Rushdie, with his usual spirited bluster, seems set on giving back to the world only the cacophony the mind is anyway subject

115

to these days, Seth is after more calculated and harmonious effects. The distance between the rock band in Central Park pushing amplification to the limits to drown out helicopters and sirens, and the tail-coated quartet entertaining a scrupulously silent, if somewhat dusty middle-class audience beneath a baroque ceiling rose, will serve well enough as an analogy for the distance between these two novelists' performances.

Vikram Seth's reputation began with *The Golden Gate*. Here, some light-hearted satire and a series of sentimental relationships were rescued from banality by being presented entirely in tightly rhyming tetrameter. The effect, at least in the opening cantos, is charming. Unlike Rushdie, when Seth approaches his readers, it is always to seduce, never to accuse, even less to browbeat. But he is careful not to challenge either. Despite occasional lapses into doggerel, *The Golden Gate* slips down like a well-made ice cream. It would be churlish to raise objections and simply unkind to hazard comparison either with Pushkin, whom Seth names as his model, or Byron, of whom the reader, despite the different verse form, may more often be wistfully reminded. Even returning to the book today, one cannot help but take one's hat off to someone who had the resources and tenacity to bring such a project to a conclusion and convince a publisher it would work.

That hat-doffing admiration – the critical faculty forestalled by wonder – is something Seth once again sought and largely obtained with his second work of fiction, *A Suitable Boy*. Much was made at the time of its publication of the distance the author had travelled from *The Golden Gate*, from a good-humoured satire of contemporary California in chiming verse, to this vast, meticulously researched drama of India in the 1950s, the crimes and loves of four extended families in over 1,300 pages. But with hindsight the similarities between the two ventures are evident enough: first, the decision to ignore current experimental trends in literary fiction, particularly Anglo-Indian fiction, in this case by resorting to a conventional narrative prose that offered a tried and tested vehicle for pleasure; then, the gently satirical delight in social trivia with here the exoticism of the mainly Hindu milieu standing in for the wit of clever rhyme, and the sheer scale and intricate extension of the plot serving to generate that same gasp of disarmed surprise.

At the thematic level, too, there was a similar concentration on affairs of the heart, again with an awareness of the dangers of passion and the virtues of traditional, in this case even dynastic, common sense. Unpleasantness and indeed horror are not excluded, but, as Anita Desai acutely remarked in her assessment of the book, Seth tends to hurry over the brutal and lurid as if such things were really too distasteful to occupy much space on his pleasurable pages.

Since a great deal of contemporary fiction seeks primarily and often solely to shock, this decision to restrict unpleasantness to a minimum will hardly raise hackles. If a problem does arise it is when we begin to feel that Seth's designs upon us are all too irksomely evident. There are readers whose antennae go up before succumbing to charm. Various Indian critics in particular suggested that *A Suitable Boy*'s complacent vision of Indian society verged on the grotesque. The desire to seduce must always be in complex negotiation with the spirit of truth. In this sense the decision, in *An Equal Music*, to encourage us to look unhappiness long and hard in the eye might be seen as an attempt on Seth's part to redress the balance.

Narrator and protagonist Michael Holmes describes himself as 'irreparably imprinted with the die of someone else's being'. Unable, in his mid-thirties, to get over his first love of ten years before, he 'lives in a numbed state of self-preservation', in a tiny attic apartment to the north of Kensington Gardens, eking out a barely adequate living playing second violin in a string quartet and teaching the trade to a variety of unsatisfactory students with one of whom he pursues an affair that offers no more than physical relief. The book's three brief opening paragraphs, which also form a separate section of their own, strike a melancholy and decidedly minor chord that is to be sustained, with variations, throughout.

> The branches are bare, the sky tonight a milky violet. It is not quiet here, but it is peaceful. The wind ruffles the black water to me.
>
> There is no one about. The birds are still. The traffic slashes through Hyde Park. It comes to my ears as white noise.
>
> I test the bench but do not sit down. As yesterday, as the day before, I stand until I have lost my thoughts. I look at the water of the Serpentine.

Immediately we recognise the familiar sadness of the lonely man in the urban scene, trapped in empty repetition, eager to forget, clearly attracted to and menaced by that black water the wind blows at him. There is nothing remarkable here. We might even want to call it creditably low key. Gone the springy step of *The Golden Gate*, gone the sprawling exoticism of *A Suitable Boy*, the style now spare, sometimes wilfully limp, Seth thus renounces the visiting card of virtuosity. When we discover that his hero is not only white and English but that he hails from the town of Rochdale, a declining industrial satellite on the edge of the Manchester conurbation, the kind of place that tends to be the butt of dismissive jokes in the sophisticated South, it becomes clear that if there is to be a gasp of surprise this time around, it must be at Seth's boldness in placing himself right in the mainstream of English fiction, doing exactly what the English do.

Michael, then, is marooned in the past, 'with inane fidelity fixated on someone who could have utterly changed'. Ten years ago, studying in Vienna, he fell in love with another student, Julia, a pianist. For a year things went well, but Michael's music teacher was a harsh master and dissatisfied with his achievements.

Despite Julia's insistence that he see the experience through, Michael fled, leaving both girlfriend and the possibility of a solo career behind. When, two months later, he began to write to her, she did not reply.

The exact dynamics of this break-up, the reasons for Julia's not replying to Michael's letters, for his not simply returning to see her, are never clear to the characters themselves and even less so to the reader. What evidently matters to Seth, however, is that it should appear an unnecessary separation in a relationship of enormous potential. Michael is thus more understandably in thrall to his sense of what might have been. To make matters worse, since he and Julia used to play together in a trio, his very vocation constantly brings him up against the memory of her. In particular there is a Beethoven trio they used to perform – opus 1 number 3 – that he often listens to but cannot play either privately or professionally for fear of being overcome by emotion. Informed, significantly enough by Virginie, his student girlfriend, that Beethoven in later life prepared a now obscure variation of this early work as a quintet, Michael becomes obsessed with tracking the piece down and getting his quartet to perform it with the help of an extra player. This will both remind him of Julia, but at the same time be different from the past. 'I know,' he thinks excitedly, 'that, unlike with the trio, nothing will seize me up or paralyse my heart and arm.'

Instead, then, of seeking a more appropriate sentimental variation with Virginie, Michael sets out to find this different and improbable version of what he remembers all too well. We are thus treated to one of those episodes, now so familiar in contemporary fiction, where someone searches for the crucial but elusive text in specialist libraries and second-hand shops, meeting with the predictable mixture of obnoxious obtusity and unhelpful helpfulness. Ironically, it is just as – at last successful – he boards a bus to bring home an old vinyl recording of the piece, 'so desperately sought, so astonishingly found', just as he prepares a decidedly sentimental, indeed potentially masturbatory (not a word Seth would use) evening with this variation – 'I'll come home, light a candle, lie down on my duvet and sink into the quintet' – that the lovelorn Michael sees, after ten years, who but Julia herself going by on a bus in the opposite direction. The variation, we immediately understand, is to be with the loved one in person. When Michael's quartet do play the piece with a fifth artist, that artist will be Julia.

But before considering how Seth tackles the revival of lost love, let's turn aside a moment to look at his handling of the protagonist's provincial boyhood, since this strand of the narrative offers in naked miniature an example of the writer's aesthetic at work.

Home of the Industrial Revolution, the north of England has a long and spirited tradition in socially engaged fiction. From Gaskell's *Mary Barton* to the novels of contemporary writers like Pat Barker and Jane Rogers, first the ascendancy of the brutal factory owner, then the desolation of industrial decline, finally the gloom of government cuts and, throughout it all, the plight of the poor, have all been passionately documented. Seth is aware of this of course and as the dutiful Michael goes to visit his ageing father at Christmas, he offers us a number of pages in line with the tradition, portraying a disadvantaged boyhood in a decaying landscape.

The handsome town hall presides over a waste – it is a town with its heart torn out. Everything speaks of its decline. Over the course of a century, as its industries decayed, it lost its work and its wealth. Then came the planning blight: the replacement of human slums by inhuman ones, the marooning of churches in traffic islands, the building of precincts where once there were shops. Finally two decades of garrotting from the government in London and everything civic or social was choked of funds: schools, libraries, hospitals, transport. The town which had been the home of the co-operative movement lost its sense of community.

The only other colonial outsider I can think of who took on the industrial North was the Australian Christina Stead in *Cotter's England*. With fantastic energy and mimetic resources, Stead achieved the astonishing feat of giving us a believable British working class chattering, suffering, living, laughing, loving and – she never forgets – hating as hard as could be. This is not Seth's project. He does not risk the local dialect. Aside from these few pages, his hero displays no interest in politics or the condition of England. Nor does Seth. Why then bother with this reductive and potentially platitudinous picture of the North? Is it necessary for authenticity?

Certainly Seth works hard to intertwine the history of the town with that of Michael's family, mainly in order to present the latter as victims. His father's butcher's shop was appropriated to make way for a road which was never built. Bereft of his profession, the father fell ill. Nursing him, the mother suffered a fatal stroke. Over Christmas, Michael plans 'to lay a white rose' on the parking lot that eventually replaced the shop and family home: 'the flat and I hope snow-covered site of my mother's life'.

Political and again poignant considerations also come into the account of Michael's early education on the violin:

Because the comprehensive I went to had been the old grammar school, it had a fine tradition of music. And the services of what were known as peripatetic music teachers were provided by the local education authorities. But all this has been cut back now, if it has not completely disappeared. There was a system for loaning instruments free or almost free of charge to those who could not afford them – all scrapped with the education cuts as the budgetary hatchet struck again and again . . . If I had been born in Rochdale five years later, I don't see how I – coming from the background I did, and there were so many who were much poorer – could have kept my love of the violin alive.

Cursory research is being made to work very hard here. Michael expresses commonplace views frequently fielded in the 'Letters to the Editor' section of British newspapers. But to respond with the standard objection that in the same period the people of Lancashire have equipped themselves with cars, TVs and computers, that the consumption of beer, cigarettes and junk food could never be described as negligible, that though one would always applaud a government that provided violins to its people, the people themselves are hardly screaming for them – to raise this objection would simply be to miss the point. Seth doesn't want to get us interested in the politics or economics of the situation. He himself is not at all interested in the question of how the north of England (where I was born and spent my infancy and sang indifferently in a marvellous choir) is to continue to produce musicians. He is careful never to give Michael any individual or thought-provoking views on the subject (Stead's characters, on the contrary, always have excitingly personal views). No, the whole 'northern thing' has been taken over – Seth is adept above all at taking over old forms to his special purposes – only for the opportunity it offers to strike further chords of poignancy, further variations on the theme, or rather mood, so clearly announced in the book's opening lines.

Deprived as it may or may not be, the North is certainly generous in this regard: it gives our author, among other poignancies, the ageing, beaten father attached to his decrepit cat, the image of Michael as a boy lying on the Pennine uplands listening to the larks, and the wholesomeness of the dying benefactress who introduced Michael to music and who lends him her extremely valuable Italian violin, without which he would be hard put to do his job. At the end of the book he will crumble some home-made Christmas pudding onto the snowy moors in her memory.

Admiring, if we will, the cleverness of this appropriation, we can now turn to the main plot with a proper sense of what Seth is up to. Everything will be arranged to generate the maximum poignancy: 'issues', whether moral, social or existential, will – like the decay of the North – be drawn on only in so far as they sustain the note on the heartstring, then rapidly dropped. Vienna will be the venue where it would be disastrous to fluff a concert. Venice will perform its traditional service as the right place to have a romantic interlude that is only an interlude. Even music itself, ostensibly the book's great theme, will be understood first and foremost as a vehicle of sentiment. Thus, after the vision of the long-lost Julia on the bus, Michael, rehearsing the now highly significant quintet, remarks:

> For me there is another presence in this music. As the sense of her might fall on my retina through two sheets of moving glass, so too through this maze of notes converted by our arms into vibration – sensory, sensuous – do I sense her being again. The labyrinth of my ear shocks the coils of my memory. Here is her force in my arm, here is her spirit in my pulse. But where she is I do not know, nor is there hope I will.

Wrong! Michael is wrong. For though on crowded Oxford Street he fails to catch up with Julia's bus in time (Seth's research letting him down here a little, one feels), the dear lady will turn up of her own free will at the end of the quartet's concert at Wigmore Hall. There are tentative, poignantly uncommunicative meetings. We discover that Julia is married, loves her husband, and has a son who goes to school only a stone's throw from Michael's flat. Thus understandably hesitant, nevertheless – for the old magic is at work and the plot must move on – she succumbs and the couple makes love. As they prepare to do so, watch how cleverly and tenderly the moral question is fielded:

> She smiles a little sadly. 'Making music and making love – it's a bit too easy an equation.'
>
> 'Have you told him [the husband] about me?' I ask.
>
> 'No,' she says. 'I don't know what to do about all this subterfuge: faxes in German, coming up to see you here . . . but it's really Luke [the son] who I feel I'm . . .'
>
> 'Betraying?'
>
> 'I'm afraid of all these words. They're so blunt and fierce.'

Indeed they are. But Julia need not worry, irony wouldn't fit in with the particular effects Seth is after here. He will do his best to make sure that both characters remain not only sympathetic, but somehow innocent. That way we can savour their sadness without any irritating distractions. After all, this is not the ordinary affair where Dionysus bursts on to a tranquil scene and the hitherto placid weavers discover a dark side to themselves that they never imagined. The sex is toned delicately down. The Bach is turned decorously up. The lovers play music together. And are they not anyway entirely justified – if justification is required (they both seem to feel it is) – by the fact that this is old and unfinished business between proven soul mates? 'I am not seeing anyone new,' Michael truthfully tells the worried Virginie.

Without recounting the whole story, there remains – as far as the plot is concerned – Seth's masterstroke to consider, the ploy that allows him to sustain his melancholy medley for the full 382 pages (the book makes much in musical terms of the problems of sustaining notes and intensity). Those awkward first meetings between Michael and Julia are suddenly explained by the fact that our heroine is going deaf, indeed is already on the brink of total soundlessness. Against all odds, she is trying to keep this disability a secret in the hope that she will be able to pursue her career regardless. Aspiring novelists will be able to profit from considering how this desperate response to personal tragedy, together with a great deal of other preparatory stage-setting, allows Seth to get away with the extraordinary coincidence of its being Julia – Julia whose whereabouts, we remember, Michael was unable for ten years to trace – who is suddenly, and without his knowledge, invited to substitute for a sick pianist who was to support the quartet at its crucial performance in of all places Vienna, where the lovers originally met.

In his author's note Seth acknowledges help from 'those who understand the world of the deaf – medically, like the many doctors who have advised me, or educationally, in particular my lip-reading teacher and her class, or from personal experience of deafness'. Fascinating here, and alas typical of so many contemporary novels, is the way the solemn appeal to research and veracity in some specialist field is actually used to mask the failure to engage a more interesting but arduous and less immediately glamorous subject. The idea of a couple with special talents and sensibilities rediscovering each other many years on and finding that their original bond does indeed challenge relationships made since, is most intriguing and immediately presents itself as a vehicle for all kinds of drama, reflection and moral dilemma. What might such a plot have become in the hands of Lawrence, or James, or Moravia, or Elizabeth Bowen? But as soon as we discover that Julia is afflicted with deafness, we have moved into the realm of kitsch. Can the film, we wonder, be far behind those quartet-accompanied readings?

Now a party to his lover's terrible secret, Michael is inevitably brought into conflict with his quartet colleagues who will be risking their reputations when they play with Julia in Vienna. The reader grows anxious over the big night. It all works splendidly in terms of narrative tension. We are well manipulated. Some will have to pull out their handkerchiefs. The downside is that it allows Seth to get away without developing the characters of the lovers or the dynamic of their relationship, which, as a result, can very adequately be summed up thus: at best diffident initially, Julia briefly indulges a tediously insistent Michael to the extent of agreeing to a few days together in Venice after the Vienna concert, then sensibly and predictably withdraws, leaving him in much the position we found him at the beginning of the book.

Of the characters in *A Suitable Boy*, Anita Desai remarked: 'They come to us extremely well equipped with easily recognisable characteristics.' The same is true of those in *An Equal Music* and in particular of Michael's fellow members in the quartet, though it has to be said that their rehearsals offer by far the best reading in the book. The ever irritable and aggressive, but also gay and vulnerable, first violinist Piers, his winsomely accommodating sister Helen, the overly diligent cellist Billy – eager to pose problems the others haven't noticed – and Michael himself, pragmatic, gruff, always in danger of distraction: this is a force field that works, and offers welcome relief from the heady monotony of the love affair. It is also the element that comes closest to evoking the uniting power of music, this picture of four people who have no special desire to spend time together nevertheless sharing the transport of the work they are playing, enjoying the pleasure of a communication beyond words, beyond deafness, and to a certain extent beyond the grave. As they perform Bach together, Michael reflects: 'Our synchronous visions merge, and we are one; with each other, with the world, and with that long-dispersed being whose force we receive through the shape of his annotated vision and the single, swift-flowing syllable of his name.'

Leaving aside the swiftness or otherwise with which the syllable 'Bach' (yes, I know it means 'stream') might be said to flow, how seriously are we to take this idea and its latent transcendentalism? Does it convince? There is a determined intertextuality to Seth's book. 'Under the arrow of Eros I sit down and weep,' Michael tells us in Piccadilly Circus having failed to catch up with Julia's bus. London's monuments and the protagonist's desperation are thus fused in an echo of Psalm 137 and its many subsequent literary adaptations. Having been treated to some gruesome Rochdale gossip on deaths, births and divorces, the sensitive Michael's mental wince is registered in a one-line paragraph: 'For better or worse, unto us a child, ashes to ashes.' Later, as he faxes Julia in German to bamboozle the husband, Walter Scott is on his mind: 'It is a tangled web that I am weaving,' he comments, reminding us of *Marmion*.

These frequent echoes, literary or biblical, are invariably deployed at moments of emotional intensity and seek to establish with the reader a community of sensibility similar to that experienced by the musicians as they play. It is a community from which the insensitive – the bank employee who refuses Michael a loan to buy a new violin, his benefactress's nephew who selfishly seeks to repossess the expensive violin – will necessarily be excluded. Towards the end of the novel, as Michael's suffering grows more intense, the literary references become more frequent and are now accompanied by a fragmentation of thought in what amounts to a stops-out pastiche of modernism. In the following passage Julia has just ushered her unwelcome ex-lover out of her house with a very decisive goodbye. The little dog mentioned is a reference to the knowing creature in Carpaccio's St Jerome cycle that the couple saw together in Venice. Shakespeare and Eliot are also present and, who knows, perhaps Mark Twain as well.

The door opens, closes. I look down from the top steps. Water, full fathom five, flows down Elgin Crescent, down Ladbroke Grove, through the Serpentine to the Thames, and double-deckered red vaporetti sputter like Mississippi steamboats down its length. A small white dog sits on the sneezing prow. Go, then, with the breathing tide, and do not make a scene, and learn the wisdom of the little dog, who visits from elsewhere, and who knows that what is, is, and, O harder knowledge, that what is not is not.

In John Coetzee's novel, *Disgrace*, the protagonist becomes aware that the literary project he is engaged in is going badly wrong, it 'has failed to engage the core of him. There is something misconceived about it, something that does not come from the heart.' We are thus given to understand that if, on the contrary, Coetzee's story is electrifying from beginning to end – and it is – then that must be because it is extremely close to its author's heart (in the same way that, for all kinds of reasons, industrial England was close to Stead's heart when she wrote *Cotter's England*). That there be something at stake in a narrative, something that engages the core of an author's being, does not of course guarantee that a reader will be convinced, but it does seem to me a sine qua non of such conviction. However eager to entrance us Seth may be, derivative artifice of the kind he is deploying here looks like no more than a tiresome literary exercise. If the subject does matter greatly to him, he has not found a way of expressing it.

Which brings us at last to the title of the book and to John Donne. Seth seeks to tie together literary reference, musical experience and metaphysical consolation by prefacing his work with a quotation from the great dean and poet:

And into that gate they shall enter, and in that house they shall dwell, where there shall be no cloud nor sun, no darkness nor dazzling, but one equal light, no noise nor silence, but one equal music, no fears nor hopes, but one equal possession, no foes nor friends, but one equal communion and identity, no ends or beginnings, but one equal eternity.

Modern ears cannot help but wonder at such confident and eloquent declarations of faith. Yet overcoming for a moment our sense of awe, it is interesting to see how the term 'equal' emerges here as the result of Donne's systematically denying all those tensing polarities – cloud/sun, darkness/dazzle, noise/silence, hope/fear – that make our mortal life what it is. In short, 'equal' becomes a word that we can use to evoke the unimaginable, something beyond tension, beyond life, beyond individuality. This is rather more radical than Michael's sentimental sense of the presence of others, even the dead, when he plays his violin: 'The attendant ghosts press down on me . . . Schubert is here, and Julia's mother. They attend because of the beauty of what we are re-making.' All the same, in the last pages of the book, when Michael has gone to hear Julia giving a solo performance of one of the pieces of music that once united them, Seth boldly attempts to clinch all his interconnections thus: 'There is no forced gravitas in her playing. It is a beauty beyond imagining – clear, lovely, inexorable . . . the unending "Art of Fugue". It is an equal music.'

But of course it is not, not in the sense Donne meant it, which is the only sense one can think to ascribe to this odd expression. What else could it mean? Only a moment later, in fact, Seth, himself all too familiar with forced gravitas, is remarking that the human soul 'could not sustain' too much of this music, whereas Donne was affirming his belief in a music that will delight the soul for all time. On closer examination, Seth's 'beyond imagining' turns out to be the merest inflation. Here we have a deaf woman playing Bach superbly, and though that may stretch the imagination, a good performance of Bach, wherever it comes from, is far from beyond imagining.

Once again, then, we have an inappropriate appropriation. Seth needs his vague transcendentalism, his lyricism and literary gesturing, his sense of community in pathos, to sugar this long, but in the end far from hard look at unhappiness. I was thus mistaken when I supposed that this work might mark a radical departure from the previous two books. It is another careful exercise in crowd-pleasing. As such, the sickly music it generates is one with which the ever vigorous, sometimes vicious Donne, the Donne for whom so much, in love and in religion, was always at stake, would have had nothing whatsoever to do.

A Chorus of Cruelty,

[Giovanni Verga]

'Cruelty,' wrote Emil Cioran, 'is a sign of election, at least in literature. The more talented a writer is, the more ingeniously he puts his characters in situations from which there is no escape; he persecutes them, he tyrannizes them, he traps them in dead ends, he forces them to run the whole gamut of their agony.'

Of no writer could this provocative intuition be more true than the great Sicilian novelist Giovanni Verga. Yet eighty years after his death the author of the 'Cavalleria rusticana' continues to be presented to the public as first and foremost a humanist worthily celebrating the passions of the ordinary man and drawing attention to his difficult lot through well-documented description of changing social conditions. G.H. McWilliam concludes the introduction to his new translation of Verga's Sicilian novellas thus:

> Verga's great merit lies in his ability to arouse compassion whilst avoiding completely all traces of sentimentality, and this is because he presents life as it is, free from the distortions of idealistic perspectives. His narratives are an unfailing source of interest, not only to those who care about good literature, but also to the historian, for whom his novels and short stories provide an invaluable record of social conditions at a critical stage of modern Italian history.

Reading such reassuring words one is bound to ask whether there mightn't be some taboo that prevents us from saying what it really is that draws us so powerfully to this man's violent and irretrievably pessimistic stories.

Yet if much of the literature on Verga is at best uneasily half true, the author himself is always the first to set us on the wrong track. Rarely has a great writer's work been so unwittingly uneven, his long and earnest reflections on his various endeavours so mysteriously distant from their impact on the reader. Sensing, at some deep level, perhaps, that the impulses driving his writing were such that they would require considerable disguise before they could be allowed to circulate in polite society, Verga's critical efforts seem to have been largely, if unconsciously, devoted to developing that disguise, not only for the world, but for himself too.

That he never managed to settle on any particular cover, ducking in the space of a long creative life from the elegant society novel, through various forms of worthy social realism, and finally to a formulation that anticipates absurdism, suggests that the real inspiration lay he knew not where. He poured his genius into many bottles, haphazardly it sometimes seems. Only in the one he initially most despised, the short and shamelessly regional novella, did it yield its full and explosive flavour. Only there, albeit with all the insipid decanting of translation, can it still produce its decidedly intoxicating effect outside the Italian language.

Born in 1840 into a family of impoverished gentry in the Sicilian city of Catania, Verga learned early about the importance of maintaining a certain reputation, the difficulty of doing so when resources are scarce. Wealthy Uncle Salvatore had inherited all the family estates on condition that he remain unmarried and use the income to assist his younger brothers and sisters. Life, Giovanni would have realised, is a tangled web and contracts are often notoriously different in letter and in spirit. Few people are naturally generous. Money was not forthcoming. His two spinster aunts, miserly beyond belief, became known as 'the mummies'.

Still, things can sometimes work out in the most unexpected ways. By the time Giovanni's elder brother Mario married Uncle Salvatore's illegitimate daughter Lidda, differences had been resolved. And this was just as well, since money doesn't serve only to keep up appearances. In 1854 a cholera epidemic forced Giovanni's parents to flee Catania to the safety of the family's country estates. Others of course were not so lucky. Years later Verga's writing would be full of figures fighting tooth and nail for the good opinion of others – their very identity depends on it – only to be defeated by illness, drought or, worse still, some irresistible passion that destroys them from within. Beneath it all runs a ferocious sense of outrage. But about what exactly?

In 1860 Garibaldi arrived in Catania. The Bourbon regime was collapsing; the state of Italy was born. Verga, who had already written a novel with the heady title *Amore e patria* joined the new Guardia Nazionale and started a political weekly under the slogan, 'Roma degli Italiani'. But far from a glorious struggle for national unity, the young novelist found himself involved in the repression of popular revolt. The harrowing story 'Libertà' tells how the people in a small village on the slopes of Etna, misunderstanding the meaning of the 'liberty' the Piedmontese state was bringing them, butchered the local nobles and began to fight over who should get what land. A few days later Garibaldi's troops arrived to restore order and butchered the villagers. In a fascinating article written in 1970, Leonardo Sciascia reveals how even Verga, the least squeamish of novelists, played down the cruelty of the soldiers of unification.

In any event, by 1865, and availing himself of another of money's advantages, Verga had bought himself out of the National Guard and sailed to Florence, then capital of Italy. D.H. Lawrence, who first discovered Verga for the English-speaking world and gave us the earliest translations, speaks of him leaving Sicily 'to work at literature'. Like everything else in Lawrence's brief introduction to *Little Novels of Sicily*, the words are

wonderfully apt. Verga was a worker. Avid, anxious, for money
and fame, he laboured at his literature, as so many of his
characters would labour doggedly in field or quarry or fishing
boat. All the same, it would be many years before he found the
form that could most successfully channel his remarkable energies.

Verga later disparagingly described his early novels as tales of
'elegance and adultery'. 'Real Italian novels,' Lawrence generously calls them, 'a little tiresome, but with their own depth'.
Casting about for something more satisfactory, Verga even had a
shot at the Gothic. But in the middle of the 'Castello di Trezza' a
hopelessly complex story of betrayal, multiple murder and ghosts
who may not be ghosts, the second wife of the cruel baron, on
hearing of the tragic death of her predecessor, finally addresses
these prophetic remarks to her terrified maid: 'Even if you took
away the ghosts, the clock striking midnight, the storm that slams
open doors and windows, the creaking weathercocks, this would
still be a terrifying story.' Whether or not the illumination came
to Verga when he wrote that snippet of dialogue, his project from
now on would be to strip the 'terrifying story' that was ever inside
him of its melodramatic mechanics and give it to us straight.

Published in a fashion magazine in 1870 'Storia di una
capinera' ('Story of a Blackcap') was halfway there. We have the
underlying play of forces, but not the milieu. Briefly: the young
Maria is taken out of her convent school to escape a cholera
epidemic and goes to join her family in the country. Her mother
died young. Her weak father remarried a rich woman who will be
interested only in the fate of her own daughter. There is no
money for Maria's dowry. She must take the veil. But during this
brief stay in the country she falls in love with rich neighbour Nino
and he with her. Needless to say Nino is intended for the sister
with the dowry.

Presented as a one-way epistolary novel, Maria writes to a
convent friend of her awakening to love, then her brutal
segregation after the romance is discovered. Heartbreaking

chapters have her shut in her room listening to merry-making down the passageway. In one brief, breathless appearance at Maria's window, the handsome Nino lets us know that he understands the cruel injustice of it all. But he does nothing to break the social ties so efficiently woven around him. Maria herself sees her love as an indulgence and a sin against her fate. Later, when she has taken the veil, she will be granted a view through the cloister grating of Nino and her half-sister who have come to announce their engagement. A final letter from an older nun tells of Maria's sickness, insanity and death.

Flawed as it is, the novel is fascinating for the contradiction at its core. Maria yearns with all her heart for society, company, love. Her essential experience is that of isolation. But the society she longs for is supremely cruel and only united in its exclusion of the individual it has no time for. Maria is poignantly attractive in her need for others, but it is this that destroys her. The reader can only conclude that she needs to get tougher. Always ready to have his work travel with forged papers, Verga allowed the first volume edition to be published with a preface by the proto-feminist Caterina Percoto who presented it as a protest against the exploitation of women. It was a big success.

But is Verga straightforwardly on the side of the victim? A few years later the short story 'Spring' would tell the simpler tale of a love affair between an ambitious but indigent young musician and a shop assistant. When the man finally gets a valuable contract, he drops the girl, who is heartbroken. The cruelty is now presented as an inevitable part of life; the man's interest in career, artistic fame and money are entirely natural. This is his destiny. One can no more quarrel with it than with a mother's desire to marry off her own child rather than her stepdaughter. Is there a sniff of justification in the air here? Or rage at life itself?

One of the few salient events in Verga's hardworking life would be his affair with a woman married to a wealthy man in Sicily. In embarrassingly naked first person, the story 'Beyond the Sea' tells of just such an affair and of the woman's return, despite all the love that has been sworn, to Sicily, and to her husband. The lover is appalled, betrayed, but, like Nino in the earlier novel, does nothing to keep her, and so he also betrays love. Verga wrote the story *before* his mistress, Giselda Fojanesi, in fact went back to her husband. He knew this would happen. He had a career to think of. He must 'work at his literature'. How fascinating all this must have been to Lawrence whose presence in Sicily in 1919 and consequent discovery of Verga was largely due to his having made the opposite gesture: he had run off with the married Frieda and abandoned society altogether.

In any event it seems only appropriate that when Verga at last found his voice, money was the stimulus, together with the felt need to maintain a social façade. It was 1874. His publisher had just turned down not one but two novels. Verga considered giving up, then fought back. A literary magazine invited him to contribute a story, something he was not in the habit of doing. But 'in order to resolve economic problems resulting from his desire to cut a fine figure in Milanese society', writes critic Carla Riccardi, he accepted. In three days he wrote 'Nedda'. 'The merest trifle,' Verga remarked, and made a point of insisting he had only written it for money.

To come to 'Nedda' after reading the earlier works is to savour the surprise of seeing the competent craftsman transformed into the great artist. Something has happened. But what? The story is simple. Nedda is a young Sicilian peasant girl travelling the countryside for work to support a dying mother. Verga, it seems, has gone back, not so much to his own childhood, but to the poverty-stricken world that surrounded it, that threatened it, a world at the furthest remove from fashionable Milanese society, and somehow a rebuke to it too, as the poor left behind to die of cholera while the rich flee the city might well present themselves to a child as a silent rebuke, and a warning.

Verga now proceeds to torture his character, and does so all the more ingeniously for the complete lack of that elaborate plotting and melodramatic language that had characterised the earlier books. In the end it takes very little to torture a Sicilian peasant girl of the mid-nineteenth century. The cards are stacked against her.

The mother dies. Nedda has exhausted her resources paying for medicines. She is criticised by the villagers for going to work immediately after the mother's death. Clumsily courted by the poor but honest Janu, she becomes pregnant. He works hard to get the money to marry her. But the most fertile fields below Etna are also those damp areas where malaria is rife. Janu falls ill. Fruit picking with a fever, he falls from a tree, dies. The girl goes through with her pregnancy, winning the scorn of the village. Refusing to give her baby to the nuns, she nurses it in the most abject poverty. As the story closes, she has a corpse in her arms: 'Oh blessed you who are dead,' she cried, 'Oh blessed the Holy Virgin who has taken away this creature so as not to have her suffer like me!'

So many elements recall 'Storia di una capinera'. The lonely individual dreams of access to society. Society is ugly and cruel. Religion is a sop and a whip. Love is sweet but always imprudent and quite unequal to economic forces and illness. Even the landscape is an enemy. Yet the story never becomes forced or formulaic. Overnight, it seems, Verga has learned the secret of narrative dispatch, of naturalness, and above all of a swift and terrible irony:

The next day being Sunday there was the doctor's visit, since he conceded to the poor the day he couldn't devote to his farms. And what a sad visit it was! for the good doctor wasn't used to beating about the bush with his customers, and in Nedda's poor cottage there was only the one room and no family friends to whom he could announce the real state of the invalid.

137

The sudden shift of viewpoint within an apparently spoken narrative would be a staple in Verga's armoury from now on. 'And what a sad visit it was!' We expect this to be followed by some compassionate remarks about the sick mother or Nedda's grief, only to be invited to sympathise with the 'good doctor' and his distaste at having to deal with patients who have neither spare rooms nor friends. The reader's reaction can only be one of protest. And so much is left unsaid. Has the doctor told Nedda the truth or not? And the mother? It doesn't matter. Knowing he has got his effect, Verga moves directly to extreme unction, the next paragraph ending: 'The priest left and the sexton waited in vain by the door for the usual offering for the poor.'

The success of the story, and of those that would follow, clearly has to do with its fusion of setting and voice. It is not that Verga is writing in Sicilian dialect, for that would be incomprehensible to his readers. But he has put together a weave of dialect inflections and colloquial mannerisms that at least suggest the speech of the poor and above all, through the narrator, the voice of a peasant community. A comparison of Lawrence's recently republished translation and McWilliam's new one will suggest how central the effect is to delivering Verga's vision and how difficult it is to reproduce.

Usefully, McWilliam's introduction quotes Lawrence as observing that a translation of Verga would 'need somebody who could absolutely handle English in the dialect'. 'Probably I shall never do it,' Lawrence says. 'Though if I don't, I doubt if anyone else will – adequately at least.' Remarking on the acuteness of observation, McWilliam then lists four or five howlers Lawrence made as evidence that his 'immodesty' was misplaced and his version not 'adequate'. But there are few translators, McWilliam included, who do not make occasional mistakes, and in any event, what matters here is that the voice be consistently and convincingly integrated with the characters; in short, the handling of

'English in the dialect'. The wonderful story 'Black Bread' opens thus in Lawrence's version:

> Neighbour Nanni had hardly taken his last breath, and the priest in his stole was still there, when the quarrel broke out between the children as to who should pay the costs of the burial, and they went at it till the priest with the aspersorium under his arm was driven away.

McWilliam gives:

> No sooner had Nanni closed his eyes for the last time, with the priest standing over him in his stole, than his children were at one another's throats over who should foot the bill for the funeral. The priest was sent packing empty-handed, with the aspergillum under his arm.'

Lawrence stays with the original by trying to find some solution for the Sicilian *Compare* Nanni (*compare* is a southern Italian term of address and respect) and above all by keeping the paragraph down to one loosely articulated sentence. But he also makes various departures with 'the last breath' being introduced for 'the closed eyes' of the original and the priest being driven off more by the quarrel than by direct command.

McWilliam also makes changes. He has the priest standing over Nanni, and introduces both 'for the last time' and 'empty-handed' neither of which are in the original. But the main difference is in the handling of idiom, and here, perhaps surprisingly, we see McWilliam using idiomatic expressions more frequently than Lawrence. We have 'at one another's throats', 'foot the bill' and 'sent packing' in just a couple of lines. At this point perhaps I can offer the nearest thing to a literal translation of the original.

No sooner did *Compare* Nanni close his eyes, and the priest still there in his stole, than war broke out between the children over who should pay the costs of the funeral, so that the priest was sent off with his aspersorium under his arm.

It's breathless stuff, colloquial, immediate, delivered by a narrator who is so much part of the scene that he explains nothing. Despite some reservations as to whether this is the kind of milieu where the implied context of 'foot the bill' is appropriate, one has to say that McWilliam's idiomatic approach makes sense. The next sentence reveals all its dangers: 'For Nanni had been sick a long time, with the sort of illness that costs you an arm and a leg and the family furniture too.'

Here the idiom 'costs you an arm and a leg' collides with the so far mysterious illness creating one of those alarmingly comic effects Beckett liked to produce to show just how ridiculous language can be: 'I have no bone to pick with graveyards' is the example that comes to mind. Needless to say it isn't what Verga was after here. Lawrence hugs the original and gives us: 'For Neighbour Nanni's illness had been a long one, the sort that eats away the flesh off your bones and the things out of your house.'

The illness is malaria. Flesh, bones and eating are the subject of the story. Peasant fare. 'Furniture' sounds like an extravagance.

Nanni caught malaria because, like Janu in 'Nedda', he needed money and went to work on the most fertile ground where the mosquitoes are. His neighbours had warned him. McWilliam gives: 'The neighbours told him over and over again "You're bound to snuff it, Nanni, on that Lamia farm."'

Of course everyone has his idiolect, but for myself the expression 'snuff it' recalls the films or playground talk of the 1960s. Again Lawrence stays close to the original, doing no more than to substitute the standard idiomatic Italian 'lasciare la pelle' ('leave your skin') for 'leave your bones': 'In vain the neighbours said to him, "Neighbour Nanni, you'll leave your bones on that half-profits farm."'

Less than a page into the story, then, it's evident that the problem is one of finding a credible voice. McWilliam does some excellent work, but his ear lets him down and we regularly find words and expressions that are out of place. A few lines further on, when the eldest son Santo goes to live in his dead father's house, we hear that he 'shifted in his movables'. Lawrence gives, 'carried across his things'. Verga wrote 'robe', 'stuff, belongings'.

Meanwhile, as far as the younger son is concerned, McWilliam tells us, 'if he wanted to eat, [he] would have to go and find work for himself away from home'. Lawrence, whose Italian was sometimes shaky, nevertheless knew well enough that Verga had written something rather different: 'Carmenio, if he wanted to have bread to eat, would have to go away from home and find a master.' One finds a 'master' in nineteenth-century Sicily, not work. The implications are considerable.

But the most amusing moment comes two pages later. With great delicacy, the narrator is telling us how it came about that Santo made the terrible mistake of marrying a penniless woman, thus compounding his family's woes. It was of course because she was beautiful, with red hair and full breasts. These features are mentioned more than once, above all at the crucial moment just before Santo declares himself, when, as McWilliam effectively puts it, the girl tucks 'in her chin above those gently heaving breasts'.

At this point nature becomes complicit with romance, the air is seductive with the scent of herbs, the mountainside red in the sunset. McWilliam finishes the description: 'She then turned to listen to the great-tits singing merrily in the sky.'

Now, it's true that the dictionary gives 'great-tit' for '*cinciallegra*', but chirping up as the creature does just seconds after the description of those ample breasts there's a problem here. Great tits indeed! Is it a howler, then, on Lawrence's part that he

141

gives: 'Then she stood listening to the night crickets rattling away'? After all, Verga's '*le cinciallegre facevano gazzarra*' does *not* mean they were 'singing merrily', but that they were 'making a racket'. These stories are never pretty.

More than just a question of conviction, Verga's choral narrative voice, as Italian critics came to call it, is central to the peculiar pathos behind his stories. He writes in an age now well aware of the atomising and alienating nature of a modern industrial society, an age already deep in its dream, at once nostalgic and futuristic, of the 'good community', the place where the individual would no longer feel alone, just another contender in a capitalistic free for all. What was the nation-building enthusiasm that had taken Garibaldi to Catania if not part of a growing desire to establish a community based on race where ties would be strong and a shared identity recovered?

By setting his stories in the Sicily of his youth and adopting this 'choral voice', Verga might appear to be making the double gesture of yearning for the past and at the same time helping to forge a united Italy in the present by bringing the Sicilian experience into the national consciousness. But ironically it is precisely the voice of traditional community that turns out to be the most cruel, the most resigned to the fact that a doctor is a busy man with no time for people who can't pay, that to marry a girl without a dowry is madness, that if having sex with your master will allow a servant girl to get the money she needs to marry her boyfriend and help her poor relatives, it's not a bad idea. While in the earlier work, reader and victim at least have the narrative voice of modern compassionate consciousness on their side, here the voice itself excludes all hope. To use Cioran's terms, Verga has found a new way of persecuting his characters.

This chorus of cruelty would ultimately be heard at its most consistently callous in the novel *I Malavoglia*: 'You have to be friends with everyone and faithful to no one,' remarks one of those who remain entirely unmoved by the catastrophe that overwhelms the Malavoglia family when their boat is shipwrecked, 'that's why each of us has his own soul and everyone must look after himself.' Never perhaps has the word 'soul' been used in such an unchristian and uncharitable sense. Indeed one of the central ironies of Verga's work is that a society so steeped in biblical vocabulary and church tradition could have remained so impervious to Christ's message of compassion. The usurer who lent the Malavoglias the money to buy the cargo they were carrying (which he knew to be rotten), and whose insistence on being repaid despite the family's imminent ruin and despite the fact that he has no legal right, is generally known in the community as 'Zio Crocefisso' (Uncle Crucified). He constantly remarks, 'They're doing to me what they did to Christ,' even when it is evident to everyone that the real victims are the Malavoglias. Disquieting as ever is the absence of any serious opposition to this kind of inhumanity. Although knowing that they are not legally bound, the Malavoglias nevertheless feel that Zio Crocefisso is right to demand his money at once. They take pride in upholding a vision of honour so crude that it hardly bears inspection. And thus are ruined.

Like a child at a computer game who finally clicks on the secret door that leads to a higher level, Verga, in writing 'Nedda', had blundered into a new world, a place at once of reality and imagination, as Wessex for Hardy, or Yoknapatawpha for Faulkner. Yet before he could explore it, he needed an alibi. For the implications of what was flowing from his pen now were scandalous indeed. It is at this point that *verismo*, or realism, comes to his aid.

Zola was in vogue. Literary circles were chattering about an objective, documentary narrative style, that might help bring about progress and social change. So in the wake of the French writer's *Histoire naturelle et sociale d'une famille sous le Second Empire*, Verga now announced that he was planning not one but

143

five novels, each covering a different social class, in a 'cycle' to be called *I vinti*, *The Defeated*. This was a worthy and most ambitious project. Meanwhile, the short stories he was putting together for money, in the wake of 'Nedda' 's success, could be considered mere studies for the great epics to come. In fact they are his finest work. 'Rosso Malpelo', a story assigned to my adolescent children at school in Verona as an account of the unhappy conditions of working children in the nineteenth century, shows how acutely Verga understood the tragic contradictions that still tense our modern experience today.

A boy with red hair, and hence known as Malpelo (evil-haired), works in a sand mine on the slopes of Etna. He has no other name but a great reputation for violence and surliness. His father, a dogged labourer, known as 'the donkey', dies in a mining accident. The engineer in charge, a theatre enthusiast, is watching *Hamlet* when it happens and reluctant to leave his seat. The mother remarries and has no time for her difficult son who will get his first decent clothes when his father's body is unearthed some months after his death.

Somewhere between Browning's Caliban and Beckett's Molloy, Malpelo differs from Verga's female victims in glorying in his alienation. Physically strong despite all deprivation, he takes beatings and gives them, to man and beast. His philosophy is as brutal as it is appropriate: when you hit, hit hard enough so that you won't be hit back. In any event you will end up like the pit donkey whose corpse the boy likes to visit, dumped in a ravine, eaten up by dogs and rats, beyond suffering. The world after death holds no secrets, no terrors, 'because nobody who has to live alone should ever be afraid of anything'. His favourite expression in the face of any adversity is the proudly solipsistic, 'I am Malpelo.' This, one feels, is how Maria or Nedda would have had to become if they were to survive. They lacked Malpelo's brutal selfishness, which in the end is no more than a grotesque escalation of the gesture the young musician made when he abandoned his shop-assistant girlfriend.

But Malpelo does have one weakness: a residual sentiment of solidarity. A cripple is put to work beside him in the tunnels. Malpelo beats him brutally: 'if you haven't the spirit to defend yourself from someone who isn't against you, you'll let your face be stamped on by anyone.' But he helps the boy when the work gets too much for him. And when the cripple is dying of consumption, Malpelo goes to visit him. The mother is weeping. Malpelo doesn't understand and asks the boy why the woman is crying over someone who earns less than it costs to feed him.

Ultimately, the pathos of Verga's stories is not the individual suffering and death of this or that person, but the collective failure – is it Verga's failure too? – to imagine the world as anything other than a long and ruthless power struggle. The victims see nothing unnatural in the avarice and cruelty of those who destroy them. Compassion is reduced to the dubious aesthetic experience of the engineer who hurries back from mining disaster to theatre to be able to see his favourite scene in *Hamlet*: Ophelia's burial.

> Once we have established that he distrusts ideals and ideologies, considered as vehicles of hidden interests . . . one may wonder whether there was anything he really cared about, anything he believed in unshakeably. To which one answers that there was at least one thing he believed in: *the struggle of everybody against everybody else.*

These words were written by the French anthropologist Louis Dumont. The man described is Hitler. But had Malpelo had an education he might well have written *Mein Kampf*. Certainly he would have made a good *squadrista* in Fascist Italy. Verga's deep sense of outrage has to do with the fact that the fine sentiments of life, love and compassion intersect with reality only when art

145

turns them into money. 'The cheers of the triumphant drown the cries of the trampled. But seen close up, isn't the grotesque gasping of those faces inevitably artistic to the observer?' These frightening words were written as part of the preface to the novel *I Malavoglia*, then cut. They would hardly encourage sales.

For Verga needed the money. He liked to cut a figure. In his mid-forties he was still borrowing from whoever would give him credit. So the terms of a loan would always be important to him. He never married, either a poor wife or a rich. But he was determined not to join 'the Defeated', not to be the object of a mining engineer's aesthetic appreciation. Denied the royalties for the opera *Cavalleria rusticana*, based on a script Verga himself adapted from his own short story, he fought a long court case and won. At last he had fame and cash together. But now the writing was going badly. He couldn't get past the second novel of the projected five-work cycle, and though those first two, *I Malavoglia* and *Mastro Don Gesualdo*, were to become classics of Italian literature, and are indeed rich and remarkable narratives, still the extraordinary impact of the short stories, novellas so-called, is dispersed in their huge accumulation of detail.

Then, in his fifties, it occurred to Verga that the principles of *verismo* were false. It was impossible to represent reality. The whole thing was a farcical charade in which words were always manipulative. All a writer could do was to explode life's fictions and be a fool to no man. So his last collection of published stories, *Don Candeloro & Co.*, gives us a grotesque rereading of the earlier work where love triangles, betrayals and the rest are now seen as the merest and most cynical manoeuvrings. But Verga had been most effective when the yearning that the world not be absurd was still intact; it had reached its greatest intensity in stories like 'Rosso Malpelo', where the boy's humanity, expressed in his compassion for his crippled companion, is still *just* there, but only as something residual, anachronistic, quite mysterious in the modern world. In 'Don Candeloro' compassion has finally been eliminated. It may be a relief, but the narrative loses its force. If, as Cioran maintained, cruelty is a sign of election in a writer, we now discover that it is so only when held in tension by its opposite.

'Poor old Verga went and died exactly as I was going to see him in Catania,' wrote Lawrence. The Sicilian was eighty-two. He had spent the last twenty years sensibly looking after the family estates in grumpy isolation, writing very little, perhaps because he could no longer find any cover for his distressing vision. Made a senator in 1920, he succumbed to a stroke in January 1922. Just nine months later, the terrifying combination he had ever described, a ruthless will to power dressed in grotesque rhetoric, stepped out onto the world stage in the stalwart form of Benito Mussolini.

But young Malpelo perished thus: ordered to explore a labyrinth of abandoned mine shafts under the slopes of Etna, he boldly took up his father's pick and lantern. 'I am Malpelo, if I don't come back, no one will look for me.' And no one did. Defiantly alone, he disappeared for ever, as though swallowed up at last in the dark logic of pure individualism and commercial exploitation. Needless to say, his ghost haunts.

Voltaire's Coconuts

[Ian Buruma]

As I set out to write this piece on Ian Buruma's book *Voltaire's Coconuts*, Italy has just come to the end of another referendum campaign. Two general elections ago a new system of voting was introduced. Instead of the extreme form of proportional representation in force since 1948, a first-past-the-post system was introduced for 75% of the seats in the lower house, while 25% would continue to be allotted on a proportional basis. The recent referendum proposed to eliminate that 25% and base voting for the lower house entirely on the British system.

The idea behind these changes is the same that was dear to Voltaire's heart and that inspires the title of Buruma's book: the notion that those institutions that have proved successful in one country, in this case Britain, might, like coconuts, be transplanted elsewhere with the same positive results. Dogged by a combination of chronically unstable governments and long-term political paralysis, the Italians hoped that by importing the British system they might also import the opposite and, as they perceive it, peculiarly British combination of stable governments coming alternately from different sides of the political spectrum.

As yet the scheme hasn't worked. Rather than being reduced, the number of parties has considerably increased. The pattern of unstable and shifting alliances, of governments held to ransom by small minorities in hung parliaments, has remained much as it was. The pressure for this new referendum, then, came from those who feel that this failure is due to the fact that the British system was not introduced in all its brutal extremity. The 25% of

149

seats still handed out on a proportional basis, they claim, has been used to keep tiny parties alive and unpresentable members of the old guard in parliament. Its elimination will finally produce British results.

Those who opposed the referendum and voted against its proposal (or in most cases did not vote at all, since without an overall 50% turnout a referendum is declared void) maintain that British stability has little to do with the British electoral system and may rather come in spite of it. The first-past-the-post system, they insist, encourages a low turnout, as those who know they can't win in any given constituency don't participate, and this alienates them from the democratic process. A totally British system, they conclude, could lead to serious unrest in Italy.

Astonishing and certainly ingenuous is the assumption, on both sides of the debate, that the results of such major changes would come sufficiently rapidly as to be perceptible after just one or two elections. For if Voltaire chose, of all plants, the coconut for his analogy of transplanting institutions, it was precisely because the coconut takes so very long to bear fruit. All the same, the lapse of time – how much time? – allows the debate to rage: are institutions universally applicable, or are they intimately related to circumstances of history and race, or to what is more vaguely referred to as 'national character'?

In *Voltaire's Coconuts* Buruma sets out to present us with the visions of a number of European intellectuals who have come to Britain over the last three centuries and reflected on its traditions and institutions. In doing so he finds himself almost obliged at some point or other to define them either as 'universalists' who believed in the possibility of exporting the best they found in Britain, or 'nativists' who either did not believe things British could be successfully exported or, perhaps more commonly, did not wish them to be so. Pierre Coubertin, founder of the modern Olympic Games, saw no reason why the ethos of the Arnoldian public school could not be profitably transported to France and indeed all over the world. The Games, for him, were to be an expression of that ethos. His ideological and anglophobe enemy, Charles Maurras, present at the first of Coubertin's Olympics in Athens in 1896, rather than acknowledging defeat, rejoiced in the observation that 'when different races are thrown together and made to interact, they repel one another, estranging themselves, even as they believe they are mixing'.

Dreaming of a future Jewish homeland, Theodor Herzl charmingly imagined it as having British institutions, an English style upper class and even Jewish cricket on trim Palestinian, or indeed – did it matter? – Ugandan lawns. This was at a time when significant sections of continental Europe were engaged in identifying Jews as alien, hostile and by nature unassimilable to the German or French cultures (logically, the extreme nativist no more believes in the possibility of someone's assimilating another culture than he does in transplanting its institutions elsewhere). The British were thus to be stigmatised for their perceived sympathy with Jewish positions. '*L'anglais est-il un Juif?*' Buruma quotes one French tract as demanding in 1895. Clearly the danger of arguing against Voltaire and his optimistic universalism is that one may open the way to the merest and most obtuse racism. It is the lure of this trap that makes it so important for us to understand what we mean by national character.

Buruma's book is largely and unapologetically anecdotal. He introduces us to a cast of prominent Europeans from Voltaire and Goethe in the eighteenth century to Nikolaus Pevsner and Isaiah Berlin in the twentieth, with the central (and best) chapters dedicated to the revolutionaries and dreamers of the mid-nineteenth century, so many of whom were to find themselves obliged to flee to the safe if perplexingly unrevolutionary climate of London. Each character's association with Britain is briskly sketched in, Buruma astutely pointing out that their positive or negative visions of the country can only properly be understood in relation to the circumstances they are coming from. Indeed much of the comedy he is eager to offer arises from observing how difficult it is for those who stay in Britain for any length of time to sustain a view initially prompted by a personal agenda elsewhere. Unable to publish an anti-clerical poem in France, Voltaire praises the English for their love of reason and liberty, their respect for the artist, but he will later be obliged to leave the country in a hurry after some ambiguous money transactions. Inspired by *Tom Brown's Schooldays*, Coubertin will need all his considerable reserves of enthusiasm to overlook the less attractive aspects of the British public schools he visits. The intellectual traveller, and even more so the refugee, lives in a constant tension between his desire to abstract what he finds abroad and use it in an argument with those back home, and the pull to engage in the society that surrounds him on its own terms. Accordingly, the long-term immigrant's vision of his host country will very largely depend on whether he genuinely chooses to stay there, or is merely physically present while spiritually embattled abroad. One of the most touching pictures in *Voltaire's Coconuts* is that of the ageing Russian revolutionary and idealist Alexander Herzen finding himself after all not so unhappy in the mercantile and irretrievably bourgeois stability of Victorian London.

Buruma's sketches, for the most part in chronological order, are interspersed with complementary anecdotes about his own family – an intriguing Anglo-German-Dutch-Jewish mix – anecdotes which allow us to understand where *he* is coming from and why the characters he speaks of are important to him. Nothing in this personal and generally engaging approach need detract from serious consideration of the matter in hand, especially since, with the present acceleration of moves towards a united Europe, the question of national character is one that is of general, even urgent, interest. Buruma has frequently shown himself to be a formidable essayist on this subject. Yet something in the whole slant of the project seems to prevent him from giving his book real weight, or even coherence. As if writing the script for some Channel Four documentary, he appears to be more interested in popping up in prima persona at Fingal's Cave, or Prince Ludwig's Walhalla, or Highgate Cemetery, than in seeking to define his terms, or push his argument on.

With regard to the debate announced by his title, Buruma's sympathies are clearly with the universalists. He rightly criticises nativists for their tedious use of the 'native soil' analogy, the idea that institutions have grown naturally from the organic inter-twining of race and place. It is a ploy that precludes argument and leads at best to immobility, at worst, as has been said, to racism. Conversely, he enjoys much humour, though always kind-hearted, at the expense of the wilder universalist dreamers, those who would see Tom Brown in Paris, or the aristocracy of a Jewish state sipping tea at four and being nice to the servants.

But despite his brilliant asides and exciting intuitions – and they are many – he seeks to offer no reasoned middle ground between the two camps, even when the authors he quotes, Tocqueville and Pevsner in particular, seem to be inviting him to do so. Less forgivably, he himself has a habit of slipping into a use of national stereotypes which inevitably detracts from establishing a more sophisticated approach to the conundrum of national character. Thus of Hippolyte Taine we read: 'In his twenties, Taine was attracted to German idealism: Hegel, Herder and so on. He grew out of that, however, and turned to more practical English ideas instead.'

Whether the disparaging 'grew out of' is to be attributed, ironically, to Taine or, more problematically, to Buruma is unclear and perhaps unimportant. To many readers it will pass unobserved. We are in the realm of received ideas where the use of 'national character' amounts to no more than a hasty appeal to presumed experience and shared sentiments before the argument is hurried along elsewhere.

153

A few pages later the need to define terms becomes even more urgently evident. Rightly remarking how Taine's nativism – his refusal to believe that one country could be a model for another – allowed him to be more candid than other anglophiles about England's shortcomings, Buruma concludes: 'He could observe the stability of the British government and contrast it to the violent upheavals in France, but if national character was indeed the key, such observation could serve no political purpose: The world is what it is, because it grew that way, like a tree, and there is nothing much we can do to improve it.'

Here it seems that national character is being used almost as a synonym of race – or at least as something necessarily immobile – with the implication that the universalist cannot admit the existence of a national character at all. 'The definition of national identity,' Buruma announces elsewhere, 'is largely the project of intellectuals and artists who wish to find a role for themselves.'

When these sweeping statements are seen together with the previous comment on German ideas – a comment that accepts not only the stereotypes regarding British and German thinking but also the spin the British like to put on them – our author presents himself as a confirmed, even dogmatic universalist who occasionally falls into a use of nativist national stereotype, perhaps because in the end it is so attractive. Like caricature, national stereotype contains an element that is immediately recognisable or felt to be so, and again like caricature it allows for the rapid establishment of a topography – Teutonic efficiency, Anglo-Saxon pragmatism, Gallic passion – within which the various parties concerned can enjoy a sense of immediate and mutually confirming identity, together with the security, which is also the comedy, of predictability: when the Brits do this, the Krauts will undoubtedly do that and the Frogs, of course, the other. Although this oscillation between opposing positions – universalism, nativism – is understandable (in the way we understand perfectly when someone says it's *only* caricature, while at the same time enjoying a secret complicity in its reductive panache), it does not really help clarify the issues under discussion.

Why has the introduction into Italy of a British inspired electoral system not given the desired results? It cannot be merely because of this or that trait in 'the Italian character', since, despite the popular image of the excitable, talented, unreliable Italian, the country clearly has as wide a range of personality types as any other. The expression 'poles apart' would seem entirely appropriate to describe such pairs as Cavour and Garibaldi, Mazzini and Victor Emanuel II, or to bring things up to date, D'Alema and Berlusconi. Thus one can no more – the reflection is obvious – be Italian (or English or French) *on one's own*, than one could be human, or indeed inhuman, on one's own, or a son without a mother.

To the extent, then, that we perceive different patterns of behaviour in different countries this would appear to have to do with a certain dynamic in the way people behave *together*. After all, what is usually most perplexing in our experience of a foreign country is not the pleasant conversation with any one individual – in that scenario we tend to be struck by how like us they are, how easy it is going to be to understand each other – but the way they behave in relation to each other. Drawing on the culture's available role models, they become themselves in a play of forces that may be very different from that pertaining in our own country. Rather than one immediately recognisable type, what we're up against is a constellation of possible types whose mutually tensing and defining energies may be even more difficult for us to grasp than those in the night sky.

Ex-prime minister Giulio Andreotti, to hazard an example, is often referred to as quintessentially Italian for his particular mixture of piety and mystery, of astuteness and ambiguity. Yet the man could only function as he did and become what he was within the special environment of Italian politics, and most particularly post-war politics, something dependant on a huge number of external circumstances. Brought up in Liverpool or Lisbon it is reasonable to suspect that Andreotti would have developed very differently.

If we accept this premise, it isn't difficult to see how we can have a 'national character' – or a series of behaviour patterns – that perpetuates itself through education (the word used here in the broadest possible sense), without assuming that this is an inevitable product of the race or the soil and without imagining that it is necessarily impervious to outside influence. By the same token, it is clear that any institution exported to another country will necessarily be absorbed into the local dynamic, perhaps be transformed by it. The end results are not easy to predict. This is what makes the experiment so exciting. And perhaps dangerous. In any event, there is no need for us to be either strictly nativist or strictly universalist.

When the Italians introduced something approaching the British electoral system, they did so after the traumatic years of *mani pulite* had led to the disintegration of the broad-church Christian Democratic Party that had dominated since the war. The decision of the old Communist Party to distance itself from the past and become the *Partito Democratico della Sinistra* also led to splits on the left. On the right the fascist-inspired *Movimento Sociale Italiano* had likewise made a move towards the democratic fold, changing its name to *Alleanza Nazionale*. Again this led to splits. The new system was thus introduced at a moment of maximum flux when the formation of two clearly dominant parties of the kind that would thrive in a first-past-the-post system was particularly difficult.

Immediately campaigning began, it became evident that an electoral tradition is far more than the legal machinery of its voting system. The Italians have a long history of complex electoral alliances of the variety that tend to nullify the clarifying effect of the first-past-the-post system. While in England one might indeed find, say, the Liberals and Labour agreeing not to stand against each other in certain seats, it is unlikely that one would see scores of parties allying with all kinds of different partners in a huge and complex mosaic designed to give each of them more or less the proportion of representation they hold across the country. Far from shunning such complications, the Italian electorate is at home with them, or at least inured. *Fatta la legge, trovato l'inganno* goes the proverb ('no sooner is a law made than the way round it discovered'). It's an old observation that a history of despotic foreign rulers has led, in Italy, to the exaltation of the anarchical model. A certain pleasure is taken in demonstrating that a system imposed by the centre doesn't work. There is nothing racial or genetic about this, nor any reason why it shouldn't change. But, as Voltaire himself accepted, it takes time.

The existence of proverbs which seem to sum up aspects of national character naturally leads to a reflection on the relationship of that character to the language its people speaks. Here Buruma is dismissive. 'The *Geist* of language,' he announces, 'is one of those foggy concepts that swirl around like dry ice on Wagnerian stage sets.' Later he takes Pevsner to task for suggesting that the difference between the English word 'chop' (as in pork chop) and the Italian word 'costoletta' shows an English love of understatement and the Italian predilection for the florid. Here one can only agree and smile. But without any further consideration, Buruma then sums up his position thus: 'The notion that some essence of Englishness, running from the middle ages to the present time, can be identified in the national language is to put it mildly dubious.'

If we imagine any group of people as organising their behaviour around available role models and a consequent hierarchy of values, it is reasonable to suppose that those values will be reflected in the language they speak and the way they speak it. This must have been even more evident when societies were smaller and more homogeneous. So while one would hardly wish to make much of the sound or length of a single word, it would equally be hard to deny that, say, the more elaborate nature of Italian sentence structures might reflect different habits of thought. And clearly there are some words 'Geist' is one – that Buruma himself will not translate because he knows that they are the product of a pattern of thinking which would be lost in translation. This is why Europeans do not translate such words as 'gentleman' and 'hooligan', or why a notion like 'omertà' needs more than a little explanation in English. What have our non-conformist writers always done, after all, if not sought to expose the pattern of thinking implicit in the language itself? When Lawrence wrote a sentence like 'she was destroyed into perfect consciousness', he was eager to subvert the normally positive loadings afforded to the concepts of both perfection and consciousness. The translation of the sentence into Italian – 'era dilianiata, perfettamente consapevole' – rejecting as it does the oddly transformative 'into' of the English, is suggestive of the Italian resistance to provocative subversion of the language within the field of *belles lettres*, something everywhere evident in Italian translations of British modernists.

Clearly the phenomenon of translation offers an intriguing instance of the extent to which any culture may or may not be open to influence from another. Again, the question is complex and ultimately impossible to resolve. Again Buruma's thinking is cloudy. At the beginning of a chapter dedicated to Goethe and the German appropriation of Shakespeare, he remarks of his own early bilingualism: 'Such a background effectively cuts off all routes to linguistic nativism.'

Buruma, then, a universalist, believes in translatability. Apparently, languages are interchangeable. But a few pages later, discussing Schlegel's translation of Shakespeare, he is offering the following typically nativist and entirely reasonable qualification: 'His brilliant translation may have been the most accurate version of Shakespeare in German to date, but it also contained echoes of Goethe's classicism and Herder's poetry. It was, in short, a German text.'

Having made this observation, Buruma would now appear to be in a strong position to make a truly pertinent statement about the way cultures may indeed be open to each other, yet transform, without necessarily nullifying, what they absorb according to their own dynamic: yes, this is Shakespeare, but Shakespeare in German. Instead, his closing remark merely betrays how little he has been enjoying his reading in this particular field: 'A famous German Shakespeare (and Goethe) scholar tried to explain this [Schlegel's translation] in the following rather tortured formulation: the universal genius of Shakespeare could be reborn in Germany only after the universal genius of Goethe had infused the German language with a German *Geist* equal to the English spirit of Shakespeare.'

Though the lofty diction of the scholar's observation may not be to everybody's taste, it is hard to see what is 'tortured' about this. That the way in which certain writers have enriched their languages then makes it possible for translators to find solutions to hitherto insoluble problems seems self-evident. How could translations into Italian of English novels be the same after Manzoni had written *I promessi sposi*? How could one not draw on Eliot for a translation of the French symbolists?

Freshly arrived in England, Voltaire thoroughly enjoyed an afternoon by the Thames and at the races; but introduced the same evening to court society his enthusiastic report was met with disdain: 'the young women he had admired so foolishly were maidservants, and the jolly young men mere apprentices on hired horses.' A century later, Tocqueville is bewildered to find that his English friends are 'still convinced that extreme inequality of wealth is in the natural order of things'. When will these people have their revolution? the Frenchman wonders. Why are they obsessed by class? Visiting the Poet Laureate Alfred Austin, Theodor Herzl was unimpressed by the man's grasp of international politics but terribly taken by his respectful manners. In general, Buruma comments, Herzl made a point, 'of mentioning that the Grand Duke of this or the Marquess of that had helped him into his coat or showed him to his coach'. How could the Jewish immigrant fail to love a country where a Jew had not only been made prime minister, but an earl too . . .

The most exciting aspect of *Voltaire's Coconuts* and its very real contribution is the way – with all the attractive diversity of the anglophiles and anglophobes it presents – nevertheless and across three centuries, a very clear consensus begins to build up as to what the conundrum of British national character amounts to, for a European. We are allowed, that is, a growing insight into how the dynamic of our own national life puzzles our neighbours.

Inevitably the difficulty is not with any single element but with the way in which they stand in relation to each other. On the one hand there is the high value put on reason and on political and religious freedoms: the Britain of the last two centuries was indeed freer than its European counterparts. On the other, and however much it may now be under attack, there is the strong sense of class belonging that continues to enshrine social and economic inequalities. There is a great and progressive drive in the areas of trade and industry, coupled with ancient, ludicrous, even Gothic traditions, usually in those areas where privilege is sacred. There is a notable lack of support for, or even interest in, extremist ideological positions, together with the most vociferous and tasteless gutter press anywhere imaginable. Above all – and on this point it seems all the bickering revolutionaries, from Ledru-Rollin to Herzen, Marx and Mazzini agreed – England was *dull*, was mediocre. Buruma never quotes Nietzsche but that philosopher's denunciation of the 'English-mechanistic stultification of the world' never seems far from the visiting European's lips.

Naturally, the more astute thinkers were eager to guess at the secret that kept these apparent opposites in equilibrium. Tocqueville noted that for all the starkness of class distinctions, nevertheless there was a possibility of upward mobility in England, something that was not true in France. 'A man could become a gentleman,' Buruma glosses, 'but you had to be born a *gentilhomme.*' The English avidity for trade and money is thus peculiarly different from the American, in that the Englishman aspires to use his cash to buy into a world of mystique and privilege, to change class. As a result he isn't eager to have his aristocracy abolished, while the aristocracy in turn is, yes, snobbish – how could it be otherwise? – but does not entirely turn up its nose to new money and new celebrity. In this regard Buruma offers some convincing remarks on the alliance between Thatcher and the Tory party.

There appears, then, to be a curious alchemy by which, in certain circumstances, the English mind turns the water of money into the wine of nobility. Intriguingly, Buruma draws on his own experiences to remark that most anglophiles are snobs. They see the English social world as offering a recognition that elsewhere neither money nor celebrity can buy. Convincingly, he points to the great many foreigners who have become English lords and gentlemen. England offers this odd opportunity. After twenty years in Italy, I have yet to see the phenomenon in reverse.

Herzen's observations on English mediocrity may at first sight seem some distance from Tocqueville's musings on the permeability of the British class system. Taken together, however, and with the help of an observation or two from Giacomo Leopardi, who was neither anglophile nor anglophobe, perhaps we can hazard a guess as to the deeper nature of the quarrel, or love affair, between England and mainland Europe, both a century ago and still today.

Herzen reflected that 'the only countries in Europe that are tranquil are those in which personal liberty and freedom of speech are least restricted'. However, not being oppressed by their governments, the British and Swiss were not obliged to develop a spirit of private disobedience and thus tended to become duller. What was more, freedom of speech actually opened the way to a different kind of tyranny, that of public opinion as expressed in a scandal-mongering press. Herzen wrote: 'The freer a country is from government interference, the more fully recognised its right to speak, to independence of conscience, the more intolerant grows the mob: public opinion becomes a torture chamber; your neighbour, your butcher, your tailor, family, club, parish, keep you under supervision and perform the duties of a policeman.' In short, Tocqueville's upwardly mobile industrialist, eager to buy into a world of British privilege, will not only have to accumulate a great deal of money, he must also avoid scandal so as to keep the public respect.

So far so good. But what was this dullness, this supposed mediocrity that Europeans, particularly the revolutionaries and above all Marx, despised? What did it amount to? Did Mazzini, for example, honestly imagine that in the Utopia he proposed – ultimately a free, democratic, one-world state – people would be *more interesting*? Surely when no longer obliged to disobey in private they too would become 'dull'.

Herzen's reaction to a representation of the battle of Waterloo is telling here. Wellington and Blücher, he complains, 'had turned history off the high road and up to the hubs in mud'. For these European revolutionaries excitement and romance had to do with a particular and basically Hegelian vision of history in which they saw themselves as high-road prophets of a future transformation at once inevitable and positive. From this they derived importance and self-esteem. It is a curiosity of the British mindframe that it has remained largely indifferent to this particular delirium, and it was this indifference that so irritated nineteenth-century revolutionaries, as today it irritates those in Europe who are eager to construct, with a similar vision of history in mind, the single European Community. Rather than appreciating, with Tocqueville, that the British, and so many of those who have been attracted to Britain, were perhaps locked into a different project, the acquisition of prestige through style and money – what we often refer to in the pejorative as snobbery – they chose, and choose, to dismiss them as mediocre.

Leopardi was among the first to suggest that in the great wreck of noble illusions brought about by rationalism and the retreat of religion, national *mores* would play an important part in helping the individual develop a strategy for dealing with the now evident, as he saw it, meaninglessness of life. Written in 1824, his *Discourse on the Present State of Italian Customs* presents 'Italianness' as almost a special condition of the spirit. In other countries public morality had survived the collapse of metaphysics thanks to a more highly developed sense of society. In England or France a gentleman 'would be ashamed of doing wrong in the same way as he would be ashamed of appearing in conversation with a stain on his suit'. As in Schopenhauer's aphorisms on honour, it is the search for the respect of one's peers, coupled crucially with the knowledge of how that respect is to be obtained, that holds society together. Leopardi thus envies the British the ridiculously high opinion they afford to each other, seeing in it a guarantee of moral behaviour.

In Italy, however, the poet claims, no such society had replaced the illusions of the Middle Ages; Italians conceded no respect to each other, indeed took pleasure above all in exchanging insults, with the result that it was clear to everyone that 'there was no reason for not behaving exactly as one wished'. Leopardi concludes by prospecting the need for collective illusions on a large scale to combat a sense of meaninglessness and the resultant cynicism. He speaks of the idea of nationhood, prophesies, long before Coubertin, that sport and its associated pageantry will become an important spiritual resource. He can hardly be blamed if Italy's great collective illusion, when it did finally come, was to take such unfortunate turns.

Ever since the Enlightenment, continental Europe has been busy producing grander and grander projects to compensate for the collapse of feudal authority and shared religion, to cover up underlying doubt and existential anxiety. Infinitely preferable to communism or fascism, the European Community is the most recent of these projects. Unlike empires seized or rigid systems merely imposed, it possesses a novel and perhaps decisive asset: a scope for seemingly endless complication, endless accommodation of minorities, interminable negotiation with new members. Not for nothing have all the national languages been maintained. Not for nothing are various tiers of membership envisaged. Quite simply, this project, which can easily be believed in as inherently good and historically inevitable, will take up *all the time there is.* Not a moment will be left for feelings of futility. At present one sure way to gain prestige in Europe is to work tirelessly to keep this ideal on the high road of history, out of the mud.

Meanwhile, and at the deepest level, the British are not so much opposed as disinterested. They have other ways of keeping meaninglessness at bay. Wasn't the fate of Diana, Princess of Wales, the possibility of her introducing a wealthy Middle Eastern playboy into an extended royal family, a much more interesting story than anything the bureaucrats of Brussels have dreamed up? And the British agony is that while they would be content to stay out of the European project, this might lead to a loss of wealth and, ever associated with wealth, the prestige they chase. But it's only a might. For, alas, the further agony is that participation and the corresponding surrender of sovereignty could equally well lead to a loss of wealth: those hellish complications the continentals keep generating are not conducive to the accumulation of capital. We'll wait and see, the British say about the Euro, blissfully unaware that this approach is as contemptible to the contemporary European with the Grand Idea as British diffidence to liberal revolution was for Mazzini and Herzen 150 years ago. Yet in or out, like it or not, Britain is part of the larger dynamic that makes up European character. It is, as Buruma's book very convincingly shows, the place where people can go when, whether as leader or victim, the Continent's grand ideas let them down.

How did the Italian referendum end? At midnight on election day, forecasts suggested 52% of the population had voted, 91% of whom supported the British system. Little over an hour later, the official result came. Only 49.6% had voted. The referendum was void. The following morning the government announced that it would persist with a project to introduce the French system of two ballots. At once, and across the political spectrum, smaller groupings announced their opposition, preferring the German proportional system with a 5% threshold. The Northern League immediately declared who they would ally with to be sure of overcoming the threshold. Even when bombarded with promising foreign coconuts, a national mindframe, it seems, dies hard.

Literary Trieste

[Svevo, Joyce, Saba]

Trieste is hardly on the beaten track for Italophiles. Almost a hundred miles east of Venice and on the wrong side of the Adriatic it seems to gaze back at the *bel paese*, instead of being a part of it. It has no great art galleries, museums or monuments. The weather is notoriously harsh. Even identity is a problem: a windswept stone's throw from the Slovenian border, Trieste is home to three distinct ethnic groups: Slav, Germanic and Italian.

'I am Slavic-German-Italian,' wrote Scipio Slataper, the first writer to claim (around 1910) that there was in fact a 'Triestine type'.

From my Slav blood I have within me strange nostalgias, a desire for novelty, for abandoned forests, a sentimentality (or sensibility) that demands caresses, praises: an infinite limitless dreaming. From my German blood I have my mulish obstinacy, my dictatorial will and tone, the certainty of my plans, the boredom I feel at having to accept discussion, my desire for domination, for exertion. These elements are fused in the Italian blood which seeks to harmonise them, to balance them out, to make me become 'classical'.

The local intellectual Roberto Bazlen was more sceptical, writing:

A melting pot is a utensil into which are put the most disparate elements, which are then melted; what is produced is a homogeneous fusion, with all its elements proportionately distributed, with constant characteristics. But in Trieste, as I know it, a fused type has never been produced, nor any type with stable characteristics [. . .] And since a unique Triestine type does not exist, so a Triestine creative culture does not exist either.

His contemporary and fellow citizen Giani Stuparich agreed:

there is something in this city of mine that blocks any initiative designed to give it a cultural character or physiognomy, not only in its disintegrative atmosphere but in its individuals, who willingly isolate themselves or go elsewhere. It has a bitter air . . .

Yet in the early years of the twentieth century, the small and troubled town of Trieste was home to three writers who would later be designated great: Italo Svevo, James Joyce and the poet Umberto Saba.

Of course writers and above all groups of writers tend to encourage mythologies about themselves, their lives and achievements: Gertrude Stein and her school, Ezra Pound, Ernest Hemingway. And readers too are often eager to surround the texts they love with anecdotes, and to attribute remarkable qualities to the authors they admire.

In Trieste, a port city with an uneasy history of difficult allegiances and blurred racial boundaries, the question of identity and ethnicity was bound to play a part in the formation of such mythologies. Hence it's hardly surprising, for example, that both Svevo and Saba are pseudonyms, and that the names should be the starting point for a great deal of literary speculation. Was Ettore Schmitz, alias Italo Svevo, who was educated in German, grew up speaking Triestine dialect and indeed lived most of his life under Austrian rule, really an Italian writer? Was his style, as some contemporaries suggested, perhaps more Slav than Italian? Would he have done better, as Umberto Poli, alias Umberto Saba, thought, to have written in German? And did Saba's own problems of identity (he changed pseudonyms more than once) arise not only out of the early desertion of his father, but partly from the curiously mixed ethnic origins of the Jewish mother and aunts and the Slovenian nurse who brought him up, and from the uncertain identity of a city he was so determined should be Italian? Finally, could it have been precisely the uneasiness of this local situation and the fierce desire of the local people to be liberated from an imperial power that made the Irish exile, Joyce, feel at home in Trieste for ten long years?

These are questions that loom large in Joseph Cary's book, *A Ghost in Trieste*. Behind them lies the more general but ever intriguing conundrum, How much does the spirit of a particular place at a particular time inform and shape the novels and poems written there, and how anyway could such influence be measured and savoured?

Yet Cary's book is slow to home in on its subject. As a guide and critic he proceeds on the principle that indirections will eventually find directions out, and although some of the consequent meandering does have its charm, it must be said that much is sentimental and self-regarding. 'I went to Trieste because I hoped to find my business there,' he tells us in his 'preliminary'.

A notion for a book, *Literary Trieste*, was in my head, and I felt that going there would translate this notion into a clear and spurring idea . . .

I drew a beautiful equilateral triangle in my notebook

and wrote 'Trieste 1905–15' beneath it. Trieste was the key.

All too soon, however, he discovers that Trieste is a modern town not unlike many others, that Joyce and Svevo's relationship was not after all very much more than that between any young language teacher and his older pupil, that Svevo met Saba only rarely and with no more than tepid cordiality, and that Saba, so far as we know, never met Joyce at all. His desire for an easy mythology, or literary salon to exhume so immediately thwarted, Cary then embarks on pages of wistful self-irony which tell us little about either Trieste or the writers whose relation to the city we are interested in, and rather more than we would care to know about Cary's sense of himself as travel writer manqué:

> In the Cinema Eden I sat through *101 Dalmatians* wondering what they made of it in Dalmatia. Ghost-wise I petered past as a pretty blonde peered through a crack in the green canvas at a tennis match on the court behind Villa Necker. For hours and hours, the louvers of my darkened hotel room cut street-lamp light into thin orange stripes across the ceiling. They rippled when a car passed.

Finally, it occurs to him to see himself as a ghost wandering through Trieste in search of an ever elusive literary past, a quaint image but hardly an encouraging one for those of us expecting to hear more of Saba, Svevo and Joyce. At other moments Cary seems to forget his literary interests altogether: 'This is a book about Trieste: its curious history, some of its residents, some of my stumbling steps to get a view of it.' How long exactly did this adventure last? 'My three weeks in Trieste have been distributed over five years with long intervals at home . . .'

If readers were puzzled by the adjective 'beautiful' used to describe the hand-sketched equilateral triangle earlier on, they will no doubt be even more perplexed by that 'long intervals at home'. More surprising still is the way it does not occur to Cary that to acquire the kind of deep sense of place and local character which might shed some light on the way the city influenced its writers, a critic might want to stick around for three months, or three years, rather than three weeks.

These irritations have to be mentioned, but fortunately, once Cary has got his self-indulgent comments on travel out of the way and begun to concentrate on this history of the city and the relationship of that history to its artists and writers, then his book becomes fascinating. We hear of Trieste's early development as a Roman garrison town, its struggle to survive through the Dark Ages and its unusual decision to offer itself to the Austrian crown in return for protection. We discover that it was the enlightened if never altruistic strategy of successive Austrian emperors that led to the city's rapid development as a southern port of central Europe, to the point where, in the late nineteenth century, it was second only to Marseilles. Most of all, Cary gradually and thoroughly establishes the huge irony that whereas Trieste's economic prosperity depended on its connection with Austria and the north, the predominantly Italian identity of its people and the rising tide of nationalism which swept through Europe in the mid-nineteenth century inevitably pushed the city towards union with Italy in the west.

Thus the first decade of the twentieth century, when Joyce and Saba and Svevo were all in the city at the same time, was a fascinating one. Trieste was at the height of its commercial success, but the very energy generated by that wealth went to feed a passionate Italian nationalism which, in achieving its end, would ultimately destroy the city's wealth by cutting it off from Austria and its hinterland. Cary is at his best here, weaving together an excellent series of quotations to show how artists, poets and novelists reflected this nationalism in their writing. From Carducci through the predictably flamboyant D'Annunzio, the rumbustious critic Scipio Slataper and the futurist Marinetti, what is extraordinary is the vehemence, eloquence and, some-times, thank God, wit, with which this nationalism was expressed. Slataper, who died fighting on the Austrian-Italian frontier in 1915, is particularly attractive when he imagines Trieste's discovery of its national and cultural identity as that of an ingenuous young Parsifal,

> who awakened one day between a crate of lemons and a sack of coffee beans thinking that, for his own good, he ought to modulate his life to another rhythm than that of a snorting or puffing engine, treat it to another melody than that of silver clinking in the pockets of some capacious waistcoat.

That is, he should look to Italy. Marinetti, on the other hand, is merely frightening. In the amazingly titled *War, Sole Hygiene of the World* (1910), he apostrophises Trieste as follows:

> You are the scarlet, violent face of Italy, turned toward the enemy! . . . Trieste! you are our sole shield! . . . Do not forget O Trieste, that the Italian peninsula has the form of a *dreadnought*, with a squadron of torpedo-boat islands.

The passage vaguely echoes, D'Annunzio's notorious 'Ode To a Torpedo Boat in the Adriatic' written almost twenty years earlier:

> Steel ship, straight, swift, flashing
> beautiful as a naked weapon,
> alive, palpitant
> as though metal enclosed a terrible heart.

By the end of the poem D'Annunzio leaves us in no doubt that that naked weapon is pointed in the very specific direction of Austrian-controlled Trieste.

But it is not so much the warmongering of the literary intelligentsia that is surprising and sobering here as the realisation that only a hundred years ago European culture was still based primarily on the written word, and a poet could still see himself as having a formidable and immediate political part to play. Just a few years before the movies would become ubiquitous, a few decades before television, the time of Joyce, Saba and Svevo in Trieste marked the last years of the word as unrivalled manipulator of public feeling. As if in valedictory homage to that power, or demonstration of the prophetic and political vocation of the poet, the transfer of Trieste from Austrian to Italian sovereignty was effectively confirmed by the arrival in the port of a torpedo boat, the *Audacious.*

So much for the fervid literary and political scene. Yet as we read through Cary's carefully chosen quotes we gradually become aware of the absence of any contribution from Joyce, Saba or Svevo. True, Joyce, while in Trieste, gave one or two lectures on Irish history where clear parallels were drawn between Britain and Austria as imperial oppressors. True, Svevo remarked that it was the coming of Italy to Trieste that gave him the inspiration to write his last and greatest novel, *La coscienza di Zeno.* True, Saba later spoke of having 'married [Trieste] to Italy for ever with my song', but he was clearly speaking more of having been the first to write poetry on the city in a 'proper' Tuscan Italian than of having contributed to nationalist propaganda. For the fact is that none of these writers had anything at all to say in their creative work about the political issues that were exciting the other writers round about them.

In his indirect style Cary thus appears to stumble on the central point of his book when remarking that a literary history of Trieste and Istria, written in 1924 by a professor at the newly established University of Trieste, includes neither Saba nor Svevo. Cary comments: 'It is the total absence of *anima patria* in the novels of Svevo . . . and in the poetry of Saba . . . that accounts for their absence from the pages of *Storia letteraria di Trieste e dell'Istria.*'

Exactly. And we begin to see that it was the creative isolation of these three writers that distinguishes them. For all their living in a very particular place at a very particular moment, they had nothing in common with the local literary scene and very little with each other. For Joyce, the most important thing about Trieste was that it was not Dublin. He arrived there by accident. He found he was able to borrow money and to work (teaching English). It was enough. He was obsessed with words, with style, with the extent to which words can evoke a world, create a world, many worlds, most of all the world of Dublin, where he never wanted to live again. To a very great extent he must have lived in those worlds of words (since in another way he never left Dublin at all). Svevo's description of his teacher, written as an English homework assignment, is pertinent here:

> When I see him walking on the street I always think that he is enjoying a leisure, a full leisure. Nobody is awaiting him and he does not want to reach an aim or to meet anybody. No! He walks in order to be left to himself. He also does not walk for health. He walks because he is not stopped by anything. I imagine that if he would find his way barred by a high and big wall he would not be shocked in the least, he would change direction and if the new direction would also prove not to be clear he would change it again.

Thus, when Trieste was closed to Joyce with the arrival of the First World War, he continued his walks in Zurich, and later Paris. Nor is there any indication that leaving Trieste affected his writing. If Molly could say of Leopold just before she decided to take him, 'well, as well him as another', certainly Joyce could have said the same of the cities he lived in after Dublin.

For Svevo, on the other hand, as Cary sensibly points out,

Trieste was merely home, a place he had no quarrel with, a place above all for work. If the city comes through at all in his novels, which despite being set in Trieste rarely mention or describe it, it is in the world of work, the shipping and commerce that all his characters are involved in, as indeed was Svevo himself. The observation points up the fine irony underlying the now traditional linking of Joyce and Svevo's names. For the two could scarcely have been more different: the Irishman living in Trieste, but meticulously describing, recreating his home town of Dublin, the Triestine happily at home but apparently uninterested in the city round about him. Joyce, the avant-garde aesthete, the stylist par excellence, was searching for new techniques, new games, new languages. Svevo, for his part, is quite embarrassingly inept as a stylist, to the point where, on reading him in Italian one occasionally has to look at a sentence very hard indeed before understanding it, and this is not because of some effect the writer was aiming for, but out of sheer clumsiness.

Was this perhaps the essential aspect of the Triestine influence on Svevo, this writing in a language that was not really his own? Certainly, of all the serious novelists I have read, Svevo seems the least interested in drawing deeply on the resources of language to enrich his vision. Rather, Italian is a medium he uses as best he can to get across a brilliantly comic and perceptive succession of thoughts and actions that continuously unravel the perversity of his characters. When Joyce apparently told Svevo that 'there are passages in *Senilità* that even Anatole France could not have improved', he was either lying (to flatter) or simply had not appreciated why he liked the book, or has been misreported. And if *La coscienza di Zeno* is Svevo's best book, it is perhaps because by adopting the first person he makes the clumsiness of his Italian, and the constant strain in it, a reflection of Zeno's own curious mix of effort and buffoonery, the confusion of a man who tries so hard, and so hopelessly, to be morally healthy. The final irony, however, of all the fashionable criticism of Svevo's Italian is that he is now by far the most readable, and particularly in translation, of all his Italian contemporaries. Their D'Annunzian grandiloquence seems so egregious beside his simple, if occasionally awkward, dispatch.

Saba (1883–1957), a lyric poet who moved to Florence to improve his Italian, but then wrote many of his poems about Trieste and eventually returned to live there, is a very different, perhaps even 'opposite' case. Towards the end of his book Cary offers translations of extracts from the writers he has talked about, plus two of Joyce's *Pomes Penyeach*, translated into Italian by Montale. One is struck how well Svevo and Slataper come across, how poorly Saba. 'Poetry,' as Paul Celan said, 'is the fatal uniqueness of language,' and for Saba the exact register and semantic range of each word, the exact rhythm of the line and arrangement of the syntax are all-important. Read in the Italian, which Cary wisely leaves alongside, the spareness and hard-earned intensity of his verse is immediately apparent. Transferred into a would-be poetic English, it disappears. The subject of the poems Cary chooses to quote is Trieste, its streets, its bars, its people, but one soon appreciates that the city is above all a mirror of the poet's mood, a source of consolation for his suffering, material for the constant reinvention of that wisely dying fall which is Saba's voice.

Apart from the space and time of Trieste and Triestine politics in the early twentieth century, another source of influence was, of course, the less provincial, more elusive world of European ideas in general. So, as Cary remarks towards the end of his book, each of the three writers was more influenced by, and influencing of, incipient literary modernism than the city they lived in. 'Conscience', 'consciousness', or the Italian catch-all '*coscienza*' are useful words here. In his poet's manifesto, *Quello che resta da fare ai poeti*, Saba speaks of the poet's responsibility as lying precisely in *coscienza*, his 'moral awakeness' as Cary puts it, his determination to write nothing and use no technique that is not profoundly felt. Hence the hard-won precision of his language, the difficulty of translation.

Svevo, on the other hand, in *La coscienza di Zeno*, seems to be engaged above all in revealing, sincerely, the impossibility of such sincerity. Every resolution his hero takes is immediately over-whelmed by an opposing appetite, every appetite is thwarted by moral awareness. In this tragicomic demonstration language need not be precise, on the contrary all the better if, being the writer's second language, it is inherently mendacious. Commenting on his analyst's ingenuousness in imagining his confessions sincere, the hyperconscious Zeno remarks: 'With every Tuscan word we use we lie. If only he knew how much we enjoy saying those things we know the words for and how we avoid anything that would oblige us to resort to the dictionary.'

Meanwhile, Joyce was inventing his 'stream of consciousness', amorally following thoughts wherever they and language would lead, during his Trieste walks perhaps. Behind all three writers one can't help feeling the presence of their near contemporary, Freud. Svevo translated him and presented Zeno as an exercise in self-analysis. Saba got himself analysed, discovered all about his identity crisis and dedicated a book of poems to his analyst. Joyce pooh-poohed Freud and confirmed his importance in everything he wrote. Trieste, as Cary points out, for the obvious reason of its daily commerce with Vienna, was one of the main entry points by which Freud's ideas came to Italy.

Party Going

[Henry Green]

We should be familiar with the scene. A major railway station in central London. It's early on a foggy evening. The office workers are returning home, a party of England's most privileged are about to board the boat train for a continental holiday. The date must be sometime in the late 1920s. Apparently we are at the very heart of the declining Empire. Waugh territory. Yet no sooner have we read a paragraph of Green's prose than we know that this is not the case. On the contrary, we feel completely disorientated, as if we had been mysteriously spirited off to some far-flung outpost, some improbable possession we could never imagine had been annexed to the Crown. Kipling in India, Lawrence in Mexico, Joyce in Trieste, they are all and immediately more central to what has become English Literature, what we expect when we open a book, than this bizarre and beautiful comedy that is Henry Green's great masterpiece.

More reassuringly clichéd, you would have thought, than the thick fog of pre-war London, one cannot get. Yet, as if the ghostly material had seeped into the writer's mind and syntax, obliging him, and us, to advance with hands outstretched in constant fear of some unexpected obstacle, we soon appreciate that Green is using exactly this meteorological commonplace as image and abettor of our disorientation. One grey matter has invaded another and everybody is bewildered. Instructing a chauffeur to deal with her many suitcases, the fabulously wealthy Julia Wray sets out to walk across the park to the station. Immediately she is in the fog.

179

Where hundreds of thousands she could not see were now going home, their day done, she was only starting out and there was this difference, that where she had been nervous of her journey and of starting, so that she had said she would rather go on foot to the station to walk it off, she was frightened now. As a path she was following turned this way and that round bushes and shrubs that hid from her what she would find she felt she would next come upon this fog dropped suddenly down to the ground, when she would be lost.

What are we to make of this sequence of relative clauses: '*that hid from her what she would find she felt she would next come upon this fog dropped suddenly down*'! Julia is not alone in being lost. What can the sentence mean? How strangely and rapidly its monosyllabic rhythm with barely a word unstressed plunges us into confusion. As we begin to read, we expect something like: *As she went this way and that round bushes that hid from her what she would find on the other side, she felt … lost*. But no, for immediately after the word 'felt', the sentence speeds up and complicates in an alarming way. The problem then becomes, where are we to put the comma that ends the temporal clause and introduces the main clause? Could it be: *As she went round bushes that hid what she would find* COMMA *she feared (felt) that she would come upon this fog dropped down (rather than staying up in the trees) in which case she would be lost*. Certainly that's possible. But ugly. It also prevents us from reading 'this fog dropped suddenly down' as a strong indicative end to the sentence.

Alternatively we might read the main clause as beginning with 'she would next come upon' thus: *As she went round bushes that hid what she would find* COMMA *or so she imagined (felt)* COMMA *she would come upon this fog dropped down, and then she would be lost*. But again the thing seems unwieldy and the attractive rhythm set up in 'what she would find she felt she would next come upon' disappears.

Only after a double or even triple take and some careful attention to those shifty 'would's, ever ready to switch from imperfect to conditional and so keep us from separating the wood from the trees in this foggy park, do we come upon a reading that gives a deeper sense to that extraordinary succession of verbs at the core of the sentence: *Julia went round bushes that hid from her what she thus discovered ('would find') that she had been expecting ('felt') to come upon on the other side, but didn't.* To arrive at this reading is to appreciate that nothing so much as disorientation will help you discover what you expected but didn't find. This isn't a book like any other.

But we mustn't be put off by a little confusion! A little disorientation. One would never, surely, break off a promising conversation merely because something the other person said didn't quite or immediately make sense. Then bewilderment can be exciting. For even if what you are going to come upon in *Party Going* is not what you expected either from this or any book, it may all the same turn out to be very beautiful and very seductive. Even illuminating. And it might even be the case that the disorientation Green imposes on us is a state that will make us peculiarly receptive to beauty, perhaps a necessary precondition of our discovering it. Would somebody so self-obsessed and silly as Julia Wray ever have noticed the beauty of leaves lit up at night if she had not been lost in fog? Here is the next paragraph.

Then at another turn she was on more open ground. Headlights of cars above turning into a road as they swept around hooting swept their light above where she walked, illuminating lower branches of trees. As she hurried she started at each blaring horn and each time she would look up to make sure that noise heralded a light and then was reassured to see leaves brilliantly green veined like marble with wet dirt and these veins reflecting each light back for a moment then it would be gone out beyond her and then was altogether gone and there was another.

Green must be the most highly praised, certainly the most accomplished, of twentieth-century novelists not to have made it into the canon, not to be regularly taught in universities, not to be considered 'required reading'. The celebrated critic Frank Kermode gives us the key to why this is so. Delivering the Norton Lectures at Harvard University in 1977, he chose *Party Going* as an example of a work that perversely frustrated every analytical tool in the hermeneutic workshop. Brilliant as it is, Kermode insists, *Party Going* cannot be made to make sense *as a whole*. Is this fair comment? Would it matter if it was? 'Life after all,' Green remarked, 'is one discrepancy after another.'

Max Adey, unpardonably rich and notoriously handsome, has invited, all expenses paid, a gaggle of bright young things to a winter house party in France. But barely an hour before departure Max himself is not quite sure if he will go. For he hasn't invited Amabel. He is trying to break up with her, beautiful, wealthy and fabulously pampered as she is. All the same, it was unkind not to invite her. Perhaps he should stay behind, then. Should he? Max has difficulty making up his mind. Actually, he has difficulty thinking at all. He invites Amabel to dinner, then leaves for the station, then phones from the station to cancel dinner explaining that he is at the airport. Then, discovering that the train has been delayed by the fog, he books one room in the station hotel for his party and another for himself on the floor above to which he immediately takes Julia with whom he plans to replace Amabel while a third girl Angela is to be kept waiting in the wings. As he and Julia settle down to possible lovemaking, Green tells us:

If Julia had wondered where Max was taking her as they went upstairs together, Max, for his part, had wondered where she was taking him. With this difference however, that, if she had done no more than ask herself what room he was taking her to, he had asked himself whether he was going to fall for her. Again, while she had wondered so faintly she hardly knew she had it in her mind or, in other words, had hardly expressed to herself what she was thinking, he was much further from putting his feelings into words, as it was not until he felt sure of anything that he knew what he was thinking of. When he thought, he was only conscious of uneasy feelings and he only knew that he had been what he did not even call thinking when his feelings hurt him. When he was sure then he felt it must at once be put to music, which was his way of saying words.

Being brutally reductive, one might say that the twentieth century excelled in two manners of representing character. There is the flattery of Joyce and Woolf, who give us a vision of individual minds constantly generating poetry, perpetually seeking to expand the spirit. How encouraging it is when we find we can identify with them! And there is the more traditional approach, perhaps of Graham Greene or Anthony Powell, that sees character primarily in terms of its response to moral struggle in scenarios social, sentimental and political. This too, like any call to duty, has its reassuring and flattering aspect, even when, as in the early and hilarious Waugh, it means pillorying people for not being what writer and reader know they should be. One could never say of such books that they do not 'make sense'.

But Green offers neither of these, nor one of the derivative combinations typical of the average novel today. Though all perfectly believable, all presented with a psychology that is ruthlessly and comically convincing, his characters are not immediately distinguishable and the reader may have a little difficulty at the beginning of *Party Going* sorting out Claire, Angela, Evelyn and Julia, not to mention Robert, Robin, Alex and Max, as if obliged, as I have been on various occasions, to watch a game of football in the fog. It's hard to see who's got the ball. But much of the pleasure of reading Green comes from just this struggle to distinguish – it seems we're being teased – and the resulting recognition that any clarity in human relationships will be a fiction won from heavy clouds of incomprehension.

The description of Max and Julia as they head towards first intimacy gives us a clue to Green's vision. The words he uses for them, symmetrically repeating 'wonder', 'take', 'thought', 'knew', suggests that they are tangled together, mutually interact-ing – who takes whom where exactly? – just as their similar manner of speaking when their wonderful dialogue begins makes it very clear that they are the product of the same society, they share the same prejudices, the same memories almost. Yet the substance of the paragraph is their ignorance, not only of what is going on in the other's head, but of their own intentions likewise. And the conversation when it gets going will be that of two people missing not only each other in the dark, but themselves too. 'All and always alone', as Green believed we are, he does not allow his characters the consolation of a Dedalus or a Dalloway that they are special individuals, or even 'individuals' at all in the way we give status to that word. They don't possess themselves. Often both action and speech come as the result of the merest compulsion. And if it is hard to 'identify' with them, this is perhaps because Green more than any novelist of his time had appreciated that 'identity' and 'character' were convenient and somewhat overgenerous fictions. '"What do we know of any-one?" said Julia,' and Green adds, 'thinking of herself'.

But do these people have a moral duty at least? Is the book a satirical account of their inadequacy? Our party gathers in the station. The fog is impenetrable now. No trains are leaving and the press of homeward-bound commuters is becoming a suffocat-ing and potentially dangerous throng. Well-connected, pockets well-lined, Max and company take refuge (for the whole of the novel) in the station hotel whence, when gossip and flirtation flags, they can gaze down on the crowd beneath. Then at a certain point, the hotel doors are locked and barred and the building sealed off from the outside world.

> The management had shut the steel doors down because when once before another fog had come as thick as this hundreds and hundreds of the crowd, unable to get home by train or bus, had pushed into this hotel and quietly clamoured for rooms, beds, meals, and more and more had pressed quietly, peaceably in until, although they had been most well behaved, by weight of numbers they had smashed everything, furniture, lounges, reception offices, the two bars, doors. Fifty-two had been injured and compensated and one of them was a little Tommy Tucker, now in a school for cripples, only fourteen years of age, and to be supported all his life at the railway company's expense by order of a High Court Judge.
>   'It's terrifying,' Julia said, 'I didn't know there were so many people in the world.'

Class distinction, social privilege, couldn't be more clearly established. Green, himself a communist sympathiser from the moneyed classes, has no illusions. Yet, there is never any suggestion that Max and company should or even could *do* anything about the situation. Nor do the crowd ever put them to some awful test. The words, 'peaceably' and 'most well behaved' are telling here. The classes are as tangled together in an overall society, mutually engendering, mutually uncomprehending, as are Max and Julia, men and women in general. The conflict and moral dilemma that a hundred years of a certain kind of literature has led you to expect won't occur. The rich young folks get on well with their servants who appear to think kindly of them in return. No, if Julia and company try to ignore the crowd locked outside it is not because of any rejection of social duty, but because the sheer anonymous size of the throng in the foggy plaza makes them think of death. 'Like a view from the gibbet,' says Alex looking down on the scene. 'Cattle waiting to be butchered' says another. Here and there in the gloom suitcases lean this way and that like headstones in 'an exaggerated graveyard'. Max steps back from lace curtains.

The perversity of *Party Going*, Kermode claimed in his Norton Lectures, was that while the core of the book is a series of dazzlingly complex dialogues, hilarious social manoeuvrings and tawdry sex games among the rich in the hotel, these bear no relation at all to a possible political interpretation of the book, which is nevertheless flung in our faces in the presentation of rich and poor inside and outside the hotel, and even less to a possible 'mythical' interpretation, equally shamelessly flaunted when the novel opens with the description of an elderly woman, aunt of one member of our party, finding a dead pigeon, washing it in the public lavatories and wrapping it in a brown paper parcel. Purification rituals? Funeral rites? The book teems with potentially symbolic figures and events: the mysterious man who despite locked doors seems able to pass in and out of the hotel, his accent changing from Birmingham to cockney to Oxbridge every time he opens his mouth; the goddess-like Amabel whose bath, after she too inexplicably penetrates the hotel's defences, is followed with awe by the other members of the party, as if she were no less than the huntress Diana herself. Then there are Julia's talismanic toys, the egg with the elephants in it, the little wooden pistol, the spinning top, not to mention Robert's memories of buried treasure in a thicket of bamboo. And yet, Kermode complains, while in Joyce or Eliot such manifestations would offer the key to an overall interpretation, this does not seem to be the case in Green.

All the same ... if we stop fussing over explanations, interpretations, and if, while enjoying the thickly planted maze of

Green's dialogues, we keep our eyes on the references to death, the characters' anxieties about death, all will become, if not clear, then at least fatally, fantastically familiar.

Where did the dead pigeon fall from? Out of the fog. Disorientated it flew into a beam. Miss Fellowes, Claire's aunt, picks it up, then, 'everything unexplained', falls ill herself, buys a whisky, she who never drinks whisky, collapses, is perhaps even dying. Thoughtful and embarrassed, Max arranges for her to have her own and separate room in the hotel. Two nannies 'dressed in granite' sit outside it, like Fates ready to cut the mortal thread. At this point, the geometry of the novel is at once more complex and more recognisable. To defend what fragile identity they may have the group has separated itself from encroaching anonymity, as any society might set up a palisade between itself and the wilderness. But before the gates could be shut the fog had slipped in from beyond the pale, in the form of the dead pigeon, the sick auntie. So the pigeon is hidden in a parcel and then the auntie in her separate room. But how to stop thinking about them: the dying soul within, the amorphous world without? Everybody is fascinated by the idea that Miss Fellowes may be dying and at the same time all hope against hope that her eventual deterioration won't prove an even greater obstacle to their escape to the 'paradise' of southern France than that 'pall of fog' which has paralysed them in this hotel where the problem is, alas, 'there's nothing to do.'

In this scenario, what is the marvellous fizz of shenanigans that makes up the bulk of the novel, if not a heroic attempt to keep death at bay? It's a situation where the abilities to flirt, to preen and to start pernicious rumours are not qualities to be lightly dismissed. Other writers, Green seems to be telling us, have not given these achievements their due. The conversation must go on. We must not be obliged to think. For at every misunderstanding, every 'strangling silence', every hiccup in the conversation (and with the amount these people can afford to drink the

187

slip-ups will be many), it's as if the fog had made a further advance into the hotel, creeping into booze-befuddled heads and threatening to have them crashing into a beam to drop down damp and lifeless. Fortunately our party are well trained. The finishing schools have not been in vain. Here is Amabel listening to Alex relaying some hot gossip through a closed door while she has her bath:

> When Alex came to an end she had not properly heard what he had been saying so she said something almost under her breath, or so low that he in his turn should not catch what she had said, but so that it would be enough to tell him she was listening.

Never, not even in Beckett's *Endgame*, has there been a greater communal complicity in that vital game of keeping the ball rolling.

An atmosphere of mockery hangs over *Party Going*, seeps into its every nook and cranny. It is the fog. It is the grey matter of the artist's mind. Both have a peculiarly corrosive quality that dissolves identity, disconnects things, above all, puts everything on the same level – people, objects, images, different parts of speech, political readings, symbolic readings – as if in some primeval soup, something far older (and if Green is dated, as some complain, the date goes back many thousands of years) than any empire or class distinction. The oddly compelling rhythms of the prose with its elimination of weak stresses and frequent use of demonstratives, reproduce the dismembering effect at the auditory level. Everything is fragmented, displaced.

> She bent down and took a wing then entered a tunnel in front of her, and this had DEPARTURES lit up over it, carrying her dead pigeon.

Departures indeed! It's a state of decomposition that cannot help but remind us of our mortal precariousness. Yet at the same time it is also the warm and fertile sea from which all life once crept. No wonder we felt we were far from home! Everything interrupted, sense perceptions blocked, the ancient archetypes are free to rise up quite naturally like dreams in a Jungian sleep. So Alex, driven through dense fog in a taxi, is transported far away from central London:

> Streets he went through were wet as though that fog twenty foot up had deposited water, and reflections which lights slapped over the roadways suggested to him he might be a Zulu, in the Zulu's hell of ice, seated in his taxi in the part of Umslopogaas with his axe, skin beating over the hole in his temple.

All Green's work is inspired by his perception of a complicity between composition and decomposition, between the creative and corrosive powers of the mind, or again by the way a disability, a misunderstanding, can unleash powerful and vital forces, or a dying auntie have the most astonishing hallucinations. He left us but one precious hint of the method this perception led him to. It comes in almost the only interview this very private man ever gave and is disguised in a sly remark that has been more often quoted than understood.

> INTERVIEWER: I've heard it remarked that your work is 'too sophisticated' for American readers, in that if offers no scenes of violence – and 'too subtle', in that its message is somewhat veiled. What do you say?
> GREEN: Unlike the wilds of Texas, there is very little violence over here. A bit of child-killing of course, but no straight shootin' . . .
> INTERVIEWER: And how about 'subtle'?

GREEN: I don't follow. Suttee, as I understand it, is the suicide – now forbidden – of a Hindu wife on her husband's flaming bier. I don't want my wife to do that when my time comes – and with great respect, as I know her, she won't . . .

INTERVIEWER: I'm sorry, you misheard me, I said 'subtle' – that the message was too subtle.

GREEN: Oh, *subtle*. How dull!

Subtle it was! Deaf in one ear though he may have been, Green could not have imagined that his interviewer, Terry Southern, was talking about 'suttee'. Indeed Southern's notes suggest that parts of the interview was as much written as spoken. In any event, Green uses the exchange to show, with typical playfulness, how from a misunderstanding, a moment of mental limbo, an ancient religion with its terrible ritual may suddenly flare up again, and immediately we are thinking of our own death and simultaneously trying to forget it with the wonderfully wry remark about the wife. After which we can safely return to the duller world of literary discussion.

It will be pointless, then, to ask what this or that image in *Party Going* means, or how this or that conversation might be interpreted. Quite simply, these are the things that people say to each other, and these are the images the mind has ever produced. You can't help recognising them. So it is that Green, unlike Waugh or Wodehouse or Wilde, can allow even the most witless characters moments of extraordinary and completely convincing beauty. Here, to close, are the incorrigibly faithless Max and Amabel nodding off to sleep together after what may or may not have been a reconciliation. As always with Green, beauty has to do with birds, with dissolution, and with death.

Lying in his arms, her long eyelashes down along her cheeks, her hair tumbled and waved, her hands drifted to rest like white doves drowned on peat water, he marvelled again he should ever dream of leaving her who seemed to him then his reason for living as he made himself breathe with her breathing as he always did when she was in his arms to try and be more with her.

It was so luxurious he nodded, perhaps it was also what she had put on her hair, very likely it may have been her sleep reaching out over him, but anyway he felt so right he slipped into it too and dropped off on those outspread wings into her sleep with his, like two soft evenings meeting.

The Enchanted Fort

[Dino Buzzati]

'Now a book lives,' wrote D.H. Lawrence, 'as long as it is unfathomed. Once it is fathomed . . . once it is *known* and its meaning is fixed or established, it is dead.' He uses the remark to launch an attack on allegory, indeed on all stories that offer a neat equivalence between their characters or settings and abstract qualities. 'A man is more than a Christian,' he protests, 'a rider on a white horse must be more than mere faithfulness and truth.'

Written in 1938, *The Tartar Steppe* is the story of a young officer dispatched to do service in a remote mountain garrison overlooking a vast northern desert. At first desperate to escape and return to the pleasures of normal life, he nevertheless falls under the spell of the place to the point that he will spend the next thirty years there, sustained only by the vain hope that one day an enemy attack will offer a moment of glory and fulfilment. Buzzati commented: 'The idea of the novel came out of the monotonous night shift I was working at *Corriere della Sera* in those days. It often occurred to me that that routine would never end and so would eat up my whole life quite pointlessly. It's a common enough feeling, I think, for most people, especially when you find yourself slotted into the time-tabled existence of a big town. Transposing that experience into a fantastical military world was an almost instinctive decision.'

Is the book, then, a mere allegory of equivalences? Buzzati had originally called his story 'The Fort' and the title was only changed on the insistence of the publishers who were keen to avoid allusions to the sensitive military situation in Europe. One

Italian critic remarked: 'The "desert" of the novel is thus the story of life in the "fort" of the newspaper which promises the wonders of a solitude that is both habit and vocation.' You can already hear Lawrence muttering, 'Fathomed and dead!'

But if it's a commonplace that something explained is very largely explained away, it is also true that faced with any phenomenon the mind instinctively sets out to construct an explanation. Here is an irony Lawrence doesn't follow up. Confronted with a story, any story, we immediately seek to fathom it out, to *know* it, even though we realise that if we succeed it will no longer be interesting, it will die. Oddly, then, the greatest pleasure we can get from a story only comes when the smaller satisfaction of having explained it away is thwarted. The mind discards, as it were, the chaff of the explicable to find real repose, or real excitement, in a kernel of enigma.

The Tartar Steppe is one of those precious novels that take the enormous risk of throwing down a gauntlet to the reasoning mind. Explain me if you can or dare, it says. Fathom me out. Provocative and frightening as the book is, we feel we must accept this challenge, put this disturbing story behind us. Who is this man who tosses away his life for a chimera, why does he seem so recognisable? Fortunately, the extraordinary clarity of the narrative, its elegant structure and straightforward execution, persuade us that it is that manner of thing for which explanation is surely available, a puzzle we can solve. Yet in the end, twisting and turning this way and that, mocking and infinitely ironic, Buzzati's story somehow denies us what we always felt was within our grasp. No, on putting the book down we cannot honestly say that we know what it meant. Quite the contrary. In this way it succeeds in evoking in its reader the central experience of its main character: in every sense life, not only his own but the whole of life, eludes his grasp.

One September morning, Giovanni Drogo, being newly

commissioned, set out from the city for Fort Bastiani; it was his first posting.

And his last . . . There is a ruthless dispatch to these opening lines which is typical of the way Buzzati works. Already he knows exactly what he is doing. In a way the whole novel will be written on the first page. Given no details of his past life, no sense of geographical or cultural location, Drogo is immediately and inevitably Everyman. He has waited for this day, this departure, the beginning of his 'real life', 'for years', but looking in the mirror now he doesn't 'find there the expected joy'. His early youth is gone, tediously consumed in books and study, but fortunately adulthood promises new satisfactions, new hopes. For the next two hundred pages, Buzzati will show us how resourcefully and how cruelly such hopes will ever sprout from the interminable erosion of Drogo's wasted days, their punctual disappointments. The wonder is that a writer should display such merciless control in elaborating a scenario of frustration and impotence.

Far from resembling the editing room of a big city newspaper, Fort Bastiani is located on the highest and most inaccessible of mountain terrains. This is Buzzati's masterstroke, the decision that more than any other will give the book its rich elusiveness. How can we not think of a medieval knight embarking on a spiritual quest as we watch Drogo urge his horse up winding paths beneath rock face and waterfall, lie down for the night wrapped in his cloak, emerge the following morning at an altitude immeasurably higher than anything he expected, onto a narrow plateau where the yellow walls of the fort rise in the cleft between towering peaks? The scene is set for some apocalyptic trial. We are anxious that our hero perform well.

But no trial presents itself, or at least none of the variety we expect. Drogo is not going to war. Nor is there a grail to recover. He will never meet the enemy, let alone be given a chance to slay an ogre or a giant. Only in routine regimental rituals will his sabre be bared, only at the endless changing of a meaningless guard will the stirring trumpet sound. This is a story of drama deferred, catharsis denied. To compensate, there are the mountains.

It is important here to say a word on what the mountains meant for Buzzati, and indeed on the place they occupy in the collective imagination of Italy in general, northern Italy in particular. Brought up in Belluno at the confluence of the Ardo and Piave rivers immediately below the majestic Dolomites, Buzzati was ten years old when Italy joined the First World War and became involved in the one military campaign of modern times that Italians will still refer to as glorious. Defending a line that ran across the very peaks of the Alps from the Swiss border to the Adriatic, the Italian troops hacked trenches in stone and snow, lived in caves and igloos at frightening altitudes, attacked machine guns in terrain where the only grave was a heap of shards. Finally routed at Caporetto in the east with the loss of half a million men, they nevertheless fought a desperate rearguard action to hold a line behind the Piave, a river north of Venice, whence the tide was eventually turned and the enemy chased north again. For an Italian the northern mountains are the locus par excellence of military glory.

And so much more than that of course. In his early teens Buzzati began to climb in the Dolomites. It would be a lifelong passion. A competent artist, he drew and painted the mountains. He never tired of it. His first literary effort, at fourteen, was called 'La canzone delle montagne', ('The Song of the Mountains'). In his first novel, *Barnabus of the Mountains*, the Dolomites were already assuming a role at least as important as that of the people in the book. So while the initial inspiration for *The Tartar Steppe* may indeed have come out of the fear that a mindless office routine was eating up his life, Buzzati nevertheless chose to set that routine in a landscape that was his chief recreation, and also something he was clearly in thrall to, a limit-experience for him, a drug almost, an endless source of exhilaration. The effect is double-edged. Against the vast backdrop of pink peaks and dark gorges, dazzling ice fields and dizzying gulfs, the rigid routine of the garrison in the puny human geometry of the fort becomes more meaningless than ever. But it also takes on a borrowed sublimity. The mountains are that place where the sheer extravagance of nature's waste and emptiness becomes sublime. And there is something sublime about the way a group of soldiers can waste their whole lives observing the severest of rules as they wait for an enemy who never materialises. Inexplicably, in the night, snow slips from a roof, a landslide alters the shape of a crag, freezing water splits a rock. There is an obscure complicity between this alpine erosion and the web of wrinkles spreading across the stony faces of the guards as they gaze out across the desolate steppe to the north. The mountains, we discover, offer a marvellous view of the void.

To read *The Tartar Steppe* is to be asked to take the idea of enchantment seriously. Young Drogo knows that he must not stay in the fort. It is isolated, futile. No sooner has he arrived than he is asking to leave. He understands perfectly that there is no hope of ordinary human fulfilment here, or military glory for that matter. Reassured by the smiles and blandishments of older officials – he doesn't want to let the side down – he agrees to stay a few months, at least until the first medical when he will be pronounced, they promise him, unsuitable for service at high altitude. Immediately we are terribly anxious for him. He slips into the routine. We feel it happening. The narrator will even insist that it is this cosy, easy, empty existence that will persuade Drogo not to leave when the medical comes along and the doctor gives him his chance. A moral failing, we are told. But we know it isn't so. Or it isn't *just* that. Drogo is enchanted. It is a spell that has something to do with the meeting of human vanities and mountain landscape, a fatal complicity between aspiration and emptiness. As the doctor who could send him back home speaks, our hero cannot even bring himself to listen, intent as he is on the view from the window: 'And it was then that he seemed to see the yellow walls of the fortress courtyard soar up toward the crystal sky, while, above them and beyond, higher and ever higher, snow-topped bulwarks rose obliquely to solitary towers, tiny redoubts and airy fortifications he had never noticed before.'

Drogo cannot tear himself away. He is doomed, seduced by this hubristic and fantastical vision of some vast engagement between man and mountain. At bottom it is an aesthetic enchantment, the terrible sorcery of the magnificent gesture. Once, when there were real enemies, bloody battles to be fought, such magnificent posturing could serve a social purpose. The glorious endeavour – swords brandished over the dramatic landscape, fortifications built with tremendous sacrifice – was still connected with the more mundane life down in the city. The military hero protected that life. Now the gesture is entirely cut off from any other reality, it lives only in the mind, entirely absurd, and paradoxically all the grander and more seductive for being so.

A pitiless psychology drives the development of the novel from this point on. Again and again, in his dealings with his fellow soldiers, with the mountains, the desert and with time itself, Drogo is outflanked, outwitted and fantastically ingenuous. Again and again he fails to understand either the manoeuvrings of those around him or the changes in his own body and psyche. There are moments when we can't help wishing that this blindness, this cruelty would stop. Yet everything that happens, every trick played by comrades, nature and fate, is entirely believable, even normal. Never do we feel that Drogo has been singled out for special punishment. At one level we even suspect that he is not entirely unhappy with his unhappy destiny. This is the book's perplexing core.

Much, far too much, has been made of Buzzati's debt to Kafka. True, he flirts with symbolism and surrealism; true, his writing is suffused with a sense of life's absurdity ('a most stupid landscape', the major assures Drogo on his arrival at the fort), but the same is true of so many of his contemporaries, Calvino, Beckett and Thomas Mann to name but three, all writers whose stories achieve verisimilitude precisely in their refusal to grant the drama we crave. What Buzzati does not share is the all-pervading paranoia that characterises Kafka's writing; as a result the horror and humour that Buzzati evokes is one, I suspect, that will prove more recognisable to the general reader than Kafka's, closer to the grain of common experience.

If asked to name the writer with whom Buzzati has perhaps the greatest affinity, one is tempted to say, Giacomo Leopardi, Italy's great poet of a hundred years before. Leopardi, an early atheist, was obsessed by the role of hope in human life, a hope he remorselessly exposed as the product of illusion, yet saw, and occasionally celebrated, as ever ready to flower again even in the most barren places, the most unexpected forms. This incorrigible inclination to hope, Leopardi felt, was both the curse and salvation of the race: it guaranteed that the defining experience of human life would be disappointment, and allowed us to press on regardless.

Buzzati's intuition is that with the collapse of the great collective illusions – religion, national destiny – and the consequently intensifying sense of absurdity (there is no common enemy to sustain the fort's purpose), the individual mind can only react with ever more frenetic attempts to generate hope, the most preposterous hopes, out of nothing, to enchant itself with whatever desert terrain is available. Certainly the final chapters of *The Tartar Steppe* present Drogo as somehow in complicity with novelist and reader to drag out a vain illusion, perhaps even a whole tradition of literary fiction, far beyond the limits of reason. There is one marvellous moment in particular when the authorities ban the use of telescopes. With the help of a powerful lens Drogo and a friend had managed to identify some tiny specks on the very edge of the visible horizon and had built around this mirage the fantasy of an approaching army that would at last bring to the fort the catharsis of war. Denied the collective pursuit of this fantasy by order of their superiors, Drogo nevertheless goes on staring into the empty desert until it seems his busy imagination, or Buzzati's, or perhaps ours, at last wills the enemy into existence.

For at the very end of *The Tartar Steppe*, the prospect of real war finally does present itself. What a huge relief! How pleased, busy, even joyous everybody is! How eagerly the rusty military machine is set back in motion, how bright the faces of the young men as they march up the gloomy valleys to the fort! And the reader is implicated too. Because you too are relieved, happy that war has come, that the wait is over. Yes, the reader too has been enchanted by the mirage of release, the fantasy that it might all have meant something.

Buzzati's typescript of *The Tartar Steppe* was submitted to the publishers in January 1939. There is no need to comment on what followed. In any event the book still serves as an alarming reminder that the century that discovered nothingness would go to any lengths, however catastrophic, to fill that nothingness up.

In the Locked Ward

[Jay Neugeboren]

'Throw away your Sigmund Freud, Mrs. Neugeboren . . . because I am going to cure your son!'

It is 1968 and Dr Cott is offering massive doses of vitamins B6, B12 and C. One of the first of a score of psychiatrists to take charge of the schizophrenic Robert Neugeboren, whose story is told in *Imagining Robert*, Cott's confidence is, alas, unwarranted. Still, the same could be said of most of those who follow him, each with his own favourite wonder cure, whether it be electroshock, insulin, Adapin, Mellaril, lithium, Stelazine or any number of others. When one doctor announces with great excitement that he is going to try 'the brand new' anti-convulsant Depakote, Robert's brother Jay, who is telling the story, has to remind him that actually Robert has already been on Depakote. He responded briefly, then relapsed.

Jay, however, is ever willing to hope and in the early nineties when a psychiatrist decides that Klonopin is the way forward, the author welcomes the decision. A little later, however, he discovers that this is the same drug that has just been prescribed to their eighty-two-year-old mother who suffers from Alzheimer's. Is it likely, then, that this will prove the promised 'magic bullet' for schizophrenia?

In the meantime Robert is frequently deprived of his phone privileges. Why, Jay complains, 'what possible *medical* reason can there be for depriving him of any contact with the world beyond the ward?' Invariably he is told that 'the staff like Robert' but that he can be 'impossible' and even 'dangerous'. 'He curses loudly,

201

screams at telephone operators, keeps demanding refunds from the phone company, spits at aides, scratches them, strikes other patients.' Reading *Imagining Robert*, it soon becomes apparent that dealing with the schizophrenic from day to day is far more of a problem than the choice of his new medication.

A novelist by profession, Jay Neugeboren is a constant thorn in the flesh of those who have treated his brother over almost forty years of mental illness. It is not that he has an axe to grind. On the contrary, he displays an exemplary openness to a wide range of points of view. No, Jay's behaviour is irksome first because he just will not leave be. He continues to visit his brother, even when those visits leave Robert more agitated than they found him, and he always insists on knowing what medication is being offered, what therapy proposed.

'Stop being so concerned about your brother,' advises Dr Laqueur, a great advocate of coma-shock therapy (this back in the early sixties). 'You should get on with your own life.' From time to time – as the years go by, the dashed hopes, the violent crises – readers of *Imagining Robert* may be inclined to agree with Laqueur. Yet at the same time they would have to acknowledge the author's constantly implied objection: 'but how can my "own" life be separated from my brother's? They are inextricable.'

For another quality of Neugeboren's that psychiatrists find unsettling is his memory. Not only does he recall every wonder drug and improbable therapy that has been tried on his brother, but he also remembers how his brother was before his illness and the dramatic family scenario in which the two of them came to consciousness. This is the story he tells in *Imagining Robert* and we cannot come away from it without reflecting that narrative and contemporary psychiatry are implacable enemies. With all its mess, waywardness and ambiguity, the well-documented narrative reminds readers of everything they intuitively know beyond psychiatry's austere vocation for separating things out into demonstrable fact and repeatable results.

The book begins with a crisis. Invited to attend his nephew's high-school graduation ceremony, the fifty-year-old Robert (schizophrenic since twenty) disappears, stays out all night, returns distraught and belligerent, and two days later has to be forcibly hospitalised. The author then goes back half a century to give us the childhood of the Neugeboren brothers and proceeds by switching back and forth from past to present throughout. The method is dense with implication. Though the author never insists on links between now and then, it is clear that he finds it hard to uncouple his brother's mental illness from the more general madness experienced in the family as a child. Is this a failing, or merely common sense?

Born in 1938, Jay is five years older than Robert. The parents are Brooklyn Jewish. Relatives are legion, likewise arguments. In thrall to a shared vision of the happy family, Mother and Father are nevertheless in permanent conflict. Mother is strong, generous, impulsive, insatiable; Father, whining, intelligent, incompetent. Infallibly, his businesses fail. Jay must remove debtors' letters from the mailbox before Mother sees them. Does she know he is in league with Father? 'Robert is my love child,' she declares cruelly. 'That one,' she points to Jay, 'who could ever love that one?'

A hospital nurse, Mother works night shifts to pay the bills, but also finds time to be involved in charities. She is greatly admired in the community, bitter and irritable at home. 'What can I do to make Momma happy?' Father asks. 'You're a bright boy, Jay . . . Please tell me what to do.' The man is desperate. He goes down on his knees before the whole family, crawling across the floor to lick his wife's shoes. 'That's how much I love her.' But why does she insist on coming to the dinner table topless, fondling her breasts with her free hand? Why does she parade around naked? Jay watches enraged as Mother paints little Robert's nails red, his mouth pink. Jay can't play in the football team because that would dishonour the Sabbath. Jay must not date a goy! It will kill Mother if Jay dates a goy.

Crushed by his wife's imperious hysteria, the father neverthe-less refuses to get a steady job. Anything to please, but not that. So there is always something for her to demand that won't be granted. The tension is extraordinary. The arguments escalate. Confused but compos mentis, Jay gives up trying to win his mother's love and starts to detach himself. He's an adolescent now. More amenable, darling Robert is entrusted with the task of keeping his parents together. Shall I divorce your father? Mother asks. No, you mustn't! Robert learns to play the clown, to do music-hall acts. He performs in public. What has he spent his life doing if not watching one splendid performance after another? When he puts on a show everybody laughs, everybody claps their hands. The Neugeborens are a happy family with a charismatic child. It's exhausting.

In short, here is a group of people who thrive on what has come to be called in the mental health profession an excess of 'expressed emotion'. Interested readers may find it instructive to turn for a moment to Julian Leff and Christine Vaughn's book *Expressed Emotion in Families* where they can observe a research team ticking off boxes on interview sheets to establish the number of times the relatives of schizophrenics speak critically of each other, or make direct eye contact, or use coercive impera-tives. Although a psychologist of the systemic school, which originally developed out of Gregory Bateson's reflections on interpersonal relationships and mental health, Leff is one of those who accept that schizophrenia is basically an organic disease, but nevertheless notes that the sufferer's families of origin tend to be characterised by high levels of confrontation and conflict, something that may trigger a crisis. In this scenario, the therapist's role is thus to seek first to measure, then reduce that level of negative engagement by teaching relatives to avoid excessive eye contact, verbal criticism, and the like. Of one young woman who had a psychotic crisis only days after returning from the hospital to live with her mother, he remarks that the decision to spend the weekend on the family's small cabin boat was fatal. Think of the constancy of eye contact in the cramped cabin of a boat!

The subtext of Leff and Vaughn's book is optimistic: this side of the schizophrenia problem is quantifiable and hence, we immediately assume, manageable. It can be tackled in an organised fashion if teams of researchers and social workers are sent out to train families to deal with their loved ones. But *Imagining Robert* reminds us that this is no ordinary form of stress whose reduction we might reasonably plan for. Here every expression of emotion is generated within the inexorable dynamic of the parents' relationship which is also the crucible in which two young personalities are now being formed. Past decisions have determined present dilemmas. Entrenched positions have been assumed. Above all the emotions expressed frequently reveal contradictory states of mind. 'How make sense of what made no sense?' Neugeboren wonders, reflecting on the way declarations of love came simultaneous with gestures of cruelty. What behaviour can one learn in such an environment?

Shortly after Jay manages to leave home – against his mother's will – Robert begins to buckle. His schoolwork becomes erratic. He leaves home, declares he is homosexual, lives with an assortment of dropouts, does drugs. Then comes home again. Then leaves again. Intriguingly it is the mother who first suggests he go to mental hospital. What but mental illness could explain her darling boy's sexual inclinations? Perversely eager to see what the inside of such an institution is like, Robert confides to his brother that he faked a test to be admitted. Jay insists he takes another. Now the doctors say Robert's fine. No problem at all. Shortly afterwards he has his first psychotic breakdown. 'You and

Mother put me here,' he tells Jay from his hospital bed in a locked ward.

'While I am not surprised,' Neugeboren remarks in a second book on his brother's fate, 'that mental health professionals disagree strongly with one another, I am startled, occasionally, by the virulence with which they attack each other.' Having completed *Imagining Robert* with the compelling story of his brother's slow decline into chronicity, *Transforming Madness* poses the question: regardless of the aetiology of schizophrenia, what if a new drug were to return Robert, and others like him, to a stable state of mind? How can such people resume 'normal life' when their identities are now so entwined around their illnesses, when, in particular, they have never formed an adult personality?

Inevitably, as Neugeboren travels the United States looking at a variety of different rehabilitation programmes, this question brings the author up against the heated controversy: therapy versus drugs, which matters most? And this in turn, like it or not, cannot but reflect back on the problem of the aetiology of the illness (organic, relationship-based, or both) and indeed on our whole sense of what it is to have a self, to be a person.

One anecdote will suffice to suggest the complexity of the issue. In 1997, fifty-four now, Robert is given the new wonder drug Clorazil. Albeit marooned in the locked ward of the Bronx Psychiatric Center, he has, mainly thanks to brother Jay, a new doctor and a new social worker. There is dedication and excitement. Fifty per cent of patients respond to Clorazil, a new generation of more carefully aimed and milder dopamine blockers. Some months into the treatment, the doctors remark 'that Robert is making "slow and steady" gains – he is learning to control his rages, he is interacting more easily with others, he is not starting fights, he is being "realistic" and "appropriate" about most things'. Neugeboren himself notes that his brother seems to have overcome his 'total self-absorption' and is now sharing food, cigarettes and money with others on the ward and showing interest in their health. Encouraged by this progress, Robert's social worker concentrates on preparing him for the move to the open ward and relative freedom. Everything seems set for at least partial recovery. But two weeks before that move is due, the social worker is abruptly transferred. Despite continuing with the drug, Robert rapidly deteriorates. He now refuses to consider moving to the open ward and becomes manic and enraged, particularly with his brother. When Jay phones, he shouts, 'You put me here, so you get me out of here, you goddamned son of a bitch cocksucking bastard!' and hangs up on him. Even when not enraged, Robert's talk degenerates into streams of childlike associations. 'When I visit him,' Neugeboren writes, 'and bring him the food he has requested, he refuses to eat it. "You eat it, Jay!" he yells, "I don't want it. You eat it. Mother made it. Can't you tell? Mother made it!"'

Questions: If the drug works, why does it appear to stop working on the departure of the social worker? Was it partly the atmosphere of 'the great attempt' that brought about Robert's improvement? Might that explain the drug's only 50% success rate? Or is the brain learning to rewire itself around the transmitters the drug blocks? Then, is the departure of the social worker the real cause of the relapse, or is this rather an excuse for Robert to avoid going to the open ward and a freedom he is afraid of? Does Robert want to demonstrate to his brother Jay, of whose authorial success he is openly jealous, that no amount of fraternal string-pulling will save him, either from the vagaries of the institutions, or his own self-destructive impulses? He is his own man. 'This is my home, Jay,' Robert insists referring to the closed ward with its harsh regulations and frightening inmates. 'Why should I go anywhere else?'

To return to Neugeboren's surprise at the vitriolic exchanges between mental health professionals, the quarrel he is referring to is, of course, that between those who support exclusively organic approaches to schizophrenia, and those who would like at least to include reflections on family dynamics and other environmental factors. Curiously, the development over the last twenty years of the theory of neural plasticity would seem to have eliminated the need for this head-on (to risk a pun) collision. This is the idea, now supported by a large body of research, that while the brain is indeed subject to genetic factors (how could it be otherwise?), it also responds and changes according to environment and experience, the latter often being crucial in the triggering and even transformation of particular genes.

In a recent paper delivered in Venice, Glen Gabbard, Callaway Distinguished Professor at the Menninger Clinic, speaks of experiments indicating how psychotherapy can be shown to have altered both the chemistry and gene expression of the brain. Referring to work by Steve Hyman, Director of the National Institute of Mental Health, Gabbard goes on to suggest that gene-environment interactions give rise to a sort of 'hall of mirrors' in which it is far from easy to establish a single source for the multiplying reflections. He looks forward to the day when an awareness of the brain's plasticity – its tendency to change in response to experience – might finally erode the 'reductionism' that has divided the mental health world into two hostile camps, the psychosocial and the neuroscientific.

Yet the conflict continues as bitterly as ever. The disagreements are so heated, one suspects – and it is the great merit of Neugeboren's books that they prompt the reader to ponder the matter at length and with plenty of material to chew over – because at the deepest level the non-organic approach threatens to undermine the very basis on which the advocate of the exclusively organic approach operates. Why so?

Neugeboren quotes Harvard Professor of Psychiatry Leston Havens as remarking that despite their reputation for vanity, many mental health professionals and medical students in particular, fail to recognise their own importance. They 'come and go among patients as if their knowledge and skills were all that counted, not their persons at all'. The remark is pertinent, for it points to the underlying vision that drives the profession. The medical students are not looking for personal engagement with the patient. They don't really want their 'person' to make a difference. That is not the 'importance' they are after. Rather they want to learn (why not?) to heal the patient with a precise and controlled intervention, the exact dosage of the exact drug chosen after an exact diagnosis based on meticulous and exact analyses of spinal fluids and brain scans. They are in thrall, that is, to the great and creditable dream of Western medicine, a dream most powerfully represented in the image of the perfect surgical incision made in sterile conditions by the absolutely steady hand. It's an idea that never fails to stir our imaginations. Not for nothing did we arrive at the aberration of lobotomy.

But to make the perfect incision one must be operating from an absolutely stable vantage point. By suggesting that the self, patient's and doctor's, is constantly both product and producer of a group dynamic (family, workplace, society, nation) and never (even with all its chemistry in place) an objective given, to imply, that is, that in the long run a patient may respond as much to a 'good morning' as to a drug, that a doctor's judgement may be unsettled by a schizophrenic's antagonistic behaviour, is to shift the ground from under the feet of those who would heal the self with a perfect intervention from a detached position without.

Again and again in Neugeboren's account of his brother's vicissitudes one senses the importance of the element of taste. Quite simply, Robert's psychiatrists retreat (and understandably!) from what would be the very bad taste of becoming involved in the patient's messy life. They don't want to know about the ugly incidents that took place some months or years or days before a psychotic crisis. They don't want to decipher the patient's incoherent obscenities or know how often he masturbates. A lower-paid social worker can be assigned the unpleasant task of sympathising and encouraging the patient to 'behave'. Meanwhile, in the gleaming laboratory of the collective imagination, through years of tasteful dedication (and massive financial investment), a cure is being prepared. The magnificent gesture of the decisive intervention is at hand.

Fascist Work

[Mario Sironi]

Translating *A Manual of Mythology* by the English pedagogue the Reverend George W. Cox, Stéphane Mallarmé made one extraordinary and surely deliberate mistake. Inverting the sense of the original, he wrote: 'If the gods do nothing unseemly, then they are no longer gods at all.' This disturbing formula that turns Christian morality on its head, nevertheless seems quite familiar when applied to painters, poets and musicians. The sins and excesses of the artist confirm his genius rather than the opposite. We do not abandon Byron because he abandoned his daughter, not to mention the other women. Our admiration of Caravaggio's stormy intensity is not marred by the reflection that his temper was such that he once killed a man over a game of tennis. Nor do we shy away from Picasso because he obliged a wife to share his house with a mistress. These men are demigods.

All the same, there is one crime that is not forgiven. The Italian artist Mario Sironi painted on behalf of the Fascist regime. That a pope should commission a painting and call the tune does not perturb us. Likewise when the patron is a rich merchant, from Florence, or from Amsterdam. But that a man should have dedicated his art to a totalitarian state, to the point of being largely responsible for creating the iconography by which we remember it, this is anathema. How should we think about Sironi? What are we to make of his paintings?

Moravia's novel *The Conformist* offers a character study of the typical servant of Fascism. Marcello is frightened by violent instincts which he fears set him apart from others. Taking

211

precautions, he does everything to conform, marries a sensible girl, settles down in the civil service; only to find one day that the state is inviting him to murder someone, asking him to indulge exactly the dangerous instincts he sought to repress. It's a stereotype Susan Sontag develops in her essay, 'Fascinating Fascism'. And, as Emily Braun shows in her intriguing account of art under Mussolini, it is entirely inapplicable to its greatest exponent, Mario Sironi. This man was no conformist. On the contrary, he was independent and controversial even when most engaged in promoting the regime. Nor, so far as we know and despite the fiercest of tempers, was he ever involved in any act of political violence. He did, however, indulge in the delirium that his art might change the world. Are not painters, along with Shelley's poets the 'unacknowledged legislators of the universe'? Rightly, Braun sets out to show what kind of world it was and how he imagined he might transform it. Context is all.

Born in 1885, Sironi was eleven when his father died. Enrico Sironi had been a civil engineer. Mario's maternal grandfather was an architect. The idea that a man can shape the environment was thus available to him from early on. Despite reduced means and six children to bring up, Mario's mother didn't forget the family's cultural pretensions. The house in Rome was always open to painters and writers, and one of those who came was Filippo Tommaso Marinetti, philosopher of Futurism and author, years later, of the notorious manifesto *War, Sole Hygiene of the World.*

Was it in this adolescent period that Sironi learned, partly from a mother's desire to *fare bella figura*, partly from the revolutionary opinions of her guests, that hatred of the *borghesia* that would accompany him all his life? But many brought up quite differently were to profess the same hatred throughout the first half of the twentieth century, extremists of both the right and the left, and even people who were not extremists at all. So much so that one sometimes suspects that this contempt for the bourgeoisie so-called had less to do with class and money than with a deep fear of spiritual complacency, of merely material well-being. The world had to be made new, because it had been found to be empty. 'Take out your pickaxes,' wrote Marinetti, 'your axes and hammers and wreck, wreck the venerable cities, pitilessly.'

Having begun a degree in engineering, the young Sironi fell into a profound depression and gave up the university for painting. A succession of nervous breakdowns stretching from his late teens to his mid-twenties would lead him to destroy almost all his early paintings and frighten his family into considering the possibility of a sanatorium. In 1910 his friend and fellow painter Umberto Boccioni would write: 'Sironi is completely crazy, or at least neurasthenic. He is always at home and closed off in himself. He doesn't move, speak, or study any more: it is truly painful.'

Needless to say the young, unhappy and, it must be said, handsome artist was reading Nietzsche, playing Wagner on the piano and modelling innumerable Greek heads in gesso. Significantly, his mental illnesses came to an end when he became a regular and successful illustrator for a cultural magazine. Sironi, it seemed, was looking for a yoke that would harness his energies. He needed a purpose that 'bourgeois' life couldn't give.

Emily Braun's *Mario Sironi and Italian Modernism* is the remarkable story of how that yoke was found; or, to put it another way, it is an account of the gradual meshing of a particular political and artistic context with a peculiar and potentially unstable psychology. Sironi himself was well aware that something was up. In 1914, almost thirty now, he wrote to Boccioni: 'In Rome there has been a general strike for two days – a violent and anarchic atmosphere – a revelation of beauty in unison with my disfigured "ego". Also, your article, the "Circle", I liked it, and the rough tone was like a caress.'

A few months after that strike, desperate to overcome another depression, Sironi finally left the family home, moved to Milan and began working alongside Boccioni and other Futurists who, together with Mussolini, were campaigning to have the ever uncertain government intervene in the war. Not that they cared particularly for one side or another. But they wanted action. They felt Italy needed action, in order to become herself. By the autumn of 1915 they had got what they wanted. They were in the trenches together. They had volunteered. But, alas, it was a world quite different from the glamorous vision of national virility depicted in their magazine illustrations. Sironi was frequently ill. Nobody was prepared for the harsh conditions of the Alpine front where machine guns cancelled each other out across a desolate landscape of stone and ice. The troops tunnelled in the snow and were often buried there. Boccioni records how on one freezing night, 'around midnight Sironi came to me, and together, with our legs entwined, we tried to sleep'.

With this anecdote in mind it is with some emotion that one stands in Il Museo del Novecento in Milan letting the eye move from a Boccioni canvas to a Sironi. There are many Boccionis, few Sironis, in inverse proportion to their output of course. For in 1916 Boccioni was dead, a death that exempted him from future sins and criticism, while Sironi was destined to survive not only this war but the next and was ever as prolific as he would remain unrepentant.

Boccioni's canvases are full of colour and bear bold, ingenuously didactic titles: *Perpendicular spiral construction: woman sitting*, reads one; *Dynamism of a human body*, claims another. Both paintings are seductive shakes of the artist's kaleidoscope, a splendid whirl of bright wedges in which the moving figure is almost lost in the exhilaration of its own or the painter's excitement.

In stark contrast, Sironi's one Futurist canvas on show, *Self-portrait* (1913), is irretrievably gloomy, a fierce stare hidden beneath the most extravagant application of chiaroscuro. Rather than the dynamic movement Futurism was supposed to hail, here the familiar technique of breaking up the image into intersecting planes is used to generate the utmost stasis and a fierce psychological tension. As always with Sironi, the catalogue photograph does all it can to make the picture look brighter than it is. But in the gallery the sense of an enormous and doomed effort of will is entirely compelling. Whence, in 1918, would that will be turned?

Emily Braun is efficient and informative as she describes Sironi's early commitment to socialism, his disenchantment with the left and adherence to the more exhilarating if directionless iconoclasm of Futurism. She gives a good picture of the general frustration with Italian parliamentary politics in the early years of the century, the growing desire for a gesture of nation-building and the way this desire was exacerbated rather than quelled by the calamities of the First World War. Her descriptions of the paintings, too, are never less than excellent, particularly the way Sironi just would not leave that chiaroscuro be, modelling figures, faces, trucks, buildings and chimneys out of a thick paste of black and white (but mainly black), and then, later in life, creating mosaics that seemed to be painted in chiaroscuro and even sculpting figures so encased in a sort of shell, or even coffin perhaps, as to create a marked chiaroscuro effect, the figure ever looming from a pool of black. The dark dynamism of the artist's psyche is clear enough. Yet nothing she says quite prepares us for the turn events were to take after Sironi came back from the trenches: his total commitment to Mussolini's camp. Here, perhaps, it may be worth reflecting for a moment on a trait that still divides the Italian mind from the Anglo-Saxon.

In 1915, claims a note in the Galleria d'Arte Moderna, the collector Riccardo Jucker made Sironi an offer for a small painting entitled *La piccola danzatrice*. He was astonished when Sironi agreed to sell but insisted on *lowering* the price. The artist did not think his painting was worth so much (notably it is one of the few Sironis that is not gloomy). And throughout his life Sironi showed scant respect for his own work, signing very little of it, often walking over discarded temperas on the floor, not bothering to catalogue it. Needless to say, his opinion of his peers was even lower. Life in Rome, he remarked, immediately after leaving the city, was 'a hell full of misery and conflict . . . where I placed everyone and everything in a heap of insult and loathing'.

Going back almost a hundred years, Giacomo Leopardi in his *Discorso sopra lo stato presente dei costumi degl'italiani* paints a picture of his country that, in concentrating on the problem of self-regard, in many ways looks forward to Fascism, and indeed is not without its appropriateness in Italy today. Leopardi starts from the premise that 'the massacre of illusions' that has swept away religion and philosophy in Europe has left no other basis for morality than the 'good taste' of 'society', by which, he makes clear, he means high society. This society existed, he felt in France and in England, where a man is 'ashamed to do harm in the same way that he would be ashamed to appear in a conversation with a stain on his clothes'. But Italy, after centuries of poverty and division, found itself without such a society, without this taste, without self-respect. Thus if 'the principal basis of the morality of an individual and a people is the constant and profound regard it has for itself', Italy, where conversation was no more than a 'school for insults', is an entirely immoral place where people do what they do out of the merest habit, laziness or selfishness, and in the most complete indifference, or even scorn, for the public gestures they make.

Leaving aside the virulence of Leopardi's attack, which is not without a certain personal bitterness, what is striking about his reflections is the value they give to illusion, above all collective illusion, at the expense of truth, and the way this value is connected with self-respect. Anticipating by many years Nietzsche's argument that morality was fundamentally a question of aesthetics, he praises the English in particular for the ludicrously high opinion they have of themselves. This illusion – for there is no real reason why the English should have such a high opinion of themselves – allows them to treat each other with great respect.

The Italians, on the other hand, living in the truth of total disillusionment, do nothing but sling mud at each other, each antagonist holding even himself in the lowest possible regard. Leopardi remarks: 'thus not only does life in Italy have no substance or truth at all, something it doesn't have elsewhere either, but it doesn't even have the appearance of the same, so that we might be able to think of it as important.'

In one sense backward (they are without a homogeneous polite society), in another very important way the Italians are hence obliged to be the avant-garde: they must create a collective illusion deliberately and consciously, something that has never been done before. This is the direction in which, whether intentionally or not, the whole of Leopardi's *Discorso* tends. A huge effort of will is required, a great act of collective self-deception. Bereft of religion ('Nor should anyone object that the Italians too have their religious practices, since in Italy, as I have said, these are usages and habits not moral customs and everybody laughs at them, nor do we any longer find real fanatics of any kind in Italy'), lacking the kind of benevolent social inertia that makes life possible in England or France, Italian society must enchant itself with its own imagined worth. Such a vision can only put enormous pressure on art and on the artistic elite from whom any such act must originate.

Back from the war, Sironi was by now all too aware of the need for self and mutual regard. Nor was he alien to enormous efforts of will. How else had he overcome his depressions? How else survived the trenches? Living in subsidised housing in the depressing suburbs of a rapidly industrialising Milan, he painted gloomy cityscapes where great masses of barren commercial architecture, windows remorselessly black, open up into deep canyon-like streets, at the bottom of which, in determined patrol, moves a tiny tram, or a small black truck. Alternatively, there are imposing nude figures in classical landscapes. The celebrated *Melancholy* (1919–20) shows a seated nude in an impossibly dramatic scenario. Like the trams or trucks of the urban pictures, she is at the bottom of a vast canyon with, in this case, a viaduct spanning distant peaks beneath a stormy sky. Knees covered with a drape so modelled in chiaroscuro as to seem carved in stone, she stares in grim determination at a marble sphere on a pedestal.

It is with some amusement, in the gallery, that one moves from Sironi's rendering of this theme to Achille Funi's *Melancholy* (1930), only a couple of canvases away. Here, despite the generous fleshiness of the seated nude, we have only a pretty wistfulness, a sweet girl who for all her colourful bulk might float away at any moment. Certainly there appears to be something like a halo above her head. Turning back to the Sironi, the essential ingredients of his vision become clear: on the one hand the immense and desolate heaviness of existence, represented either in the flesh or the landscape, whether natural or urban; and then the equally immense effort of will, visible in furious face or dark truck, needed to focus it, to impose on it, to overcome it. Later, Sironi would be ridiculed for the huge feet that began to appear in his paintings. So much so that he would be known as 'Il piedone' – big foot. Braun quotes as sarcastic the advice given to Sironi by the Minister of Education Giuseppe Bottai: 'Tell your critics you make the feet of your figures so big so that they can kick them in the ass.' Sarcastic he might have been, but close to the truth one suspects. Ever ready to kick out, those huge feet bring together the heaviness of the painter's vision, and the effort required to overcome that weight.

In 1919 Sironi married Matilde Fabbrini. 'Their mutually abrasive relationship,' writes Braun laconically, 'would continue until his death.' Marriage too, then, was to be a conflict requiring a constant exercise of will. At the beginning Matilde didn't even want to leave Rome to be with her husband in Milan. But Sironi won this first round and soon she had borne him a daughter, Aglae, whom Mussolini managed to sit on his lap and promptly drop. For the little girl's father was moving in very particular circles now. He was a close friend of Margherita Sarfatti, art critic of Mussolini's newspaper *Il popolo d'Italia* and companion of his bed. How fitting that the first man to come to power through a modern use of propaganda should have an art critic for his mistress! Sironi, as sole and daily illustrator for *Il popolo d'Italia* from August 1921 through to 1923, was to be an essential instrument of that propaganda in the moment of crisis that brought Mussolini to power.

They were heady years. The First World War had brought the country to the brink of collapse. In a wave of industrial unrest the socialists were trying to push it over that brink. The workers occupied the factories. The Fascists claimed to represent the working class, but opposed the socialists, the factory occupations and the government. Theirs would be a 'third way' between capitalism and communism. The Futurists sided with the Fascists, then broke with them. It was all very confusing. Of his illustrations in that period, Sironi wrote to his wife just before she came to Milan:

The dance has begun again and so has the nausea [. . .] Every time it becomes more difficult – and I have the same sensation this time – darkness and complete emptiness and I know well where it comes from! To do philosophy in caricature! And not knowing where to begin. For control or none, for the end of the world or for Turati [the leader of the socialist party]? Total mystery and indecision. In addition, to think about all of these present and future problems makes me anxious, bewildered and sick to my stomach!

Clearly the situation demanded someone who knew his mind.

The flamboyant poet D'Annunzio had shown the way, taking, on his own initiative, a small private army to occupy Fiume on the northern Adriatic coast, a territory the allies had denied to Italy after the war. Though the mission ultimately failed, it captured the imagination. Sironi, in a rare concession to the occasional, dedicated a painting to the event. One of his typical industrial scenes is just readable as the docks at Trieste, thanks to the masts of a ship rising above a wall. In what is a shallower canyon than most of his streets, a powerful figure sits on a vigorous white horse in, as always, dramatic chiaroscuro. For the first time one has the impression of the effort of will being superior to the weight it opposes. This is heroism. For the first time Sironi's private preoccupations are clearly identifiable with a contemporary political figure.

Very soon, after the March on Rome, it would be Mussolini who embodied that heroic gesture. In the huge mosaic of 1936, *Fascist Work*, for example, the big foot definitely belongs to the Duce. As for the ubiquitous black truck of the earlier paintings, all too soon it would be unmistakably the vehicle of the Fascist *squadristi*, the thugs. And however complicated Sironi might have found politics throughout two decades of Fascism, he would never have any difficulty in offering a positive image of the exercise of will, the imposition of a decision, whatever it might be. In the thousands of pugnacious political illustrations he produced, the gesture is triumphant, almost an infantile fantasy of domination and control. In the paintings, it is for the most part thwarted, at best gloomily steadfast. 'Will to power, will to life, will to grandeur,' he wrote in 1933, 'these passwords, these majestic words of Fascism, also express the style of our art.' The private and political worlds had meshed.

But what was that style? Only a year after Sironi wrote those words, the musician Ildebrando Pizzetti commented:

Every time I come across a book, a brochure and article about Fascism and Fascist art, I read it from top to bottom, carefully, applying my intelligence to the utmost, and every time with renewed desire, the renewed hope, that I will come away from it having finally understood what is meant by Fascist art. No doubt it's my own fault if I haven't quite grasped what I read, but that desire, that hope, remains unfulfilled.

The question as to the existence or not of a Fascist style occupies the central pages of Emily Braun's book and is intimately tied up with the question: How far was Sironi's work the result of political expedience, acceptance of a group line, and how far was he his own man creating his own work? Did he really believe, as he claimed, that artistic genius was 'the foremost quality of our race' and Mussolini 'the Man who will know how justly to esteem the force of our world-dominating art'? Or were these statements part of an exercise of group self-deception of the kind foreshadowed in Leopardi's *Discorso*, though Leopardi, no doubt, would have found them even more grotesque than we do?

Some facts must be briefly stated, if only to grasp how complicated the issue becomes. Sironi supported Mussolini from beginning to end, from the March on Rome to the sad puppet show of Salò. He was personally responsible for the artwork at the huge *Mostra della Rivoluzione Fascista* which turned the tenth anniversary of Fascist power into a quasi religious festival and deliberately distorted the facts about how Mussolini had come to power (Braun gives impressive and frightening photographs). Sironi was likewise responsible for official Italian pavilions at international exhibitions in Paris and Milan. By 1933, he had actually renounced easel painting as 'too monotonous and trite for the complex orchestrations of modern life, too weak to capture the attention of men in this age of great myths and gigantic upheavals'. In short, by turning to the large-scale mural and mosaic, he identified even his 'serious' work, as opposed to the merely journalistic illustrations, with the Fascist cause.

On the other hand, it must also be said that his work for *Il popolo d'Italia* became sporadic after the alliance with Germany. He never publicly supported (but never spoke out against) the anti-Semitic campaign. Incredibly and inexplicably, he did not become an official member of the Fascist Party until 1936. He did not grow rich through his support of the regime, was always underpaid, took no bribes. He was never admitted to the Reale Accademia d'Italia, an honour Mussolini extended to both Marinetti and Pirandello. Throughout the thirties he was constantly under fire from the right-wing Fascists, notably the arch-xenophobe Farinacci, who accused Sironi of polluting Italian art with foreign and Jewish influences.

Above all, though, it has to be said that there is a remarkable continuity to Sironi's painting that seems to go beyond immediate political circumstance, or indeed artistic fashions. For although a cursory glance through the illustrations in Braun's book will make it clear how much Sironi owed to the major artists and movements of his time, from Futurism, through metaphysical painting and the various phases of Picasso's work, nevertheless to look at the paintings more carefully is to appreciate how completely his personal vision transforms each of these approaches into something immediately recognisable as his own. So much so that in its description of the canvas *Drinker with Cup*, the catalogue of the Museo del Novecento is unable to decide whether it was painted in the early 1930s or the 1950s (when Sironi returned to easel painting), so consistent is it with the artist's manner throughout his long career. Which brings us back to the question of Fascist style: when there is no gesture to the iconography of Fascism it appears there is no distinctive Fascist style to help date the work.

The secret to these apparent contradictions no doubt lay in the ambiguous nature of Fascism itself, an ambiguity that suited

Sironi. At first revolutionary, then reactionary, formed by socialists who became conservatives, Fascism prided itself on being an 'anti-ideology' whose only *raison d'être* was the grandeur of Italy. It spoke of breaking decisively with the past, but also of a return to the greatness of Rome. Essentially, it was gesture without content, tension without consummation.

This vagueness was never more evident than in the establishment of the so-called Novecento movement into which Margherita Sarfatti gathered a number of the country's foremost painters, including Sironi, immediately after the First World War. The declared inspiration of the movement was the desire to shift from criticism to construction. Futurism had been merely iconoclastic. Now the artist would play a privileged part in building a new social order, shaping a new and united national consciousness. But it was never clear what that order or consciousness would be and there was little homogeneity between the painters involved. 'True Italian tradition is that of never having any tradition,' was the kind of equivocal explanation often given, 'since the Italian race is a race of innovators and constructors.'

There is a curious mixture of authoritarianism and anarchy here, elitism and laissez-faire. Thus Sironi would have agreed with Gentile, Mussolini's minister for education, when he declared that the artist needed to be involved in the moral, political and economic life of the nation, creating myths and building consensus, putting in motion 'the forces of sentiment and will'. But it was equally important that the content of what one painted never be imposed. And indeed Sironi met the stiffest criticism of his career over his organisation of the mural paintings at the 1933 Milan Triennale exhibition, with the critic Papini claiming that the sheer variety he had admitted created a 'sense of anarchy' giving the impression that nineteenth-century individualism was alive and well at the expense of Fascist discipline. But hadn't Mussolini himself declared that he had no intention of creating an 'art of the state' since art was 'the domain of the

223

individual'. 'It would have indicated a scarce awareness of the aesthetic phenomenon,' Sironi answered his critics, 'to have demanded the representation of a given obligatory subject.'

Thus Sironi could invite De Chirico to paint a fresco in which, as was De Chirico's way, the juxtaposition of classical and modern iconography generates an amused irony about the possibility of absolute meaning, while only a room away Sironi himself produced a fresco which, taking its title from Hesiod's *Works and Days*, sought in a huge amalgam of classical and industrial figures to weld together past and present in a positive and emphatic dynamic. Alas, the impression of monumental permanence that Sironi always sought was belied by the very poor preparation of the murals' surfaces. Before the exhibition was over the images were already flaking off.

But technical problems aside, was it really possible to separate style and content in this way, something no other totalitarian regime has ever tried, to allow freedom of content and insist only on a certain 'style' that, after all, no one could define, to the point that Mussolini ultimately stated that all he wanted of artists was that they produce works that were 'strong and beautiful'?

Braun, along with others, suggests that this non-insistence on content was Mussolini's astuteness. He gave artists enough freedom, not to mention subsidies and sweeteners, to prevent them from attacking him. And certainly there is an element of truth in this. After all, it was precisely the lack of any content behind Fascism's gesturing that allowed even such an astute commentator as Benedetto Croce to say, as late as 1928 and after the assassination of Matteoti, that he saw in Fascism only 'an episode of the post-war period, with some juvenile and patriotic traits, which would be dissipated without doing any harm, but on the contrary leaving behind some positive effects'. All the same, it is also true, I suspect, that the fact that no strict content was ever imposed on artists, tells us something about the ultimate weakness of Italian Fascism as compared with its tougher Nazi counterpart. The point can best be understood when we come to the perplexing question of the Fascist 'exploitation' of myth.

A myth, of course, is a story. It distinguishes itself from other stories by forming part of a larger group of intertwining narratives that, taken together, form the spell, as it were, under which a community lives. Nobody in particular invented these stories, rather all are in their thrall, until, with Leopardi's 'massacre of illusions' they are cast off. Significantly, when the unhappy idea occurred that mythology might be at our beck and call and that it might be conjured up again to 'manipulate the masses', what is notably lacking is the narrative element. Sironi, but not only Sironi, created endless images suggesting the primacy of Italy and drawing on mythic figures and symbols. But all is static. The figures are rigidly separate. We can never say, this is the story where St Peter did this, or this is the story where Apollo did that.

Thus *Fascist Work*, the impressive mosaic for the 1936 Triennale gives us a huge central figure of Italy – seated, powerful, determined – and then two tiers of symbolic figures: above are images from an antique past, an Etruscan priestess, a Roman horseman; below are representatives of modern Italy, a mother and child, a helmeted soldier. The only figure to break the division between the layers is a stalwart Mussolini busy with a spade. While the sense of awe, and solemnity, the 'aesthetic aura' Sironi said he sought to communicate, is certainly present and powerful, there is no narrative here, nor any sense of where all this might be going. It is rather as if we had a group of figures waiting for a story to happen to them. Or alternatively, for someone like De Chirico to alter one symbol, introduce just one incongruity, and reveal the whole thing as ironic. My Italian father-in-law assured me that nothing was more common, on the parade ground, than for a word or two of a Fascist song to be replaced by some rhyming absurdity, so that everyone could burst out laughing. The eventual narrative, on the other hand, when someone finally put these static figures in motion, would be no laughing matter.

Less than two years after Sironi completed *Fascist Work*, the Racial Laws were introduced, armies began to march, Mussolini was under Hitler's thumb. In one of the strangest gestures of his life, when his close friends Carlo and Eloise Foa decided to flee to the States, Fascism's official artist gave the departing Jewish couple his private papers for safekeeping. Despite 'Italian supremacy' Sironi was not convinced of victory in the forthcoming conflagration. Of reality and illusion, he wrote: 'All of the Italians represent a centuries-old vortex of wilfulness, so much so that one can well say that they have generated an antinatural nature, a creative reality outside of and contrary to common reality.' But now it seemed the dream of Italian Fascism and the reality of European history were on a calamitous collision course.

The papers Sironi gave to his friends told mainly of his unhappy marriage. Separated from his wife in 1930, only two years after the birth of a second daughter, he had begun an affair with the much younger Mimi Costa. Sironi was a misanthrope, Mimi a flirt. During preparations for the 1933 Triennale he locked her in his car for several hours rather than have her meet his colleagues. Painting murals for the masses now, he worked alone at night because he didn't want the masses to see him. How hard to be the lonely genius underwriting a populist regime! Meanwhile the passion with Mimi couldn't last. And the argument with his wife could never end. 'I've told you over and over again,' he writes to her in 1936, 'that I just don't earn very much.' Proclaiming the innate genius of the Italian spirit, he despaired of incompetence all around him. 'Why aren't all Italians like me?' he demands in a letter to his daughters.

Throughout the war he continued to be a vegetarian, wrote of his love of animals, most particularly his dog, and condemned hunting, an activity he must have seen endlessly revered in the ancient artworks he ransacked for images of a noble Italy. So it is not surprising that he was carrying his exhausted dog when he was finally hunted down himself; he had walked thirty miles to Como from a heavily bombed Milan. Lined up for execution with other loyal Fascists, he was recognised by a young art student among the partisan executioners. Having preached since early socialist days that the artist was no different from any other worker, his special semi-divine status was recognised at just the right moment. They couldn't kill a painter. Freed, he sketched his fellow Fascists' execution.

Or perhaps it was just the wrong moment. For it is with some awe that one tries to imagine what Sironi's inner life must have been in those post-war years. He was sixty now and everything had changed. In 1948 his second daughter committed suicide. Partly as a result, the first daughter broke off all communication. His reputation was gone, his very name a scandal. But doggedly he painted on, appropriating abstract expressionism now, the same way he had previously appropriated every other style. As steadfast and isolated as the figures he had always painted, there were no confessions and no explanations. When he died in 1961, he used his will for one last act of will. His wife Matilde was barred from attending his funeral.

To see the mosaic *Fascist Work*, one has to make a telephone call. Transferred to the wall of an upper room in the Palazzo dei Giornalisti, Piazza Cavour, Milan, it looks down on a conference hall run by the Hilton Hotel organisation, representatives, surely, of that international bourgeois capitalism Sironi so hated. How solemn and gloomily powerful his figures are! And how strange to think of this thing being created for the masses to unite the Italian people and being seen now mainly by privileged foreign businessmen glancing up from their lists of statistics.

When I ask a disgruntled Hilton executive if people often ask to see the mosaic, he tells me 'fortunately not'. Clearly he hardly notices it himself. But out on the street a Benetton advert showing a man on death row continues the Italian tradition of a radical split between rhetorical gesture – this sham international piety – and banal reality – a manufacturer's need to sell its products. And in the Stazione Centrale too, one of Fascism's finest pieces of architecture, the old imperial insignia high up on the lofty arches are barely noticed beside the bold and colourful images society now raises one after another in extravagant and solipsistic praise of itself. A boy's huge grim frown on the left is altered, by a particular brand of sunglasses, to a huge bright smile on the right. As Emily Braun remarks in laconic conclusion to this excellent book, when it comes to creating social cohesion and shared vision, Sironi and company simply hadn't grasped 'the power of consumerism, whose persuasive myths would prove far more effective than Socialism or Fascist ultra-populist nationalism'.

Ferreting through my bag on the train I find the glossy Hilton brochure someone put in my hand as I left what is now called 'Lo spazio Sironi'. 'For an unforgettable stay,' it invites me, 'in an oasis of refined efficiency'. Above an illuminated computer screen, a beautifully stern face from Sironi's *Fascist Work* dominates the cover. The title of the mosaic is not mentioned.

Sightgeist

[José Saramago]

How many proverbs and clichés would have to change if everybody went blind? Could you say, 'I know the place like the back of my hand,' if the back of your hand were something you never saw? Could one usefully speak of 'the blind leading the blind', if other options were no longer available? Such considerations, you might think, would hardly be of the highest priority in a world suddenly and terribly afflicted by a loss of sight, yet of all the obstacles that Saramago has his characters blunder against in the dark world of his novel *Blindness*, language is perhaps the most frequent and the most perplexing. 'Just imagine,' remarks one girl stumbling in the entrance to her old apartment block, 'stairs I used to go up and down with my eyes closed . . .' In radically changed conditions, the inertia of common usage constantly generates absurdities. Not only is the shin scraped in contact with cement, but the mind humiliated as its mindless habits are exposed.

That standard visions of reality are enshrined in standard language is itself a commonplace. Saramago, along with a multitude of writers past and present, is eager to increase our sensitivity to the contingency of the one upon the other, and the contingency of identity on both. A major change occurs in the world: people go blind, or the Iberian peninsula detaches itself from the European mainland, or some key historical fact is reversed, or the central tenets of our religion inverted. In dramatising the aftermath of such upheavals, Saramago mercilessly satirises those whose investment in the old status quo makes it impossible for them to adapt or even understand how obsolete their vision of the world has become. In this respect, his political sympathies as a Portuguese communist come predictably to the fore. The reaction of the government to the epidemic of blindness in the novel, suggests nothing more than the brutal clumsiness of thirties Fascism. On only the second day of the epidemic, sufferers are locked in a disused hospital without so much as a shovel to bury their dead. No radio, no medication. Anyone venturing more than a few yards from the door is summarily shot. One frequently feels one is reading a book about the death camps. In *The Stone Raft*, American and European capitalism become the butt for ridicule as the Pyrenees split from east to west and Spain and Portugal drift away into the Atlantic. The rich abandon hotel for helicopter, the US president wonders if he will be able to include the ex-peninsula in an American sphere of influence, the European Community is glad to be shot of two of its poorer members, etc. In *The Siege of Lisbon*, when a humble proof-reader radically alters Portuguese history by negating a verb in the book he is checking, the bewildered indignance of the publishers again suggests the inflexibility of a status quo that would gladly dispense with the unpredictability inherent in life itself, indeed that finds any manifestation of the will outside the conventional (here enshrined in the rules of proofing) distasteful.

Fortunately, satire is only one of Saramago's many suits and hardly his strongest. He lacks the accuracy in establishing his target that makes the ruthlessness of a Cervantes, Swift, or in modern times and different ways Beckett, not only acceptable, but admirable, even necessary. Faced with a recognition problem – is this target really so guilty? – the reader begins to suspect an excess of rancour in relation to the misdemeanour (so much so that the placing of that rancour becomes one of the most intriguing challenges in reading Saramago's work). Meanwhile, though, as the powers that be behave badly and in such a way as to keep the reader ever aware of the circumstantial nature of old certainties, others – notably the humble and the womenfolk – are adapting to change and all kinds of positive developments are occurring.

Saramago is not a simple author, but such simplifications will perhaps allow us to get a grasp of what is a repeated structure in his novels. Thus the upheavals caused by the Iberian peninsula's sudden vagrancy lead the protagonists of *The Stone Raft* to discover love of the most traditional and romantic variety, and the same is true for the hero of *The Siege of Lisbon*: his apparently perverse impulse in altering received history attracts the attention of an intelligent woman who, in encouraging him to reflect on what he has done and to write an imaginative history of the siege, allows him to discover a vein of creativity he never imagined. Again, the two fall in love and are splendidly happy in bed and out. More movingly and far more convincingly, the atrocious experiences of the central characters in *Blindness* lead them to a profound and generous awareness of their now radical interdependence which is very beautifully portrayed in the closing pages of the book.

To understand the link between these negative and positive sides of Saramago's work, the satire and the generous sentiment, may be the swiftest way to get a fix on a writer who will frequently seem professionally elusive, cheerfully, often wittily stating everything and its opposite in a very short space, sometimes retelling an anecdote that he used in another book, but in such a way as entirely to invert the values it appeared to propose. Such an understanding may even help us to explain the relationship between his portrayal on the one hand of a realistic and immediately recognisable world and then his introduction of those provocatively unrealistic events that criticism has come to refer to as 'magical'.

Saramago is on record as saying that, 'I cannot save anything but what I can do is write about what I think and feel and the anguish of seeing a world that could already have resolved a large portion of its humanitarian problems, but which not only has not solved any, but which in fact aggravates many of them.' Surprising here is the opening gesture. Did anybody expect or imagine that Saramago could 'save anything'? 'Nobody saves anybody,' Cioran reminds us in one of his caustic corrections of, as he puts it, 'the obligatory optimism' of modern political thought. Clearly Saramago, like many genuine political idealists of whatever persuasion suffers considerable disappointment at having observed over the years how the development of increasingly sophisticated technical skills has not made it possible to resolve all 'humanitarian' problems. (One presumes here that he is referring above all to diet, disease and conflict, since the word 'already' suggests a reference to progress in time, whereas it is difficult to imagine that our deeper existential problems will ever be susceptible to resolution.)

Our author gives us the impression, then, of a man reluctantly emerging from the peculiarly Western delirium that a perfection of technique at the service of good will might lead to the triumph of happiness. And like anybody disappointed, he tends to exaggerate. It is surely not true, for example, that we have 'not solved any' of our humanitarian problems. All kinds of things have been achieved. On the other hand, who could disagree that the race has a perverse habit of generating problems where none need exist and how confident can we feel of our powers of dealing with them if even our sense of self and identity, as Saramago insists, and with it our whole moral make-up can easily be shown to be contingent on merest circumstance? 'Do you love your husband?' one character asks another in *Blindness*, 'Yes, as I love myself, but should I turn blind, if after turning blind I should no longer be the person I was, how would I then be able to go on loving him . . .' Though he never says as much, it is hard not to feel, as the bleak scenes of this book get bleaker and bleaker, that Saramago is approaching, albeit kicking and screaming, the position Thomas Bernhard's hero reaches in *Concrete* when, suddenly weary of oppressive feelings of socialist guilt, he brusquely declares, 'Poverty can't be eradicated, and anyone who thinks of eradicating it is set on nothing short of the eradication of the human race itself and hence of nature itself.'

Whose fault is this? In *The Siege of Lisbon*, with his realist and political satirist's cap on, Saramago remarks, 'it is always the same, we blame the gods for this and that, when it is we who invent and fabricate everything, including absolution for these and other crimes.' But elsewhere he offers us the despairing formulation: 'God does not forgive the sins he makes us commit.' While the statements are contradictory, the world they refer us to is at once recognisable and grim: a place where men and women are locked into ever repeating cycles of crime and guilt. Often one feels that the departures into the 'magical', which usually occur around those falling in love, indicate a yearning at once to remove the debate from the merely political arena, where hope has proved a cheat and satire become routine, but without as a result finding oneself trapped in a gloomily deterministic, perhaps theistic vision where there is nothing to be hoped at all. (In this respect it may be worth noting that most 'magical realists' come from an area of communist or socialist persuasion, their political positions as predictable as their fictions are fantastic.) 'The possibility of the impossible, dreams and illusions, are the subject of my novels,' says Saramago. The attentive reader will notice the sleight of hand by which the contradictory, indeed meaningless, first entry in that list, optimistically shifts the status of the second two. Perhaps the word 'love' would have done for all three, since again and again it is love and only love that redeems human experience as presented in Saramago's world.

Let us take the example of the two novels that are at once the strongest and, since they make no reference to the Iberian experience, the most accessible to the reader with little specialist knowledge: *The Gospel According to Jesus Christ* and *Blindness*. As a retelling of the Bible story, the curiosity of *The Gospel* is that, while setting out with intentions clearly hostile to established religion, Saramago does not merely debunk the supernatural by giving us a realist or psychological account of Christ's life. Rather he invents all kinds of supernatural occurrences that are not present in the Bible story as we have it. In rapid synthesis: at Jesus's decidedly non-virgin conception God mixed his seed with Joseph's. There is thus some ambiguity as to who actually fathered the boy. Jesus's youth is drastically conditioned by the fact that his father, who had got wind of Herod's planned slaughter of the innocents, saved his own baby, Jesus, but did not warn the other parents. His guilt over this terrible failing will lead him, Joseph, to pointless self-sacrifice and ultimately meaningless crucifixion at the hands of the Romans. When Jesus discovers all this he is deeply shocked and feels profoundly guilty for being alive at all.

Saramago is extremely able, here and elsewhere, in the way he takes, twists and weaves biblical events into a narrative that now fits together in an entirely different way. But if this opening prepares the reader for a psychological explanation of Jesus's fascination with guilt and sacrifice, it is immediately contradicted by the introduction of the figures of God and the Devil, who are revealed as in cynical collusion in a plot to use Jesus to extend their mutually enhancing influences outside the limited area of Judea and ultimately over the whole world. The powers given to Jesus must serve to convince the world that he is the Son of God, in order that his sacrificial death can then create the illusion of a loving and caring divinity who gave himself for others. Any benefits accruing to those healed or helped are entirely incidental. In the event, most of the miracles backfire. In helping one group of fishermen rather than another, Jesus upsets the market for fish; in exorcising the man with many demons by sending them into the Gadarene swine who promptly jump over the cliff, he deprives a number of swineherds of their legitimate livelihood.

And so on. In this grotesque comedy of evil and errors, whether on the political plane or the metaphysical, the only real miracle to emerge in the story is the love between Jesus and Mary Magdalene, or again the love of Jesus's mother for her children, the love of the disciples for their leader.

The technique the book deploys is that of making us constantly uncertain what reality Saramago wishes to attribute to any character or event. While the debate revolves resourcefully but interminably around the old chestnut that if God exists he must be fallible or evil, the narrator never allows us to settle on a particular point of view, or reading of his text, or even vision of the characters. This can be stimulating and meshes perfectly with a voice that demands that the reader be constantly exercising discrimination at every level. The lack of paragraphing and absence of any punctuation aside from the comma and fullstop (typical of all Saramago's fiction) oblige you to work hard to keep track of who is speaking to whom, while at a higher level the narrator's tendency to fall back on received ideas, or to engage in bizarre speculation, or wander off into the most inconsequential rambling, serves both to entertain and to keep us on our toes. These lines come from the period when Jesus is living with Mary Magdalene and the fishermen beside the sea of Galilee:

How true, the saying which reminds us that there is so much sorrow in this world, misfortunes grow like weeds beneath our feet. Such a saying could only have been invented by mortals, accustomed as they are to life's ups and downs, obstacles, setbacks, and constant struggle. The only people likely to question it are those who sail the seas, for they know that even greater woe lies beneath their feet, indeed unfathomable chasms. The misfortunes of seafarers, the winds and gales sent from heaven, cause waves to swell, storms to break, sails to rip, and fragile vessels to founder. And these fishermen and sailors truly perish between heaven and earth, a heaven hands cannot reach, an earth feet never touch. The Sea of Galilee is nearly always tranquil and smooth, like any lake, until the watery furies are unleashed, and then it is every man for himself, although sadly some drown. But let us return to Jesus of Nazareth and his recent worries, which only goes to show that the human heart is never content, and that doing one's duty does not bring peace of mind, though those who are easily satisfied would have us believe otherwise. One could say that thanks to the endless comings and goings of Jesus up and down the river Jordan, there is no longer any hardship, not even an occasional shortage, on the western shore . . .

What a genial little minefield of propositions this is: the naive quotation of an old saying, 'misfortunes grow like weeds beneath our feet', the bizarre reflection that such a saying could only have been invented by mortals, thus begging the question, by whom if not by mortals? Do we believe in immortal beings? Have we ever reflected on how inappropriate our proverbs would be for their happy state? The complacent description of our difficult lives: 'obstacles, setbacks, and constant struggle'. Then suddenly the mad decision to take 'weeds beneath the feet' literally, leading to the odd thought that there is a category, that of sailor folk, who might reasonably take issue with this saying. So now we get the leisurely account of what we already know very well, the precariousness of the fisherman's life, but with the ominous suggestion that 'gales [are] sent from heaven' – deliberately? – this culminating in the wonderful 'sailors truly perish', as if there were any other way to perish, or as if perishing were the only truth, followed by the rhetorically savoured and again otiose, but also confusing, 'between heaven and earth, a heaven hands cannot reach, an earth feet never touch'. Oddly, we are reminded, there are indeed occasions when we refer to the sea as the earth. This digression on the sailing life, or death, naturally returns the narrator to the Sea of Galilee, pronounced normally tranquil, 'like any lake' (but those of us familiar with other climes will know of lakes that are rarely tranquil), yet occasionally, the narrator then remembers, dangerous, indeed vicious. And here we have the marvellous non sequitur: 'and then it's every man for himself, though sadly some drown', where the word 'sadly' in particular parades all its inadequacy. Then, out of nowhere, we have a direct address to the reader 'But let us . . .', followed by the depressing aside that doing one's duty (but what is one's duty?) doesn't bring peace of mind – this now an attack on received ideas rather than their repetition – and finally the speculative 'One could say' (but presumably one might well not) introducing an entirely economic appraisal of Jesus's fishing miracles, the benefits of which, we notice are limited (sadly?) to the western shore . . .

All this is at once extremely astute and very good fun; the protean nature of the narrator forces the reader to work at establishing his own position, the echoes of Beckett's droll narrative voices, at once pedantic and perplexed, are clear and welcome. Unfortunately, the project breaks down at those points where Saramago is so sure of what he knows, and feels so strongly about it, that instead of leaving the reader this space for discrimination and for the relishing of life's mysteries, he plunges us into the most crude and coercive of satires. Here is the long delayed 'annunciation' when, with Jesus now a man, an angel is finally sent to inform Mary of the details of his conception.

Know, Mary, that the Lord mixed his seed with that of Joseph on the morning you conceived for the first time, and it was the Lord's seed rather than that of your husband, however legitimate, that sired your son Jesus. Much surprised, Mary asked the angel, So Jesus is my son and also the son of the Lord. Woman, what are you saying, show some respect for precedence, the way you should put it is the son of the Lord and also of me. Of the Lord and also of you. No, of the Lord and of you. You confuse me, just answer my question, is Jesus our son. You mean to say the Lord's son, because you only served to bear the child. So the Lord didn't choose me. Don't be absurd, the Lord was merely passing, as anyone watching would have seen from the colour of the sky, when His eye caught you and Joseph, a fine healthy couple, and then, if you can still remember how God's will was made manifest, He ordained that Jesus be born nine months later. Is there any proof that it was the Lord's seed that sired my firstborn. Well, it's a delicate matter, what you're demanding is nothing less than a paternity test, which in these mixed unions, no matter how many analyses, tests, and genetic comparisons one carries out can never give conclusive results.

While one agrees that the Bible story is absurd (but then so do many Christians, starting with the Apostle Paul), it is difficult not to feel that Saramago is falling into the merest flippancy here, something hardly distinguishable from a Monty Python script or a new and only slightly more daring episode of *The Hitchhiker's Guide to the Galaxy*. This occurs with every divine manifestation in the book causing an unevenness that seriously mars the whole effect and leaves us with the disturbing impression that for all the ostentatious rhetoric of epistemological doubt, Saramago, unlike others who have reflected on the biblical absurd – Kierkegaard, Nietzsche, Lawrence, Beckett, to name but a few – feels entirely, even smugly sure of himself when it comes to matters religious and metaphysical. The problem may go some way to explaining the curious reaction that this reader at least had on approaching the end of *The Gospel*: that of agreeing entirely with Saramago's sentiments, admiring much in his writing, yet feeling a deep and growing antipathy to the project as a whole.

The first achievement of *Blindness* is to be rid of all this, of all, or nearly, those mannerisms of method that dog the earlier books and have didacticism and satire descending into empty verbosity or worse still facetiousness. From page one, *Blindness* takes itself entirely seriously, and rightly so. A man sitting in his car at a traffic light goes blind. His blindness seems to pass from person to person, at a glance, as it were. Within a few days everybody in the city, which in this book is the world, is blind. Everybody, that is, but one woman, the wife of the optometrist who examined the first blind man. It is on her and the group who gather around her that the narrative focuses, and it is through her eyes, for there are no others, that the drama is observed.

Curiously, the phenomenon of universal sightlessness quickly clarifies the question of how much we can expect of political intervention and how far human suffering is inevitable. While the optometrist repeatedly comments on the need 'to organise', it becomes clear, as the narrative catalogues the painstaking efforts needed to achieve even the simplest ends, that no amount of organisation will ever be enough to guarantee the most basic requirements of food and hygiene. Blind, the human race can at last be forgiven for not solving all its humanitarian problems. The optometrist's wife observes, 'here no one can be saved,' and continues, 'blindness is also this, to live in a world where all hope is gone.'

In such crisis conditions, as *The Gospel* reminded us, 'it's every man for himself'. So the novel sets out to chart, effectively enough, that descent into anarchy and bestiality that we have all read about and shuddered at elsewhere: the thefts, the rapes, the gang terror, the humiliation, the murder, and this in a world where every technical aid has failed, where every room and street is swamped in excrement and filth. A dignified sense of self, we are made to see, prerequisite of moral behaviour, has very much to do with our being able to keep an eye on each other.

But what distinguishes Saramago's story from other cataclysmic tales of human degradation is the quality of the drama that builds up around the one seeing character, wife of the optometrist. The account of how the dynamic of the marriage alters, how

239

her personality grows as she assumes both political and moral authority, is at once psychologically convincing and rich with possible analogy. She becomes willy-nilly a mother and a god to her companions, husband included, and as such is faced with appalling choices: in particular, her discovery that there comes a moment when it is a moral obligation to kill another human being is daring and in narrative terms totally gripping. But finest of all is the way, despite the growing distance between the minds of the sighted and the blind, despite the horror and filth to which she is constantly exposed, this woman develops a growing physical tenderness towards the other members of the group, a sort of desperate respect for the human body, her own and others', which she transmits to her companions by simple acts of practical love.

Towards the end of the book, when in the derelict city, without power, water or food, the group has finally found an empty apartment to sleep in, the wife is woken in the middle of the night by the sound of rain. She rushes out onto the balcony: 'Don't let it stop, she murmured as she searched in the kitchen for soap and detergents, scrubbing brushes, anything that might be used to clean a little, at least a little, of this unbearable filth of the soul. Of the body, she said, as if to correct this metaphysical thought, then she added, it's all the same.' She gets the two other women in the group to help her wash the clothes – 'we are the only woman in the world with two eyes and six hands' – and then themselves.

there are three naked women out there, as naked as when they came into the world, they seem to be mad, they must be mad, people in their right mind do not start washing on a balcony exposed to the view of the neighbourhood . . . my God, how the rain is pouring down on them, how it trickles between their breasts, how it lingers and disappears into the darkness of the pubis, how it finally drenches and flows over the thighs, perhaps we have judged them wrongly, or perhaps we are unable to see this the most beautiful and glorious thing that has happened in the history of the city, a sheet of foam flows from the floor of the balcony, if only I could go with it, falling interminably, clean, purified, naked. Only God sees us, said the wife of the first blind man, who despite disappointments and setbacks clings to the belief that God is not blind, to which the doctor's wife replies, Not even he, the sky is clouded over, Only I can see you. Am I ugly, asked the girl with the dark glasses. You are skinny and dirty, you will never be ugly, And I, asked the wife of the first blind man, You are dirty and skinny like her, not as pretty, but more than I, You are beautiful, said the girl with the dark glasses, How do you know, since you have never seen me, I have dreamt of you twice . . . I too see you as beautiful, and I never dreamt of you, said the wife of the first blind man, Which only goes to show that blindness is the good fortune of the ugly, You are not ugly, No, as a matter of fact I am not, but at my age, How old are you, asked the girl with the dark glasses, Getting on for fifty, Like my mother, And her, Her, what, Is she still beautiful, She was more beautiful once, that's what happens to all of us, we were all more beautiful once, You were never more beautiful, said the wife of the first blind man.

More daring and more disturbing here than all the metaphysical high jinks of *The Gospel* is the notion that full humanity is achieved only through suffering, which thus becomes, and this idea is provocative and entirely alien to Western political idealism, necessary. When shortly after these and other manifestations of tenderness, people begin, one by one, to see again, it is both a relief, and not so. Do we really have to pass through every sort of horror, before we can open our eyes?

A Prisoner's Dream

[Eugenio Montale]

Concluding his poem 'To Silvia' in 1828, Leopardi turns on the abstraction that had been his childhood companion: hope. The lines of that bitter address were to become some of the most quoted in Italian poetry:

> All'apparir del vero
> Tu, misera, cadesti: e con la mano
> La fredda morte ed una tomba ignuda
> Mostravi di lontano.

> When the truth dawned
> You faded wretchedly; and raising
> A hand showed me cold death
> In the distance and a dark grave.

Dwarf-like, ugly, hunchbacked, the figure of the unhappy Leopardi dominates his country's poetry throughout the nineteenth century, and the central intuition of his work, its driving force, is his compelling awareness of the nothingness behind all human illusion, the fact that if there is one thing that will not help us to live it is the naked truth. His writing fizzes with the excitement of what may best be described as negative epiphany – a horror made a little less unbearable only by the thrill of its revelation, the eloquence of its articulation.

A scholar of immense erudition, Leopardi wrote frequently of the need to elaborate some collective illusion that might save

243

society from the corrosive effects of a futility now evident, he imagined, to all. But he was too clear-headed a man to offer illusions himself, nor in the end could he admire the susceptibility of others. One of the last entries in his enormous diary suggests three things humankind will never accept: that they are nothing, that they achieve nothing, that there is nothing after death.

Born in 1896, Eugenio Montale begins his work in the immediate shadow, not of Leopardi, but of a poet who did have a vocation for illusion on a vast scale, a man whose fantastic pantheism and extraordinary mastery of the Italian language produced the most purple celebrations of the world, humanity, nature and above all himself. It is not surprising that D'Annunzio would find himself in tune with the aberration of Fascism, nor can Leopardi be blamed if the enthusiasm for collective illusion that characterised the first half of the twentieth century should end so badly. Growing up in provincial Genoa, writing his first lines in the atmosphere that would bring Mussolini to power, Montale's first concern, then, is to establish his distaste for the still rising star of D'Annunzian grandiloquence and the grotesque complacency that is its inspiration. Perhaps necessarily the young poet looks back to Leopardi, as much on a personal level as anything else. He feels alienated, where D'Annunzio epitomises not so much integration as the very spirit that coalesces the crowd. Montale hates crowds. Like Leopardi, he feels emotionally, perhaps sexually inadequate where D'Annunzio likes to appear as the nearest thing to Pan himself. But what Montale cannot share with his role model Leopardi, or indeed with a poet like Eliot to whom he has frequently been compared, is the thrill of that negative epiphany. He will not indulge in grand gestures of apocalyptic despair. Rather he begins on the stoniest of ground, carefully measuring his distance from those who precede him, rejecting intoxications whether positive or negative. As can happen with the greatest of artists, voice and direction are all there in the first stanza of the first poem of the first collection.

Enjoy if the wind that enters the orchard
brings back the tidal flow of life:
here, where a dead
tangle of memories sinks under,
was no garden, but a reliquary.

Deprecating, apparently trapped in a domestic backwater, oppressed by a moribund past, the young Montale is frequently obliged to define his early vision by negatives. The second stanza of this poem 'In limine' ('On the Threshold') warns, perhaps reassures: 'The whirr you're hearing is not flight.' The collection's closest thing to a manifesto tells us:

Don't ask us for the phrase that can open worlds,
just a few gnarled syllables, dry like a branch.
This, today, is all that we can tell you:
what we are *not*, what we do *not* want.

('Non chiederci')

Cuttlefish Bones was published in 1925. Its arid landscape is oppressively illuminated, bleached even like the bones of its title, by the scorching sun of Ligurian summers. The sound of the sea, in turns threatening and reassuring, is never far away. Inside the confining walls of his *orto* – the Italian kitchen garden, locus of unchanging domestic subsistence – the protagonist is starved of life; outside, along the seacoast, he is thrilled, overwhelmed, frightened, humbled. At first glance, the subject matter of the collection would appear to be a yearning for epiphany, for some way out of confinement that would not mean destruction. Barriers suggest a beyond and thus encourage yearning, but turn out to be insuperable. Montale differs from his nineteenth-century predecessors, however, in his implicit acceptance of this condition. He never rails. The underlying stupor at the nature of existence that informs the whole collection could never be characterised as angry surprise. He seems old beyond his years.

> And walking in the dazzling sun,
> feel with sad amazement
> how all life and its torment
> is here in following this wall
> topped with broken bottle-shards.
>   ('Meriggiare')

Rapidly, the poet establishes a variety of approaches to the idea of limits and epiphany, approaches which, with endless ingenious variations, will be the staple of a lifetime's production. Another figure is in the kitchen garden, a girl, a loved one perhaps. Is epiphany possible for her if not for him? Can he help her escape? In this scenario the protagonist's life might at least have the sense of an oblatory gesture:

> Look for a broken link in the net
> that binds us, you jump through, run!
> Go, I've prayed for this for you – now my thirst
> Will be mild, my rancour less bitter.
>   ('In limine')

Or again:

> Before I give up I'd like
> to show you this way out,
> unstable as foam or a trough
> in the troubled fields of the sea.
> And I leave you my scant hope.
> I'm too tired to nurse it for the future;
> I pledge it against your fate, so you'll escape.
>   ('Casa sul mare')

One young female figure does escape, it seems, with a splendid dive into the sea while the poet, at once too dreamy and too rational can only yearn, admire, reflect:

> At the end of the quivering board
> You hesitate, then smile,
> And, as if plucked by a wind,
> Plunge into the arms of your friend
> And god who catches you.
>
> We look on, we of the race
> Who are earthbound.
>
> ('Falsetto')

Later, it seems that the beloved figure can offer as well as receive, help rather than just escape. 'Pray for me then/that I may come down by another route/than a city street/in the wasted air, ahead of the press/of the living.' ('Incontro') But more often than not, at least in this early collection, the yearning for epiphany is temporarily appeased by a fleeting Keatsian experience not so much of ceasing 'upon the midnight' but of feeling one's confined selfhood dazzled out of its limits in a flood of Mediterranean light.

> Like that circle of cliffs
> that seems to unwind
> into spiderwebs of cloud,
> so our scorched spirits
>
> in which illusion burns
> a fire full of ash
> are lost in the clear sky
> of a single certainty: the light.
>
> ('Non rifugiarti')

'Disappearing is the destiny of destinies', the poet tells us in another poem, apparently aspiring to the inanimate peace of his cuttlefish bones on the beach, and he concludes:

> Bring me the plant that leads the way,
> to where blond transparencies
> rise, and life as essence melts in haze;
> bring me the sunflower, crazed with light.
>
>   ('Il girasole')

At such moments, it becomes evident that Montale's deeper subject is the relationship of self to other, the possibilities of some real exchange, perhaps even communication, between the two, which would be epiphany. His concern is how far it is really possible to speak of such things, in Italian, at the moment he writes; for beneath the surface of his enterprise lies a fear that speech itself may generate the limitations he wishes to overcome. 'Don't ask us,' he says, 'for the word that squares/our shapeless spirit on all sides.' ('Non chiederci'). Elsewhere he declares with the angst of a Beckett or Cioran: 'The deeper truth belongs to the man who is silent.' ('So l'ora'). Hence, along with the vocation 'to wring the neck of the eloquence of our old aulic language' as he once put it, there is also a fascination, if not for imprecision, then for all that must elude precise definition, all that must be allowed to remain shadowy, Protean, on the borders of self and other. Everything is in flux, above all consciousness; and poetry, Montale claims in his essay 'Intentions' is 'more a vehicle of consciousness than of representation'.

The genius of *Cuttlefish Bones*, then, and indeed much of the poet's later work lies in an ever denser play of delicate, indefinable but always convincingly authentic states of mind, which record an individual spirit's long negotiation with the other: the world, women, poetry, the past. Needless to say this will lead commentators into all kinds of difficulty when it comes to establishing the content of many of the poems, while presenting translators with what often looks like a worst-case scenario. Here is one of the 'easiest' lyrics from *Cuttlefish Bones* as it appears in Jonathan Galassi's new translation.

Haul your paper ships to the seared
shore, little captain,
and sleep, so you won't hear
the evil spirits setting sail in swarms.

In the kitchen garden the owl darts
and the smoke hangs heavy on the roofs.
The moment that overturns the slow work of months is here:
now it cracks in secret, now bursts with a gust.

The break is coming: maybe with no sound.
The builder knows his day of reckoning.
Only the grounded boat is safe for now.
Tie up your flotilla in the canes.

We have an address to a boy launching paper boats, apparently in danger from evil spirits at large. That familiar kitchen garden is full of ominous portents. The last stanza is ambiguous as to whether grounding those boats will prevent the disaster occurring or not. Is the builder the boy who built the boats? Probably not. But at least sleep will guarantee unconsciousness. Here is an earlier translation by William Arrowsmith.

Haul your paper boats
to the parched shore, and then to sleep,
little commodore: may you never hear
swarms of evil spirits putting in.

The owl flits in the walled orchard,

a pall of smoke lies heavy on the roof.
The moment that spoils months of labour is here:
Now the secret crack, now the ravaging gust.

The crack widens, unheard perhaps.
The builder hears his sentence passed.
Now only the sheltered boat is safe.
Beach your fleet, secure it in the brush.

Aside from the cohesion of assonance, rhythm and diction which is very much on Galassi's side (and this is true throughout his new translation), actual differences are minor, though sometimes intriguing. Presumably Galassi goes for the unusual 'paper ships' to achieve alliterative effects with 'paper', 'seared' and 'shore'. Arrowsmith's standard collocation 'paper boats' sits closer to the familiar tone of the opening address. But these are the inevitable small swings and roundabouts of translation. Something of the same thing is going on with the apparently irreconcilable versions 'putting in' and 'setting sail', to describe the activity of those evil spirits, Galassi concentrating once again on achieving assonance (notice also 'seared', 'hear', 'here', or again 'sound' and 'grounded'). But what are these evil spirits up to, are they arriving or departing? Are they only going to 'spoil' the work of months, as Arrowsmith's version weakly suggests, or 'overturn' it altogether, as Galassi more dramatically announces. And looked at syntactically, what is the 'it' of Galassi's 'now it cracks in secret' – the work, or the moment? What, overall, is the poem about? Here is the original.

Arremba su la strinata proda
le navi di cartone, e dormi,
fanciulletto padrone: che non oda
tu i malevoli spiriti che veleggiano a stormi.

Nel chiuso dell'ortino svolacchia il gufo
e i fumacchi dei tetti sono pesi.
L'attimo che rovina l'opera lenta di mesi
giunge: ora incrina segreto, ora divelge in un buffo.

Viene lo spacco; forse senza strepito.
Chi ha edificato sente la sua condanna.
E' l'ora che si salva solo la barca in panna.
Amarra la tua flotta tra le siepi.

Even those who cannot read Italian will immediately be aware of the poem's careful rhyming, almost chiming, which finally breaks with the very last word 'siepi', the boat, the lyric, being brought to prosaic ground at last. Montale loves to end on a dying fall and Galassi is astute here to close not with Arrowsmith's alliterating 'brush' but with a word quite outside his translation's sound pattern: 'canes'. The original also has a great deal of internal rhyming, some of it at least potentially, significant: *cartone – padrone* (cardboard – master), *rovina – incrina* (destroy – crack), and the weighty half-rhyme, *svolacchia – fumacchi*. These latter words are difficult to translate. The rare 'svolacchiare', borrowed perhaps from D'Annunzio, whom Montale at once rejected and ransacked, suggests sudden clumsy flight, while a 'fumacchio' is a fumarole or a smouldering log, the one suggesting an infernal connection with those evil spirits, the other giving us a picture of the domestic roofs as themselves alight, the houses slowly burning themselves out from within, as almost everything in Montale's world consumes itself in fire.

While you can't expect a translation to measure up to a rhyme pattern, it's odd that both English versions ignore the implications of 'fumacchi'. In any event, internal rhyme is ubiquitous in Montale's verse and usually in combination with enjambment. It transmits an uneasy sense of an imprisoning mesh, or a series of short circuits, the poem being brought to sudden halts, often in mid-line. The reader will frequently have the disorientating sense that something connects, while remaining uncertain as to where and with what, for often the inner ear picks up the rhyme without immediately finding its earlier partner.

There is no place here to examine the complex mix of Montale's diction, its weaving back and forth between literary and prosaic, but one or two observations on how the poem achieves its deprecating resonance are apropos. For consistency of metaphor, 'fanciulletto padrone' – 'little boy master' – has to be translated as 'little captain' or 'little commodore', but read in Italian the line cannot help but recall the Wordsworthian idea that the child is father to the man. The lines invite the boy to retreat, to sleep, not to risk it, not to grow up perhaps. For those spirits are not just 'evil' they are 'malevolenti', they *wish* him evil. And the 'tu' of the first stanza is important. Redundant in standard Italian syntax, the personal pronoun is introduced (in the most prominent of positions) for emphasis and contrast. The idea is 'sleep, so that *at least you* may not hear those ill-wishing spirits', who, rather than 'setting sail' or 'putting in', 'veleggia-no'. This is a word that can mean to 'soar in flight' or to 'sail about' and it allows Montale to maintain his nautical image while increasing the sense of menace: the air is full of swarming spirits. But if the boy is to be spared hearing those spirits, who will hear them? The poet? The builder? Or the adult whom the child will give birth to as he sleeps? Even with this simplest of lyrics, the essential nub winds off into a cloud of possibilities.

There is more. A few pages earlier, in a poem dedicated to fellow poet Camillo Sbarbaro, Montale imagines his friend as a boy launching paper boats – his poems – and invites a kind passer-by to pull them safe on shore with his walking stick. So this later lyric cannot help but gather whimsical associations from the first. Is Montale suggesting that these early years of Fascism are not a moment for poetry, but for keeping one's head down? Delicate verses have little chance out there. Haul the boats in, they're only paper. Or is he talking about youth coming to consciousness, addressing his younger self perhaps? Or simply expressing a momentary loss of confidence?

Whichever way we read the poem, the line that takes on the most rhetorical and rhythmical force, to a large extent lost in the translations, is the very last line that rhymes: 'E' l'ora che si salva solo la barca in panna' (literally: the hour has come when only the grounded boat will be saved). This pessimistic invitation to inaction pulls together the odd collage of images which, while still refusing to be pinned down, establish an all too recognisable cocktail of emotions: fear, inadequacy, desire to sleep, desire to spare another's disappointment, or see one's own disappointment destroy another. From all of which Montale extracts himself with the quiet skill of one who knows that the poem's poignancy is generated precisely by its refusal to insist too much, its capacity to remain as light and precarious as a paper boat. The translations, which are probably as good as translations can be of such a poem, remind us that for all Montale's determination to distance himself from Italian's aulic vocation, a poem nevertheless remains a felicitous event above all in its own language. The little boat bobs and dips and is eventually beached into prose rather more convincingly, more attractively, in the original.

It is generally agreed that the core of Montale's work consists of three major collections: *Cuttlefish Bones* (1925), *The Occasions* (1939) and *The Storm, etc.* (1956). Galassi chooses to publish all three together, separating them from a body of work of almost equal length that came later. He defends this decision in an inspired afterword that offers the best short account I have yet come across of the nature, import and elusive content of Montale's work. Above all he has a firm grasp of its bewildering interconnectedness both inside itself and within Italian and European culture as a whole. This is the key not so much to understanding Montale – 'understanding' is the wrong word –

but to appreciating his vision of what contemporary poetry might be and do.

The passage from *Cuttlefish Bones* to *The Occasions* is crucial. At its simplest, Montale drastically reduces a first-person presence in the poems together with any obvious autobiographical reference, concentrating on constructing small groups of images, events, exhortations which will generate a complex emotional state without revealing the personal situation that sparked it off.

Since the poet is living in Florence now, the vivid coastal landscape that gave an easy homogeneity to the first collection is gone. Everything is more fragmented, harder to get the mind round. The change in direction inevitably led to accusations of hermeticism, while critics, and for that matter Montale himself, theorised at length about objective correlatives and the like.

Such talk seems less interesting now than reflections on the whys and wherefores of the change and the direction it would ultimately lead Montale to take. Perhaps if poetry is to be a vehicle of consciousness and if the poet's own consciousness is the only one immediately available to him, the twin problems of retaining privacy and of making the poems carry weight for a wide audience were beginning to make themselves felt. Montale is older. There are various relationships. Poems are addressed to different women. Then political considerations are growing daily more serious: while preparing this collection the poet would lose his job for failing to join the Fascist Party. So one might remark that any artist whose form of expression requires a semantic content will take steps to preserve that double life without which it often seems any life at all is impossible. Certainly in his essays on Dante and D'Annunzio Montale is attentive to such problems, pondering at length on the extent to which poets hide or fail to hide the biography behind the verse. No doubt his decision, as the work progresses, to draw on the Renaissance convention of a sequence of poems to an ideal beloved is taken partly because it will serve to cover tracks. Actually, I can think of no major figure who, without resorting to the provocative, almost showy secrecy of contemporary writers like Pynchon or Salinger, has more successfully and unspectacularly kept the exact nature of his private life out of the public domain. Although we now know their identities, the roles played by the two women addressed in his poems as Clizia and Volpe, or by the woman with whom he lived while addressing poems to those others, remain quite obscure.

Such reflections are, I hope, appropriate, but inevitably reductive. Montale remarks that in writing *Cuttlefish Bones*, 'I felt I was close to something essential. A subtle veil separated me from the definitive quid. Absolute expression would have meant breaking that veil . . . but this remained an unreachable goal.' Yet, referring to *The Occasions*, he then claims, 'I wanted to go deeper.' How can one go deeper if, while being able to think of the world as a veil, one can never penetrate it? What does Montale understand by 'going deeper'?

Galassi's afterword presents Montale's work as an autobiographical novel. What initially are relatively simple constructs in which man or woman are seen as involved together in a search for some form of overcoming, become progressively more complex. Montale loves a Jewish American, Irma Brandeis, a Dante scholar, who leaves Italy at the outbreak of war. The poems to her, or to her memory, slide from intense personal pain and pleasure to visions of individual, then even universal salvation, drawing on the symbolism of centuries past and Christian and Jewish traditions, not to mention relatively obscure heresies such as Nestorianism.

Here, in a constant construction and deconstruction of fantastic allegory, clearly fuelled by the catastrophic events occurring all around him, each poem is built on those that have gone before, to the extent that it is hard to read any one of them separately. Later, arriving at the work addressed to Volpe, a younger woman whose sensuality usurps, though never completely, the position of the more spiritual Clizia, it will be impossible to read the poems without a thorough knowledge of *all* that has gone before and indeed without some wonderment as to the nature of the poet's relationship with Mosca, the lifetime companion he eventually married.

Meanwhile, Montale's contact with Florentine and later Milanese literary circles, his enviable familiarity with a huge range of European and American literature, his personal difficulties with Fascism and mass culture in general, are all drawn together in work that, in his role as translator, Galassi despairingly describes as characterised by a remarkable 'over-determination'. That is, a single reference may take us back to Dante *and* Browning, or Baudelaire *and* D'Annunzio, another to the contemporary inferno of war *and* a girlfriend, or compound of girlfriends, while almost everything will gain resonance from its connection with any number of earlier poems.

Thus intensity is achieved not through revealed meaning, or lyric flight, but via a prodigious density that encourages the reader to grope for ever more complex levels of consciousness, evoking the finest shadings of emotion coloured by every variety of thought. This is what the poet meant by going 'deeper'. The strategy and its effects are difficult to summarise and if Montale is always interesting but never exceptional when he writes about poetry in prose, it is no doubt because he senses that poetry presents ideas which, as he laconically puts it in 'A Dialogue with E. Montale on Poetry' 'are acceptable only in that form'. As a result the following brief lyric, 'The Fan' from the collection *The Storm, etc.* merits more than a thousand words in Galassi's excellent notes.

> *Ut pictura* . . . The confounding lips,
> the looks, sighs, days now long since gone:
> I try to fix them there as in

the wrong end of a telescope,
silent and motionless, but more alive.
It was a joust of men and armaments, a rout
in smoke that Eurus raised, but now the dawn
has turned it purple and breaks through those mists.
The mother of pearl gleams, the dizzying
precipice still swallows victims, but
the feathers on your cheeks are whitening
and maybe the day is saved. O raining blows
when you reveal yourself, sharp flashes, downpour
over the hordes! (Must he who sees you die?)

The notes begin:

Another highly allusive 'pseudosonnet' (Montale to Contini,
June 6, 1942) (Op, 943), its title drawn from the 'éventails' of
Mallarmé (Greco, 142–43, finds parallels with Mallarmé's first
'éventail' – Avec comme pour langage, which is also an
Elizabethan sonnet). Its occasion is another 'Petrarchan'
attribute of Clizia's, drawn from her war chest of jewelry 'a
holy relic in time of war' (Cary, 312). (According to Macrì – 2,
11, the poem describes the disastrous rout of Italian forces at
Caporetto in October 1917.)

I quote this snippet with no satirical intentions, but in an
attempt to tease out what the experience is of reading this
collection, what it might mean for someone to have composed
the original work over the course of a lifetime, for another to
have dedicated years of his life to the unbelievably painstaking
and ill-paid task of translating and annotating it. Like Arrowsmith's translations, and indeed most serious contemporary
translation of poetry, Galassi presents his version side by side with
the original. This is no more than an honest admission of defeat
from the outset. 'Poetry is the fatal uniqueness of language,'

Celan remarked. Montale himself spoke of the untranslatability of poetry in essays that Galassi himself has translated. Here nostalgia for the original is overwhelming. Yet bravely the translator proceeds. Indeed, precisely as poetry in this century has become more cryptic, more private, more untranslatable, translations have multiplied. Why?

In Montale's case it is very much as if the translator were seeking to continue and expand the poet's work of interconnection, introducing into another language and tradition, with all the new connotations this inevitably opens the way for, the immense spiderweb of the man's thought. And the voluminous notes Galassi provides – absolutely indispensable for a fruitful reading of Montale – the frequent quotations of critics and sources and letters, make us aware of a huge joint effort in which the reader is invited to take part, an effort to put everything together, to understand it all in a flash. It is in this way that the yearning for epiphany is exorcised. With each new lyric the mind is momentarily appeased, dazzled out of limits, not by the Mediterranean light, but by the complex expression of its own and by extension everybody else's experience.

In his book *Ka*, Roberto Calasso tells how the first Indian god, Prajapati, did battle with Death. On the point of succumbing, he was consoled by the reflection that if he went under the connections his mind had made would nevertheless survive, for how can a web of thought be killed? Later, when his body had been broken and dispersed into all existence, the same Prajapati taught the younger gods that to overcome death they must construct the altar of fire. The bricks required numbered the hours of the year. It was a task that would take all the time there was. So much so that, moving onwards to historical time, the brahmans of the Vedic texts were still involved in the same enterprise. Calasso comments: 'By creating an edifice of such connections, the brahmans imagined . . . they had beaten Death . . . And thus died the more serene.'

Reading Montale, watching with what admirable stubbornness he sets out to arrange and rearrange the same elements over and over again, to thicken his web, and then observing the translators and critics as they minister about him with the commendable solemnity of priests, one cannot help feeling that the altar of fire is still under construction. Why not? And as the eye moves from original to translation – Arrowsmith's, Galassi's, but Charles Wright's too, and Edith Farnsworth's, an uncanny connection floats to mind. The original stands to these translations as the impossible communion of self and other to the young Montale. Each translation re-enacts the yearning the poet expressed, the frustration of another attractive but not quite successful attempt to overcome barriers – in this case that between Italian and English.

Yet the absence of the definitive version at least allows us to fill our time by trying again. One of the great pleasures of reading a bilingual edition is that you can allow yourself the liberty (as I have in the first quotations in this essay) of imagining different approximations to the impossible perfect solution. Montale's third and most ambitious collection, *The Storm, etc.*, closes with a poem whose title, 'The Prisoner's Dream', might well be applied to all his work. In Galassi's version the last lines are as follows:

> Slow-witted, sore
> from my sharp pallet, I've become
> the flight of the moth my boot
> is turning to powder on the floor,
> become the light's chameleon kimonos
> hung out from the towers at dawn.
> I've smelled the scent of burning on the wind
> from the cakes in the ovens,
> I've looked around, I've conjured rainbows
> shimmering on fields of spiderwebs
> and petals on the trellises of bars,

> I've stood, and fallen back
> Into the pit where a century's a minute –
> And the blows keep coming, and the footsteps,
> And I still don't know if at the feast
> I'll be stuffer or stuffing. The wait is long,
> My dream of you isn't over.

In 1985 Arrowsmith offered:

> I've risen only to fall back
> into that gulf where a century's a second –
> and the beatings go on and on, and the footsteps,
> and I don't know whether I'll be at the feast
> as stuffer or stuffing. It's a long wait,
> and my dream of you isn't over.

In 1978 Charles Wright tried:

> and still I don't know when the banquet is finally served,
> if I shall be the eater or the eaten. The wait is long;
> my dream of you is not yet over.

In 1970 Edith Farnsworth hazarded:

> The waiting lasts a long time, my dream
> Of you has not yet found its end.

It often seems translations tell us more about poetic sensibility in our own language than in the original. What about:

> and still I don't know who'll be eating whom
> when I get to the table. Time is long,
> I'm not through dreaming of you yet.

Unlocking the Mind's Manacles

[Gregory Bateson and Valeria Ugazio]

The paths by which one mind may come to influence another are curious indeed. Thus a new book by Italian psychologist Valeria Ugazio exploring the family backgrounds of those suffering from phobias, obsessive-compulsive disorders and anorexia begins by drawing on observations made by the British anthropologist Gregory Bateson during his work among the Iatmul Indians of New Guinea in the late 1920s. Behind both authors the anti-conformist inspiration of the English poet William Blake is frequently apparent, while between them lies the rise and fall of one of the most controversial adventures in psychotherapy, the so-called 'systemic approach'.

Bateson was born in 1904 into a family with a history of scientific controversy. His father William, a distinguished naturalist, was responsible for giving the study of genetics its name and was both translator and vociferous champion of Mendel's work on hybrids and heredity. Gregory was named after the Austrian monk, no doubt with the hope that he would follow in his footsteps. Ironically, while Bateson never sought to belittle the study of genetics, his legacy has been to stress the importance of the social environment in activating, or not, the potential available in any individual's genetic make-up.

Explaining to his disappointed father that he was giving up zoology for the relatively new subject of anthropology, Bateson spoke of his need for 'a break with ordinary impersonal science'. He had grown up in a house where Blake's pictures hung on the walls, where art and poetry were revered as the acme of human

261

achievement yet at the same time considered 'scarcely in the reach of people like ourselves'. Gregory's elder brother, Martin, who aspired to become a poet rather than a scientist, argued bitterly with his father and eventually killed himself in a scenario that might have been invented to demonstrate the limitations of 'ordinary impersonal science'. Infatuated with a girl who never gave him the slightest hope, he shot himself by the statue of Eros in Piccadilly Circus, a suicide note and a poem in his pocket.

Although in her book *Storie permesse, storie proibite* (Stories allowed, stories forbidden), Valeria Ugazio draws only on Bateson's ideas and not his biography, one can't help feeling its relevance to her thesis. Her title is that the way family members talk about themselves and others, giving particular importance to certain qualities and achievements, will make some 'life stories' (or ways of seeing one's life as narrative) available to a child while denying the possibility of certain others. Clearly, after his brother's suicide, an artist's life was a 'story forbidden' to Gregory. On the other hand it was the achievement to which his family attached the greatest value, and there can be no doubt that they were ambitious for their son. His choice of anthropology and its specifically, as he always insisted, 'human' element, can be seen as a way of combining the scientific and artistic and hence resolving the particular career conundrum his parents had created for him. Significantly, on the opening page of his first book, *Naven*, Bateson would be reflecting on the advantages of a novelist's eye when it came to describing a foreign culture.

> The artist . . . can leave a great many of the most fundamental aspects of culture to be picked up not from his actual words, but from his emphasis. He can . . . group and stress [words] so that the reader almost unconsciously receives information which is not explicit in the sentences and which the artist would find it hard – almost impossible – to express in analytic

terms. This impressionistic technique is utterly foreign to the methods of science.

At once it was clear that Bateson's project was to grasp, as an artist might, a sense of the wholeness and interrelatedness of a culture, rather than to report particular facts. But family background demanded that this be done in a scientific way. It's not surprising, then, that his second project, in Bali, undertaken with his wife Margaret Mead, was the first to make systematic use of photographs in an ethnographic study. True to his resistance to the analytic and reductive, it was important that the photographs not be seen separately: Bateson wrote of the book that came out of his work in Bali,

> In this monograph we are attempting a new method of stating the intangible relationships among different types of culturally standardized behaviour by placing side by side mutually relevant photographs. Pieces of behaviour, spatially and contextually separated – a trance dancer being carried in a procession, a man looking up at an airplane, a servant greeting his master in a play, the painting of a dream – may all be relevant to a single discussion; the same emotional thread may run through them.

In the late twenties when Bateson began his career, British anthropology was dominated by the figure of A.R. Radcliffe-Brown who was fond of describing societies using the analogy of the organism. The life of a people was to be viewed as an active system of functionally consistent, interdependent elements where social phenomena 'are not the immediate result of the nature of individual human beings, but are the result of the social structure by which they are united'.

Though he originally found it exciting, Bateson had a number of objections to this view. He felt its stress on the functional was reductive and left no space for the aesthetic; it also suggested that there was no tension between the 'interdependent elements' of the society, and, related to that, it deduced all individual behaviour from social structure in a suffocating determinism, to which Bateson with his own family experience, must have felt an instinctive repulsion. It was in opposition to this that he developed the first of the ideas for which he will be remembered, his so-called 'schismogenesis'.

Bateson had been observing the radically different behaviour patterns of men and women among the Iatmul Indians. The more the men were exhibitionist and boastful, the more the women were quiet and contemplative. It was clear that the one behaviour pattern stimulated the other in a process that led to strong personality differentiation within an overall group ethos. The process of reciprocally stimulated personality differentiation, schismogenesis, could be complementary or symmetrical. Among the Iatmul men the process is symmetrical: they are involved in a dynamic of escalating competition, each seeking to outdo the other. Between the men and women of the tribe, however, the process is complementary, each becoming ever more the opposite of the other.

Schismogenesis, as Bateson saw it, was a powerful process and could be damaging, not only because it tended to violent extremes, but also because it could deny an individual any experience outside that promoted by this social dynamic. Bateson called his book *Naven* because this was the name of the bizarre series of rituals which he saw as 'correcting' the schismogenetic process and guaranteeing stability. In these ceremonies men dressed up as women and vice versa. The women now assumed, with great excitement and relief, what was the traditional behaviour of the men while the men were abject and passive, even submitting to simulated rape.

What Bateson was suggesting, then, was a complex process of interaction, which did not deny the possibility of individual behaviour, but nevertheless saw it as taking place within a social process underwritten by a fundamentally conservative tendency that would always seek to counterbalance any movement away from the norm. Bateson had not heard of the word cybernetics when he formulated these ideas, but when he learnt of the concepts of feedback and closed self-corrective circuits, it was evident that this would offer him an analogy that could substitute for Radcliffe-Brown's unitary organism.

Almost twenty years after Bateson's death, Ugazio, who lectures in psychology at the University of Turin, approaches schismogenesis with the same combination of respect and dissatisfaction that Bateson brought to Radcliffe-Brown. Bateson had expected that complementary and symmetrical schismogenesis would be found in personal relationships, in cases of psychological disorder, in contacts between cultures and in political rivalries. Hence there is nothing revolutionary in Ugazio's considering the process as essential to personality development within the family, or suggesting that character is formed by how people place themselves in relation to others in a group. But what Bateson did not do is speak of the 'content' of a process of schismogenesis. For Ugazio, on the contrary, this is essential. Reciprocal differentiation between family members, she claims, takes place along lines of meaning, or 'semantic polarities'.

Consider, for example, a family that tends to talk about itself and others in terms of the polarity 'dependence-independence':

Family conversations will tend to be organized around episodes where fear and courage, the need for protection and the desire for exploration play a central role. It is within this critical semantic dimension that schismogenetic processes will take place. As a result of these processes, the members of these families will feel and define themselves as shy and cautious, or, on the contrary, courageous perhaps even rash; they will find companions who are willing to protect them or alternatively in need of protection [. . .] Admiration, contempt, conflict, suffering, alliances, love and hate will all occur around the themes of dependence/independence. In these families there will be some who – like the agoraphobic – are so dependent and so in need of protection as to require that someone be beside them in even the most ordinary day-to-day situations. But there will also be some members of the family who, on the opposite side of the polarity, provide examples of extreme independence.

Every family, Ugazio maintains, will 'converse' and thus 'compose itself' around a number of semantic polarities. The family mentioned above, for example, might also talk about themselves and others in terms of winners and losers, or generosity and meanness. Nevertheless, one polarity will tend to dominate. The position a child assumes along that critical line will be crucial for the formation of his or her personality.

Ugazio's second addition to Bateson's theory of schismogenesis is her insistence on the importance of what she calls 'the median position'. Bateson had seen the complementary and symmetrical processes he described as necessarily leading to extremes, but in a fascinating reconsideration of *Naven*, Ugazio draws attention to a number of men Bateson mentions only in passing who do not engage in male theatricals, nor become part of the admiring audience. In the general schismogenetic process, there will be some, Ugazio claims, who react by insistently readjusting their position this way and that in response to the excesses of those on either side of them. In certain polarities, independence/dependence for example, such a process might be positive, approaching a golden mean, but in others it could lead to all kinds of anxiety. For where the dominating polarity is saintly self-denial against 'evil' self-indulgence, there is little middle ground to be had. Here, a child seeking a median position in an already established play of opposites, is likely to find himself oscillating between a pleasurable indulgence that arouses guilt and a virtuous denial that provokes a sense of yearning and loss.

Again, Bateson's own background would have provided Ugazio with a good example. David Lipset's biography of the anthropologist gives us an adolescent who determinedly sought out a median position between his 'poetic' brother Martin and 'scientific' father William. In a scenario where poetry was considered an indulgence legitimate only for the most gifted and science a self-denying crusade to further human knowledge, an equilibrium was hard to find, as Bateson's frequent feelings of guilt when embarking on his first anthropological projects suggest. His lifelong obsession with mechanisms of self-adjustment, transforming, as it were, his personal difficulties into his science, would seem to confirm this reading, which also allows apparently minor details of his working methods to take on unexpected meaning. Talking about Bateson's research on schizophrenia at the Palo Alto Veteran's Hospital, Lipset remarks:

> Although the project's interstitial position between disciplines and between institutions had meant a degree of financial insecurity, Bateson often remarked that he protected his scientific freedom in this way, sheltering it under 'three umbrellas'. His project was housed in a hospital, was funded by grants from independent agencies, and these were administered through the Anthropology Department at Stanford University. 'When you have three bosses,' he was fond of saying, 'you have none.' Each institution maintained that the other was supervising. Or, as one of Bateson's colleagues remarked 'Nobody knew what the hell he was doing.'

Well, what the hell *was* a British anthropologist doing in the psychiatric ward of a California hospital? It's a question to which

Ugazio addresses herself at length, and one whose answer will bring us to her own most important innovation in *Storie permesse*.

Fascinated by the relationship between his own work and the fast developing communications theory, Bateson accepted an invitation to join a study of 'human communication in psychotherapy'. It was a period when he immersed himself in both the harsh realities of psychiatric medicine and the theoretical complexities of 'digital' and 'analogic' forms of communication in verbal and non-verbal speech, developing the idea that all messages imply a hierarchy whereby one element – perhaps literal meaning – is placed in context by another – perhaps body language. The latter allows the recipient to contextualise the former. It was out of this area of study that his most famous concept, the idea of the double bind, was developed.

Bateson was working with schizophrenics, who frequently fail to appreciate the sense in which a message is to be understood. A routine question from a waitress – 'How can I help you?' – might be understood as a sexual proposition and elicit a most inappropriate response. Or again, to be told by the same girl that a dish on the menu is not available might be contextualised as part of an elaborate international conspiracy and lead to an angry scene. Rather than looking for the cause of this disturbance in the isolated or traumatised psyche (as psychoanalysis tends to do), or in a specific organic dysfunction (as traditional medicine demands), Bateson suggested that the schizophrenic has rather 'learned' to 'live in a universe where the sequences of events are such that his unconventional habits of communication will be . . . appropriate'. His disorder, that is, is part of a larger system.

What were these 'sequences of events' and the system they implied? We can imagine a child who from birth receives contradictory messages from the figure most involved in his upbringing, usually the mother: the content perhaps seductive, but the body language discouraging, or vice versa. Bateson's example of such behaviour in the paper 'Toward a Theory of

Schizophrenia' (1956) has often been quoted: a young man recovering from an acute schizophrenic episode was visited in the hospital by his mother.

> He was glad to see her and impulsively put his arm around her shoulders, whereupon she stiffened. He withdrew his arm and she asked, 'Don't you love me any more?' He then blushed, and she said, 'Dear, you must not be so easily embarrassed and afraid of your feelings.' The patient was able to stay with her only a few minutes more and following her departure he assaulted an aide.

The example is followed by a two-page analysis in which Bateson remarks, among other things, on the fact that the schizophrenic's apparent state of subjection does not allow him to comment on his mother's contradictory behaviour. She rejects affection, demands affection, then criticises her son for an inhibition she herself has just induced. Ultimately, Bateson claims, the patient is up against the impossible dilemma: 'If I wish to maintain my relationship with my mother, I mustn't show her that I love her, but if I don't show her I love her, I'll lose her.'

Bateson maintained that a lifetime of such behaviour would induce a structural trauma, as if the mind were constantly put before conundrums of the variety 'All statements on this page are false'. Faced with this 'double bind', the child himself begins to communicate in the same way, wildly dissociating verbal and non-verbal communication, literal and metaphorical levels. As a result, conversations with a schizophrenic can often follow the pattern of a bizarre series of non sequiturs where the 'normal' party to the dialogue frequently suspects that he is being made fun of.

It would be hard to exaggerate the enthusiasm which Bateson's double bind aroused. For those in psychotherapy who had begun to suspect the limitations of an exasperated delving into the individual psyche, the idea that a mental illness was part of a system of communication and might thus be treated by altering the way people operated *together*, rather than dealing with them individually, was extremely exciting. No complex histories need be elicited, no insight painstakingly imparted. All you had to do was change their behaviour in such a way that the schizophrenic response was no longer 'appropriate'.

A school of therapy rapidly developed which involved getting a whole family together to be interviewed by one or two therapists while others watched, taped and even filmed the session through a one-way mirror. After discussion at the end of the session, members of the family would be ordered to perform some task or follow some instruction designed to alter the way they behaved together. A hyperactive, domineering mother, for example, might be ordered to spend a month in bed. In 1975, reviewing a crop of books published on the back of the movement, Elsa First remarked in the *New York Review of Books* that: 'Many in the family therapy movement prefer to think of themselves as anthropological consultants to very small tribes in distress, rather than as doctors who cure individual "cases" of psychological illness.'

Yet all was not well. As Ugazio points out, Bateson soon realised that the connection of his theory of a special kind of communication problem – the double bind – to an illness as complex and intractable as schizophrenia had been a mistake. The theory didn't suggest why one member of the family was affected rather than another, it didn't explain the difference between the pre-schizophrenic and the schizophrenic, or why some double binds might be damaging and others, as Bateson believed, therapeutic. But the worst blow to the theory came in 1966 when the original members of Bateson's team were invited to consider material presented to them by psychiatric patients and their parents and to pronounce on any eventual double binds. Faced with numerous accounts and audiotapes of family conversations, their disagreement was complete. Apparently, they had no criteria for identifying what was a double bind and what was not.

To complicate matters, a conflict had arisen between Bateson and Jay Haley, his most talented collaborator. Haley was a practical therapist and eager to use the ideas the project had been developing to get results. While Bateson would spend weeks chatting amiably to schizophrenics and taking notes, Haley wanted to save them, transform them. Bateson, however, was uneasy about his manipulative and invasive methods. The whole thrust of Bateson's work had been that social behaviour is part of a delicate interacting ecology and that the mistake of traditional science was to believe that it could isolate areas of study and act upon them from a stable position without. However well meaning, intervention into something so complex as a schizophrenic's family might feasibly make things worse. It is hardly surprising then that just as Haley's hands-on manual *Strategies of Psychotherapy* appeared in 1963, Bateson abandoned the Palo Alto project to study patterns of communication among dolphins in the Virgin Islands. Nobody could reasonably expect him to change the lives of dolphins. His real goal in Palo Alto, he explained rather defensively, had never been therapy, but research.

Valeria Ugazio does not disguise the fact that she came to Bateson not directly, but through the influence of her first mentor, the Milan-based psychotherapist, Mara Selvini. For precisely as the 'systemic approach' lost its intellectual father in the USA, it gained a new and charismatic champion in Italy. Selvini came to international notoriety with one of the earliest studies of anorexia, *Self-Starvation*, in later editions of which she offers a Batesonian model for 'the anorexic family': the disorder was to be seen, that is, as the result of a system of relationships and patterns of communication in the family.

271

Basically, Selvini connected the rapid rise of anorexia to the process of transition which was then so radically altering the Italian family, eroding the old imperative of group solidarity in favour of a philosophy of self-realisation. The situation was particular disorienting, Selvini claimed, for women who, from being expected to sacrifice everything for husband and children, now saw themselves as potentially equal players on the family stage. The result, at least in the families she was dealing with, was a sort of covert, never-to-be resolved power struggle where each individual was chiefly bent on self-realisation but nevertheless obsessively determined, in deference to the old ethos, to disguise every personal initiative as a gesture of self-sacrifice. A typical discussion in therapy runs thus: Mother: 'I have forbidden her [the patient] to wear miniskirts because I know her father doesn't like them.' Father: 'I've always supported whatever my wife forbade the girls in my name. I felt it would be wrong to contradict her.'

Ultimately, Selvini claimed, the contradictory desire to think of oneself as the person who has sacrificed most while in fact seeking to control everybody else could lead to a situation where authority is only acceptable when it springs from a pathology and is thus apparently beyond the individual will. Not for nothing, she claimed, does the refusal to eat combine an apparent gesture of self-sacrifice with a disorder that will demand attention and confer control as the family begins to function entirely in relation to the patient's symptom.

Systemic theorists never sought to explain the exact shift in the chemistry of the brain when a neurotic or psychotic symptom is first manifested (an achievement that has so far eluded the most advanced medical research), but rather to look for consistent patterns relating a disorder to the surrounding system of relationships. Thus, aside from the general transition across the social scene, Selvini concurred with other observers in finding that the families of anorexics tended to be characterised by an extremely strong mother complemented by chronically weak father (the dialogue above is again typical in this regard). In such a situation the 'sacrifice' of not eating, a weapon directed far more at the mother than the father, could be justified by the anorexic at a subliminal level as an attempt to redress the balance of power, while in fact amounting to a determined attempt to take over the man's role for herself.

Selvini's work offers an effective response to Elsa First's ironic remarks at the expense of an 'anthropological' approach. Her most brilliant book *Paradox Counter Paradox* presents, among scores of others, the example of the young anorexic, Mimma, who claims that her problem has to do with her fear of food poisoning. In general discussion with the family it emerges that to accommodate this fear her parents have transformed their kitchen into a sort of operating theatre: all cutlery and utensils are sterilised and before sitting down to eat everybody puts on a white surgical coat, sterilised rubber gloves and a surgeon's cap. The therapist suggests that given this state of affairs Mimma is perhaps not the only unbalanced member of the family. There is a collective craziness at work here. This interpretation is immediately and vigorously denied by parents and siblings alike. Only Mimma is 'mad'. From a systemic point of view, however, Mimma, in line with the general search for power, is running the whole show and at the same time truly suffering more than anyone else.

Selvini's undoubted success with anorexics led to her achieving almost guru status in the late seventies. Very much in the tradition of Haley, she got her results by heaving a weighty therapeutic spanner into the tortured mechanisms of such families through a process of intuitive provocation and paradoxical prescription. 'At what point' – a young anorexic might be asked after three or four sessions – 'did it occur to you that by not eating you could finally show your lily-livered father how to bring Mother into line?' Or, at the end of another session a patient might be told that the therapists had come to the conclusion that her disorder was absolutely necessary for guaranteeing the equilibrium of the family, and that until other changes occurred they could advise nothing better than that she continue to eat as little as possible. At this point the patient's spirit of antagonism might be relied upon to function in her own interests rather than against them.

Having emerged, then, from a study of schizophrenia, the systemic approach was giving its best results with a quite different disturbance. Significantly, however, when Selvini turned her attention to schizophrenia and attempted to satisfy Bateson's hope that there would one day be an elaborate model describing the family relationships underlying the disorder, she could not repeat her success.

In 'Toward a Theory of Pathological Systems' (1969), Jay Haley had sought to save the idea of the double bind by extending it to include three players in a so-called 'perverse triangle', this as a result of his observation that schizophrenics tended to be deeply involved in their parents' relationships. In her book, *Psychotic Games in the Family*, Selvini elaborated on this, painting a picture of stalled and embattled marriages where a child is drawn by one parent into a covert alliance against the other, only to realise at a moment of crisis that the favoured parent is in fact exploiting him or her as a strategic element in the ongoing marital struggle. Not only is the child shocked and betrayed, but he also finds himself unable to protest, because the alliance itself is the source of feelings of guilt.

Selvini's innovation here was to introduce the element of history into the systemic approach. Her portrayal of the anorexic's family had been largely ahistoric, an ongoing never-declared power struggle across the board. Now, however, there was a precise series of events, a development that went some way to countering the objection that the double bind did not explain why a symptom broke out at a particular moment. One could not appreciate how to alter a system of relationships and communication patterns, Selvini suggested, nor what resistance such an attempt might provoke, until one understood what events underlay it.

As a method both of research and therapy, Selvini proposed that the therapist dismiss the children, including the patient, from therapy, see only the parents and instruct them to announce to other family members that everything that happened in therapy was a secret they would not betray. After which they were to begin a series of unannounced evening disappearances designed to create the impression that a marital complicity had been re-established.

The results of the approach were explosive. The frequency with which members of the family would complain that they were being excluded from the parental relationship, to the extent of calling the police because 'he would never go out with her without telling me first', convinced Selvini that the model she was developing was accurate. She also claimed dramatic improvements in patients whose parents had managed to put together at least a façade of complicity, thus liberating the child from the anxiety, excitement and dilemmas of involvement in their parents' relationship. Unfortunately, however, she could provide few statistics for lasting transformations. Even more crucially for the fate of her ideas, she made the mistake of describing these relationships in 'the schizophrenic family' as 'giochi sporchi' which, translated into English, produced the even more unfortunate-sounding 'dirty games'. It seemed she was not only blaming the parents, but accusing them of callous indifference to the welfare of their children.

Psychotic Games in the Family was published in 1986, but even before its appearance its preliminary presentation was violently attacked by Carol Anderson on the pages of the *Journal of Marital and Family Therapy*. Anderson (who is presently editor of the influential review *Family Process*) rightly took Selvini to task for her cavalier approach to documentation and statistics, but in the end her objections were more emotional than methodological. 'I thought,' she writes, 'of the pain experienced by the families I've known as they struggled with their problems. How would they feel if they heard their desperate patterns of coping being described as "dirty games"?'

The position of outrage adopted by Anderson and others was testimony to a deep swing in opinion that no doubt went far beyond the borders of psychiatry and clinical psychology. However, in the particular area of family therapy, her stance consolidated a growing alliance with mainstream psychiatry which has always insisted, despite, it must be said, the absence to date of any conclusive results, that schizophrenia is mainly organic and genetic in nature. As Ugazio points out in her book, with regard to schizophrenia the systemic approach had not proved to be an easy alternative. It had also raised innumerable hackles. Even if Selvini was right in her analysis of the family systems surrounding schizophrenics (decades of literature on such families suggest she was not entirely wrong), nevertheless, their resistance to change, unlike that of the anorexic's family, went far beyond the powers of a therapist with a few spanners to throw. For a child who from earliest consciousness has been lured into a triangle in which the parents are perpetually at daggers drawn, it will be hard to believe that Mum and Dad have suddenly resolved their problems and chosen to exclude you. At a moment of psychotic crisis, the tranquillisers and dopamine blockers, though never a cure, are a more reassuring alternative than a long and perhaps agonising re-examination of tangled relationships.

From this point on, then, family therapy largely threw in the towel in the area of schizophrenia. Or at least, where such therapy is still used, it seeks less and less to achieve a 'cure' through a radical reorganisation of a family's way of communicating, and concentrates instead on helping families live with a symptom to be treated primarily through drugs. 'Often one has the impression,' wrote Selvini in her reply to Anderson, 'that the times of Gregory Bateson and his colleagues are only a glorious memory.'

It is in the light of this defeat that Ugazio's decision to exclude schizophrenia from her book must be understood. In recuperating and re-elaborating Bateson's theories, as well as drawing on a huge range of reading in psychology and philosophy, she seems determined to give back to systemic therapy an intellectual dignity compromised by the many books that have told scarcely credible tales of dramatic cures, unsupported by theory or methodology. Basically, she seeks to produce an overwhelming combination of argument and evidence to demonstrate that the well-defined disorders she has chosen to discuss – phobias, obsessive compulsions and anorexia – are indeed the result of the way sufferers have reacted to particular family situations. Her implication is: once we have established that ground, perhaps we can get back to 'the stumbling stone for every psychological interpretation of mental illness': schizophrenia.

The crucial innovation of Ugazio's book is the way she combines Bateson's theories of schismogenesis and the double bind. It is the schismogenetic manner in which character forms around semantic polarities in the family, she claims, that can, in special circumstances, place certain members rather than others in that position of intolerable dilemma known as the double bind.

Ugazio's reformulation of the latter idea, designed to meet all the objections described above, is complex and draws heavily on the work of communications experts, Cronen, Johnson and Lannamann. As well as insisting on the importance of the personal history of the eventual sufferer, Cronen et al suggested a certain ingenuousness in Bateson's original formulation. It is not that one side of a given message is true but hidden (a mother's antipathy) and the other false but apparent (her veneer of affection), but rather that the 'social reality', and with it the very epistemology of the eventual sufferer, is constructed around a lifetime of contradictory but equally 'true' (in the sense of sincerely meant) messages. In this scenario there is no question then of isolating a single message that would present a double bind for everybody. Context is all.

Let us return to the family who put a high price on independence. This is the kind of family, Ugazio maintains, whose schismogenetic dynamics can lead to one member suffering from a phobia. How? We can imagine an adventurous, entrepreneurial father, frequently absent, a mother who assumes a 'complementary' position, very much attached to her husband, admiring his spirit, but thinking of herself as at the other extreme of the polarity dependence/independence. A first son is encouraged to occupy a position symmetrical to the father's and does so. He will compete for the palm of independence. The mother at once admires and is concerned, perhaps a little lonely. A second son becomes extremely attached to her. She finds consolation in his presence while never withdrawing her love and admiration from her husband and first son. As he reaches a higher level of consciousness, the second son senses that to win the kind of regard afforded to the others, he must be as radically independent of Mother as they are. But in detaching himself from her, he will lose the privileged position he has occupied to date and around which he has constructed his identity.

Without there being any single contradictory message, or anybody 'behaving badly' in any way, an environment has been created where both the self-esteem of independence and the gratifications of attachment begin to seem at once absolutely desirable yet mutually exclusive. What life story can such a person construct for himself?

Ugazio gives detailed case histories showing the kind of strategies a person who has grown up in such a situation will develop: thirty-year-old Alberto has a proudly independent lifestyle counterbalanced by a series of superficial relationships which allow him to put off any serious emotional commitment; Elisa, on the contrary, has married an independent man, but has so successfully presented herself as fragile that, despite his ambitions, he has agreed to their living next door to her parents where she remains very closely attached to her mother. Both of these eventual patients can be seen to be occupying one side or the other of the dependence/independence polarity while yearning for the other.

Ugazio describes the situations that may undermine such strategies and lead to the development of phobias. Alberto comes for therapy because he is no longer able to use an elevator and suffers severe panic attacks when he travels on planes. His claustrophobia developed shortly after the death of his father, and his being dropped by a recent girlfriend. It is not, Ugazio remarks, the bereavement or new responsibility resulting from the father's death that has led to the crisis, but the intense intimacy that was established with the father during his sickness. This, together with the unexpected loss of a girlfriend, is forcing Alberto to acknowledge an intense need for attachment, but for him to succumb to that need would bring an unacceptable loss of self-esteem. As he seeks to ignore and repress the issue, the claustrophobic symptoms, the horror of the enclosed space – and in particular those enclosed spaces he needs to use if he is to continue his independent lifestyle – become a powerful meta-phorical reminder of his aversion to and yet need of the tightly enclosed relationship. Though he has no plans to enter therapy with his family, Alberto chooses a systemic therapist because he feels that this will not involve the development of a close relationship of the variety associated with traditional psychoanaly-sis. Thus, even while gritting his teeth and admitting a problem, he is simultaneously seeking to reinforce his independence. In the first session he demands to become like 'a tower that will not fall'.

With a 'strategy' diametrically opposed to Alberto's, giving more importance to attachment yet yearning for independence,

Elisa's crises are agoraphobic rather than claustrophobic. They force her to stay at home. The first came as she stepped on board the cruiser for her honeymoon. Ugazio remarks: 'Going to Greece meant a decisive move away from the protective relationship with her mother . . . not to go meant damaging her marriage and the independence and self-esteem that went with it.' In her case, the ensuing mental disorder does not so much resolve the problem as remove it from discussion. Her husband will give up the cruise, and many other adventurous projects over the decade before they enter therapy, not because Elisa isn't genuinely enthusiastic and supportive, on the contrary, but because she is ill, she can't go out.

While those suffering from phobias face a double bind that makes self-esteem and long-term attachment mutually exclusive, the obsessive-compulsive, in Ugazio's model, has the more profound problem of being obliged to choose between opposite and equally unacceptable visions of self. Here the patient's family constructs its conversation around the opposites sacrificial renunciation/selfish indulgence. The sufferer is a child adopting a median position, not unlike the position Bateson occupied between his father and brother. A huge appetite for life, stimulated by those in the family occupying the selfish side of the polarity, makes a path of self-renunciation unbearable to contemplate. But the label of selfishness placed on almost any engagement with pleasure destroys self-esteem, which, for reasons of early attachment, largely depends on the judgement of someone occupying the renunciatory side of the polarity.

The classic symptoms of the obsessive-compulsive are of two kinds: compulsively repeated actions like washing hands or checking that a door has been locked (Ugazio recounts the case of a man who stopped his car every few hundred yards to see if he had run over a child or an animal). These may be seen as the neurotic reactions of one for whom every adventure into life generates guilt. The obsessions, on the other hand, take the form of the invasion of highly erotic or violent images over which the mind has no control. These can be seen as the repressed yearnings of one who is determinedly seeking self-esteem in renunciation and repression.

Again Ugazio offers examples suggesting how the condition can arise in particular family scenarios and the strategies developed to deal with it. Particularly intriguing is her account of the tendency to cultivate a hierarchical vision of 'evil' which allows a 'selfish' self to flourish just so long as it remains under the control of a superior 'sacrificial' self. The case history of a hard-working priest living with his mother but allowing himself homosexual adventures in third world countries is instructive here. At the age of thirty, the priest had been hospitalised for two months with an acute obsessive-compulsive disorder. After decades of relative health his symptoms recur when he is fifty-nine. Usually on return from his 'holidays', his mother (decidedly on the renunciatory side of the critical polarity), though not privy to his secret, had been extremely severe, giving a welcome sense of punishment and facilitating his renewed acceptance of his 'higher' self. But after the most recent trip the elderly lady was indulgent and spoke of her 'not always being there to look after him'. Suddenly the priest feels that the guarantee that his homosexuality will remain strictly circumscribed is gone. The conflict between selfishness and renunciation is renewed with obsessive erotic images, insomnia and extreme anxiety as the result.

Ugazio makes it clear that her book is to be seen more as an analysis of the causes of the disorders she discusses than a manual of therapeutic approaches. There are no prescriptions, no large claims. On the contrary, she recognises that by linking these disorders to the very process by which the patient's character has been formed, her model demands that successful therapy achieve nothing less than a reconstruction of the patient's deepest epistemology. All the same, and despite these sensible caveats, it seems only legitimate that the reader ask what hope her new systemic model offers for the sufferers she describes.

The issue of therapy is finally, if rather unsatisfactorily, addressed in the book's last chapter. Ugazio clearly does not favour the dramatic forms of intervention proposed by Haley and Selvini. But nor does she take Bateson's pessimistic line that such matters are too delicate to be interfered with at all. Rather she suggests that, having established the critical semantic polarity which dominates the patient's life and within which he is unable to find a satisfactory position, the therapist can begin to look for other polarities around which the family of origin composed itself, since, as she insists, no family, however fierce the schismogenetic process, will be limited to just one polarity. In so far, she claims, as she has alleviated and in many instances eliminated the symptoms of the patients described in the book, this has been achieved by gradually playing down the importance of the critical polarity and building on any others available in the patient's experience to generate self-esteem in different ways and lead him or her to contemplate an entirely different life story. In this process, the original double bind does not so much disappear – after all, most of us are aware of, for example, a certain incompatibility between complete independence and close attachments – as become less urgent and all-determining.

In line with this approach, Ugazio concludes by remarking that one of the great dangers of therapy arises when therapist and patient concede the same importance to the same semantic polarity. Obsessive-compulsives, she claims, will tend to go to traditional Freudian analysts, because Freud himself saw the world in terms of indulgence and repression. This explains why, while offering such brilliant accounts of the disorder, Freud himself lamented his limited success in curing it. He could not move patients away from a vision he shared. Any inflexible approach to mental disturbance thus runs the risk of becoming, as Blake put it, another of 'man's mind forg'd manacles', and may lead to situations where the therapist is actually exacerbating the patient's difficulties. It is with this caveat that Ugazio bows out by suggesting that 'With respect to this [her own] as to other models of mental disturbance I believe the therapist must maintain a wise irreverence.'

The modesty here is admittedly exemplary, yet after the brilliance of her analysis of how double binds and illnesses can occur, one cannot help wishing that Ugazio had spent longer describing the process by which they may be eroded. And since various asides in *Storie permesse* indicate that she has worked with schizophrenics for many years, one likewise wishes that she had thrown caution to the winds and told us straight whether or not she believes her model is applicable to that most intractable of disorders. But perhaps these are to be the subjects of other books.

Christina Stead: Our Luck

[Christina Stead]

Aside from all the betrayals and broken friendships, the abortions and depressions, and, in old age, two decades of inertia and alcoholism, the real scandal of Christina Stead's life, one feels on reading Hazel Rowley's fine biography of the Australian novelist, is that right up to her death in 1983 she remained not only a hard-line communist but a declared Stalinist. In the teeth of the evidence, this brilliant and supremely gifted woman, who spent much of her life toing and froing between Europe and the United States, neither relented nor retracted.

The great scandal of Stead's novels, on the other hand, at least as seen by those who shared her political views, was that they could not have been more damaging to the cause of communism, or indeed any reformist position. Invariably and with lavish ferocity these works attack the prophets and spokesmen of the political ideals Stead claimed to hold dear. Such people are greedy, self-serving and sexually dishonest. The very notion that society might be organised on behalf of the masses and the weak is blown away by the fury and rapture of individual appetite. Yet outside the novels Stead remained a loyal Soviet Marxist and was outraged by all defections. What is going on?

'I don't know what imagination is,' says Letty Fox in the eponymous novel, 'if not an unpruned, tangled kind of memory.' Though the claim comes early on in this long book, and is made what's more by one of the flightiest narrators fiction has ever produced, nevertheless the reader will immediately take it as confirmation of what he has already suspected: flagrantly unpruned and tangled beyond any unravelling, the six hundred-plus pages of *Letty Fox: Her Luck* are the seductive and savage reworking of an apparently inexhaustible memory, its author's as much as its narrator's.

Christina Stead certainly had much to remember by the time she came to this, her sixth novel. Born in a southern suburb of Sydney in 1902, her literary ambitions, radical politics and difficult love life brought her first to London, then Paris, then New York. She had known success and failure, romance and rejection; she had worked for the Communist Party and collaborated, simultaneously, with corrupt financiers. But however complex and contradictory her career and relationships may have become, Stead's memories still tended to organise themselves around the two great stories that had shaped her life: the story of the bizarre Australian family she grew up in, and the story of the Jewish American community she ultimately became part of. The first was a horror story with comic interludes, the second a romance with recurrent nightmares. The five novels before *Letty Fox*, all equally extravagant and daring, had kept the two stages of her life apart; they dealt with either the one story or the other. Published in 1946, after she had been resident in New York for nine years and when her literary reputation at last seemed established, *Letty Fox: Her Luck* contrives to tangle them both.

Stead's early unhappiness is easily understood. The plain, big-boned daughter of a pretty mother who died when she was two, Christina soon found herself an unwanted extra in her father's second family. 'My stepmother was kind to me,' she later conceded of Ada Stead, 'until her first child was born.' Five more children would follow. From the beginning, Stead's writing would always convey a sense of life's exhausting excess. 'Living is too much for me,' says Letty Fox, who is herself more than a handful for those around her. It is as if Stead were telling us that her own explosive vitality was no more than a necessary defence against the world's threatening profusion.

Self-taught biologist and pioneering socialist, a man of immense energy and greater vanity, Stead's handsome father contrived to complicate his adolescent daughter's isolation by making Christina his confidante in what had now become the epic struggle between himself and his wife. David Stead had made this second marriage at least partly for money. The couple had moved into an extravagant mansion immediately after the wedding. But when Ada's father died, her family was found to be as deeply in debt as it had previously appeared to be swimming in wealth. Reduced to poverty, obliged to make do with ramshackle accommodation, Ada sulked. The charismatic David found her plain and dull. Christina, on the other hand, was intelligent beyond her years. How sad, however, as he never tired of reminding her, that she was also 'a fat lazy lump'.

On research trips to Malaysia and Paris, David Stead, a staunch supporter of women's rights and a great believer in eugenics, wrote his daughter long letters sharing his enthusiasm for the superior and slender beauty of the women of those countries. Bulky Christina yearned to travel. When she was seventeen her father fell in love with a sixteen-year-old girl, Thistle Harris, and would eventually run off with this pretty junior. Again he made the ugly duckling of his brood his confidante. Twenty years later, from the distant fortress of Manhattan, his daughter took her revenge. I know of no account of father and family more generously observed or more irremediably cruel than the auto-biographical novel *The Man Who Loved Children*. Published in 1940, it remains Stead's most frightening and ruthless work. At the height of her powers, she was thus able to begin *Letty Fox* with the worst of that old bitterness exorcised. She was ready to have fun.

The passage from family of origin to partner of election is the story at the core of *Letty Fox*. In that sense, albeit with a completely different milieu and a whole new gallery of characters, the novel takes over where *The Man Who Loved Children* left off.

In the earlier work the heroine leaves home only on the final pages, here instead she is decidedly out of the fold and on the make. For Stead herself, as one learns from Hazel Rowley's biography, this period of young adulthood was marked by the most intense yearning and frustration. It was also the period in which the contradiction that shaped her novels, or rather that extended them beyond any immediately perceptible shape, first becomes apparent.

Stead's final school exams won her a scholarship to university, but she was ineligible for an arts degree because she hadn't studied Latin. The daughter of a biologist and man of action isn't encouraged to grapple with fossil languages. She could have chosen a science course and had her higher education financed by the state, but decided against it, apparently because she had come to associate women in science with dowdy and frustrated spinsters. The Darwinist determinism she had learnt from her biologist father had apparently convinced Stead that in the struggle for survival, which was always a struggle to win the right mate, a science degree would not be a winning card, for a woman. The more biology a girl knew, it seemed, the more she appreciated that it was not biology a girl needed to know.

This disturbing lesson was reinforced, in Stead's case, by the fiercest erotic longings, desires which, if only because they couldn't be talked about in the puritan society she grew up in, she often feared would drive her mad. Would a plain girl find a lover and husband? 'Hunger of the stomach can be confessed,' she later wrote in a note for the novel *For Love Alone*, 'but not sexual hunger.' In *Letty Fox*, Christina Stead would make it her business to be alarmingly frank about that hunger. From earliest adolescence, Letty lusts. 'This fox was tearing at my vitals,' she tells us. Hazel Rowley remarks that 'Stead liked the hint of bawdiness' in the title's combination of the words 'fox' and 'luck'.

Unable to study the arts and unwilling to take up science, the nineteen-year-old Stead settled on teaching, making the long journey back and forth to training college in Sydney every day. Rising at dawn, she wrote down stories of great fantasy that nevertheless show an acute awareness of what was the most urgent reality of her life: she was a highly sexed young woman after her man, a caricature almost of the traditional gal.

But she was also a socialist and a radical. Here come the complications. At Sydney Girls High School, Christina had been enthusiastic when a teacher told them about the Communist revolution in Russia. Throughout the First World War she was staunchly pacifist. These controversial positions were again things she had taken from her atheist but far from clear-headed father. As he saw it, you discovered the hard facts of the biological struggle, facts that in Europe were preparing the way for a book like *Mein Kampf*, but then paradoxically, idealistically, you used that knowledge, or said you were using it, not for your own personal fight, or even for that of your race, but to further the cause of mankind in a spirit of solidarity. David Stead, for example, had established which fish off the Australian coast were fit for human consumption, where and how they could be caught. It was an important contribution. It also made him, if only briefly, an important man, the sort of man a bright young girl might run away with.

There was an irony to this of course: the altruism of the common cause had proved an efficient way for the individual male of the species to get what he wanted: a young woman. But would the same be true for the female? Attending a politicised evening course at Sydney University, a course whose object, according to one student, was nothing less than 'the reform of the Universe', Christina Stead fell determinedly in love with the left-wing lecturer Keith Duncan. Alas, she was not in a position to offer him either what her father could offer Thistle Harris, or what Thistle could offer her father. Perhaps it was at this point that Stead began to appreciate the hypocrisy and contradiction in her father's position. Certainly the comedy that everywhere galvanises *Letty Fox* is the mismatch between the idealistic rhetoric of radicalism and the biologically driven power game between men and women. Both Stead and Letty dream of the grand individual career, the generous altruistic gesture *and* traditional romantic love. Since such romance notoriously involves feminine submission, the combination proves arduous. What was required, it seemed, was an improbable stroke of luck.

Stead failed to become a teacher. In the classroom she lost her voice, arriving at the school gates she panicked. Again the problem was the fear of a virginity prolonged into old age. School was a place where 'a woman was not a woman'. Bound over to teaching for five years to pay for her training, she had to struggle hard to escape without a heavy fine. She was lonely now. Keith Duncan and other radical friends had left for England and the wider world. They had travel scholarships. But for Stead there were no such handouts. She worked for two years as a secretary to save the money to follow Duncan. He wrote to encourage her, then to put her off. Would they ever become lovers? Every day she walked miles to save tram fares. A special kind of feminism was developing in Stead. She wasn't interested in rights and equality as ends in themselves, but in relation to the struggle to marry one's man.

Then, at last in England, aged twenty-five, Christina Stead did get what she would always consider her one great piece of luck in life: she met the man with whom she could combine both career and romance. It wasn't Keith Duncan. Duncan had led her on, but wouldn't commit himself. He wouldn't even take her to bed. It was Christina's new employer, ten years older than herself, who finally relieved his young secretary of her virginity. In a letter home announcing imminent marriage, Stead described him thus: 'William James Blech is a German Jew of American upbringing, small, very loquacious, very astute in business and literary affairs and art, highly educated and original.' Some years later, as a precautionary measure against arrest for fraudulent bankruptcy, William Blech changed his name to William Blake. It was a gesture typical of his innocent charm and considerable presumption.

In fact Blech, like Stead's father, was entirely self-taught. Like her father he was a radical, indeed a communist, though he worked for a decidedly shady banking company. Like her father, he had boundless energy and optimism. And like her father, alas, he was married. He had a wife and daughter. Wedding bells were far from imminent. Once again, Stead was an anomalous creature on the edge of a family that didn't quite know what to do with her. The second story of her life, the second great struggle had begun. Having gratefully given herself to this man, she must now persuade him to persuade his wife to agree to a divorce. Stead's staunch communism, her unquestioning support for Bill's unceasing political endeavours, would be a crucial part of that struggle.

I can think of no author for whom milieu is more important than for Christina Stead, no author who works harder to create the social settings of her novels and to convey the sense that character and background are inseparable. She appreciates the irony that although the individual struggles above all for himself, and although his primary experience is that of being alone, nevertheless he does not create or even possess that self, but is very largely a product of his own milieu.

No doubt this knowledge came from being so frequently forced to change milieu herself. Having met Blech in London, so soon after arrival from Sydney, she at once agreed to his moving her nearer to his wife and daughter in Paris. She loved it. In Paris, well dressed, speaking French, she decided she was not so plain after all. Place changes you. Over the next few years she lived in London again, then New York, Spain, Belgium, London and – at last a few years of stability – New York.

She made copious notes on every community she came in contact with. She changed languages, accents. She wrote books set in Australia, England, France, the USA, set in the lower class, the middle class, among expatriates. Each work was testimony to her own determination to adapt and survive, to fit in; or perhaps one should rather say, to shine whatever the milieu, whatever society she chose to write about or style she chose to use. Her first novel, *Seven Poor Men of Sydney*, rediscovers and reproduces the Australia of her youth. Moving back and forth from London to Paris, her second, *The Beauties and Furies*, shows an intimate awareness of the Englishman and his relationship with France, but also a readiness to measure herself with Lawrence, Joyce and the most innovative fiction of the century. *The House of All Nations* is entirely at home in the international banking community of northern Europe, while *The Man who Loved Children* and *Letty Fox* are both written in a determinedly American idiom. Later in life, after a spell in Newcastle, Stead would produce a completely convincing novel of the English working classes: published in 1966, *Cotter's England*, was a feat far beyond mere mimicry and suggests an extraordinary facility for penetrating an alien group psychology.

But in the decade that led up to the writing of *Letty Fox*, Stead was above all determined to fit in with Bill Blech's family, with the German mother, the expensively educated American daughter, the wife whom she must never meet, and, in short, with the whole Jewish American community and its cosmopolitan traditions. It was here that her penetrative eye must go deepest. How else could she hope to win through, to arrive, if not at the altar, then at least the registry office?

Letty Fox: Her Luck was the fruit of those long years of adaptation, an exuberant muddling of Stead's own girlhood memories, with her meticulous observations of Blech's now adult daughter, Ruth, who was a frequent visitor at the Stead/Blech ménage in New York. Ruth becomes the model, or one of the models, for Letty. She is given all the contradictions that formed the core of Stead's experience: the erotic charge, the romantic longings, the left-wing politics, the desire to be both beautiful and brilliant, to be admired and feared, to love with feminine faithfulness and submission and with masculine presumption and promiscuity. It's an explosive cocktail.

The relationships around Letty are likewise a retangling of those Stead knew best. So the heroine is given a father who, like Bill Blech, is a businessman radical, still married yet living with a mistress, who thus becomes, at least potentially, a portrait of Stead herself. Then Bill Blech, of course, was not unlike Christina's father, David Stead, another radical who left his wife for a mistress. The book is a hall of mirrors as far as possible identifications are concerned. Certainly when it was published all of Blech's extended family would see themselves in it. The only character who was unrecognisable was Letty's father's mistress: cool, level-headed, beautiful and practical, Persia was as different from Christina as her exotic name suggests.

Wasn't this blatant mixture of fiction and reality a risk for Christina? Couldn't it perhaps lead to a break-up with Bill, to whom she still wasn't married, particularly if his daughter was to be presented as wild and promiscuous and Bill as an ineffectual father who kept wife and mistress happy by lying to them both? Reading Rowley's biography one becomes aware of an unspoken pact between Stead and Blech. She would never disagree with him politically and he would never take an offence at what she wrote in a novel. It is to Blech's immense credit, after all, that he was the first to appreciate Stead's talent. Discovering his secretary's ambitions, he had asked to see a manuscript and, an able writer himself, recognised at once that it was remarkable. Her genius, perhaps, would excuse his betrayal of his family. It must be given full reign. 'Dear Bill said once to me,' Stead recounted, 'that he would like to be to me what G.H. Lewes was to George Eliot . . . I was not very pleased, because G.E. was not a pretty girl.'

Stead would also one day remark that she only felt truly 'moral' when writing, and again that she had only 'felt herself' when writing. Perhaps what she meant was that in this supposedly fictional space she was free not to adhere to certain ideals, not to be coherent, to tell a truth or two. 'Radicalism is the opium of the middle class,' announces an incensed Letty. Stead is enjoying herself. What luck to be able to say such things! And if this was the only space where she could be herself, where she could say she loved a man but found him unforgivable, or alternately that she loved a man but yearned for other men, or again that she was deeply attracted to women, but found lesbianism abhorrent, then little wonder she made the books long, and furious. The novels would express all the wild life no orthodoxy could embrace. 'He had some wonderful vision of the future,' Letty remarks of a black man who falls in love with her, 'where no hate would exist, only love between peoples and races, this was fine enough, but I live too much in the here and now; this is my great weakness.' It was Stead's strength as a novelist.

The here and now of *Letty Fox* is overwhelmingly New York. Stead is determined to demonstrate that she has gained full command of Bill's world. It opens thus:

> One hot night last spring, after waiting fruitlessly for a call from my then lover, with whom I had quarrelled the same afternoon, and finding one of my black moods on me, I flung out of my lonely room on the ninth floor (unlucky number) in a hotel in lower Fifth Avenue and rushed into the streets of the Village, feeling bad.

Letty is always flinging out of rooms, rushing across streets. She is always full of energy and always on the edge of depression. Above all, she always needs money. The long first paragraph finishes:

Beyond such petty expenses, I needed at least two hundred and fifty dollars for a new coat. My fur coat, got from my mother, and my dinner dress, got from my grandmother, were things of the past and things with a past, mere rags and too well known to all my friends. There was no end to what I needed.

Immediately, we have the picture of Stead's America, a place where love and money cannot be separated, where relationships are talked about in terms of investments and cutting losses, where people enjoy the illusion that the marriage game can be managed, and evaded, like an income tax return. It's savvy, cynical, full of corrupt life. But no sooner has Stead seduced us with the bubbly frankness of Letty's voice than we are to be repulsed by the brutal consequences.

Acting on the principle that the greatest asset a girl has is her availability (for men), Letty decides she must have an apartment of her own. On 11th Street she sees the signs of a family moving out. However, a haggard woman informs her that she has already taken the place, she needs it desperately for herself, her husband and three children. 'I went down half a block,' says Letty, 'saw the woman had left the railings and was rounding the other corner. I, at once, went back, had an interview with the superintendent's wife, promised her thirty dollars (the old woman had promised twenty dollars) to hold the place for me, agreed to paint the place myself, exterminate vermin, and to move in in less than a week, and so forth. It was discussed and concluded within the hour.'

The needy woman with first claim on the apartment is never again mentioned. No compassion is shown her. Needless to say, Letty is a left-wing radical. America, as Stead sees it, is that place where the struggle of everyone against everyone else is most visible and the rhetoric of concern at its absolute thinnest. Yet it is impossible not to appreciate the gusto with which Letty enters the fray. Wondering whether she should accept a job offer in return for sex, Letty tells us: 'I do not even see a scandal in this, for wide-awake women. In other times, society regarded us as cattle or handsome house slaves, the ability to sell ourselves in any way we like is a step towards freedom.' Later in the book the terms are reversed, but the principle the same: 'I had the feeling that he could have been bought,' Letty remarks of one reluctant lover, 'if I had had a little more money.'

Having given us just a dozen sparkling pages on the twenty-three-year-old Letty's life in wartime Manhattan, Stead then goes back to reconstruct her narrator's childhood. It is here that the reader will first boggle at what Angela Carter referred to as Stead's 'almost megalomaniac ambition'. The 'almost' was unnecessary. It is the sheer scope of the enterprise that is so extraordinary. Stead, an Australian, goes right back to the beginning of the century to reconstruct the rich New England family of Letty's maternal grandmother, the notorious Cissy Morgan, then the German Jewish family of her paternal grandmother. Uncles, aunts and cousins, marry, divorce and remarry. We have their foibles, ambitions, views on education and endless improprieties. None of these are mere vignettes or anecdotes, but highly developed studies integrated in a tangled series of interlocking stories that could well fill a book of their own. What they establish beyond all dispute is that Letty, like so many modern children, knows far too much far too young.

The satire is vast, fed constantly by the ancient struggle between the sexes and the modern American woman's discovery of alimony. At great length we learn of the unhappily complex relationship between Letty's father Solander and her mother Mathilde, then his passion for the younger woman who becomes his mistress. Eagle-eyed, always excited, Letty wants to know what all this means. By the time her father leaves home, she and her younger sister Jacky have already learnt how to present themselves as victims and make the most of it. They know that compassion is a harbinger of gifts, hopefully cash.

The daughters are moved in with relatives, they are taken to England, to Paris, they write extremely long, witty, passionate letters in highly individual voices, seeking to impress their father, or calm their mother. Slowly and with complete conviction, Stead shows the two sisters becoming distinct as they react first to the overall situation and then to each other's response to it, seeking individuality through complementary or competitive behaviour. We see character in the making.

Meanwhile, stories you thought must have ended, start again. An uncle you imagined married and forgotten reappears with debts and a mistress. He tries to seduce a niece. A cousin is becoming a whore, or a saint. An aunt turns up with a child, but without a husband. The book smoulders, flaring up where you thought it extinguished, smoking where you had seen no fire.

But where is the whole thing going? If every form of narrative representation is essentially a convention, a pact between writer and reader as to how experience can be talked about, then it is only natural that the finest authors should be uneasy with some aspect of that convention, eager to bend it closer to the grain of their own lives. What Stead most resisted in traditional narrative was any easy formulation of shape and direction, any neatness, 'the neatly groomed little boy in sailor collar', she called it, speaking disparagingly of the fiction the publishers liked most. In contrast, the exuberance and manic extension of the world she depicts in *Letty Fox* denies any possibility of order. The work is rich and capricious, its descriptions dense, vital and highly particularised; its only overall drift is that of Letty's growing up.

Not surprisingly then, it is with the depiction of Letty's adolescence and young womanhood that Stead achieves her most impressive effect in this book. For perhaps three hundred pages we have been given a dazzling social satire, a tragicomic picture of a modern society where, with all traditional hierarchy broken down, the only possible relationship between people, above all between men and women, is competition and conflict; it is the mirror image at a social level of the political war that is raging in Europe as Stead writes her story. Yet up to this point, the reader feels, the whole book, bar the opening dozen pages, might well have been written in third person; for Letty is retailing stories she has heard, or overheard, stories she understands only in the most superficial fashion. She feels superior to these people with their incomprehensibly muddled lives. There is a consequent narrative distance. And, as with most satires, the reader too feels a certain smug, if uneasy, detachment. There is something slightly grotesque about all these Morgans and Foxes with their interminable passions. Letty feels sure she will do better.

But the moment Letty too becomes subject to sexual desire, everything changes. It is as if a sane psychiatrist, chuckling over the antics of his lunatic patients, had himself gone mad. Suddenly it is no laughing matter. Or it is, for there is still plenty of comedy, but the nature of the laughter has changed. It is full of pathos, where before it was constantly on the edge of caricature. What had appeared to be an essentially political book is overtaken by existential concerns: the compassion Stead arouses now is not for the victims of poverty – the usual objects of public piety – but for those of desire.

Moods of blackness and suffering passed through me, of fierce, fierce intercourse such as no flesh could bear. I got up and the fever that raged through my body was intolerable. Yes, this is the love that nymphs knew on afternoons when Pan chased them, I thought, this is the meaning of all those stories. I thought I was passionate; now, I know what growing up is. I thought, if it is going to be like this, this suffering and madness, I will kill myself now, for in the difficulty of getting married nowadays and of getting a child, that cooling cold stone of a child which stands in the hot belly and makes a woman heavy and tired, forgetting all her cruel fervours, that thing that drags her to the doors of the death-house and away from the intolerable ardours of the sun, in this slow world for women, I cannot live, I will kill myself.

Letty does not kill herself. She goes out and finds another lover. And another. Sexual conquest brings with it a gust of energy. Letty studies hard, works hard, she goes to meetings to discuss socialism and reform, achieving the 'cheerful feeling that a lot is wrong with the universe; and it's marvellous to be able to discuss it all over a Martini'. Political militancy thus emerges as no more than a by-product of sexual happiness. Or as a way out of distress: ('Everyone forgot . . . my troubles and we all began to discuss . . . the African problem.') In one of the most powerful scenes in the book, Letty seduces her father's radical and philandering friend, Luke Adams, while the older man is selfishly trying to get her to take in a Hispanic orphan boy whom he himself, in a moment of weakness, had agreed to look after. Letty remarks: 'One not only felt that, in love, this dangerous man consulted his own pleasure and had no morals, but with him, all altruism vanished like smoke.'

As fully drawn as any character in literature, Stead's Letty is marvellously talented, bursting with energy and youthful optimism. What is to become of such vitality, the book wonders? And so does Letty. How is it not to be spilled? In her biography, Hazel Rowley feels that this is a question Stead could not answer. The blurb to the Virago edition of 1982 shows all the feminist publisher's uneasiness with the answer that, on the contrary, the novel very frankly offers, marriage: '*Letty* is a "powerful portrayal",' the blurb writer says, 'of a woman who might have been independent, but chose otherwise.'

But could she really have been independent? What Letty most profoundly learns from her promiscuity, from her growing fear of herself and of her appetite, is that marriage is not, as her

299

profligate family had led her to believe, merely the legally regulated collision of sex and economics. Something else is going on in the long-term union of man and woman, something to which she is inexorably drawn.

> I sometimes wondered at the infinite distance between the state of not being married . . . and the state of being married . . . I couldn't figure it out; perhaps I was too young, anyway; but it savoured to me of magic, and I felt very miserable that in this modern world something so primary, this first of all things to a woman, smacked so strongly of the tribal priest, the smoky cult, the tom-tom, the blood sacrifice, the hidden mystery. It didn't seem fair. We should have abolished all that with enlightenment.

It is in the novel's savouring, over so many pages, of Letty's growing belief, or obsession, right or wrong, that her energies must be 'husbanded', that *Letty Fox* becomes more than a brilliant satire. Watching a poor working girl give birth to her illegitimate child, she muses: 'I wish I were a mother too. Cornelis and all the men I had played round with seemed far away. This was the reality, and this was, truth to tell, what I, in my blind ignorant way, was fighting for, trying to make shift with one and all of them. But what chance has a smart, forward girl to be innocent or maternal? That's a dream.'

How are we to take this? No doubt Letty is in earnest, but then she is perfectly capable of earnestly maintaining the opposite point of view on the next page. All the same, as the chapters accumulate and with them Letty's frustrations, we sense the growing seduction of that traditional dream, the pull of the marriage bond and maternity. Sooner or later Letty will succumb. In her case, it does not seem to be a question of choice.

The conclusion to *Letty Fox: Her Luck* is at once mockingly traditional and strikingly new. It is, I believe, one of the first novels to offer what we might call catharsis through exhaustion. Like many modern writers – Verga, Lawrence, Kafka, Faulkner, Beckett – Stead faced the problem: if our vision of the world is that it is perpetual struggle, if there is no state of harmony and propriety to which we can be returned after the disturbing events of our story (for however necessary she might have believed it was for herself or her characters, Stead never viewed marriage as such a state), then how is a novel supposed to end? Where can it leave us? Her answer, like Thomas Bernhard's after her, is to bring characters and reader to such a state of plenitude, or weariness with events, that the thing simply has to stop.

Letty moves from job to job, man to man. She is getting nowhere. A fiancé goes off to be a war correspondent, writes to say he has married somebody else. Another suitor backs out during the crucial discussion with her parents. She goes on vacation for a 'trial honeymoon' with the perfect American, Wicklow; it lasts five days. Men promise to leave their wives. Out of curiosity, she seduces the elderly professor her sister is in love with. But she is getting tired of it. She throws some extraordinary tantrums. She is more and more manic, more frequently depressed. She is appalled by herself. Without a husband 'a woman as strong as I am can also be strongly, wickedly lazy, and for ever'.

But finally she, like her author, does get her one piece of luck. In the summer of 1945 she meets an old lover as tired of the game as she is herself, as tired as Europe then was with its interminable war. Everybody is quite quite worn out. Ring the wedding bells. It is not a Jane Austen ending. 'Will this last?' Letty asks. And she muses: 'It is a question of getting through life, which is quite a siege, with some self-respect. Before I was married I had none.' At last pregnant, she concludes: 'The principal thing is, I got a start in life; and it's from now on. I have a freight, I cast off, the journey has begun.'

Are these closing words sardonic? Are they romantic? Or simply practical? Or has Stead somehow managed to make them all three? Rather than merely ambiguous, the novel contrives to go beyond any possible resolution. It constantly invites the act of discrimination, but only to repel it, to humiliate the critical faculty. At the end of the day Letty is both a romantic girl and a promiscuous opportunist, a happily married mother-to-be and a left-wing militant.

However we are meant to take them, Letty's final words must have echoed in their author's mind with increasing poignancy over the coming years. All too soon after the publication of the novel, Stead too would be embarking on a journey, casting off from New York's docks, but without her heroine's long-desired 'freight'. In the early days with Bill Stead had twice aborted. While writing *Letty* she had suffered a miscarriage. Now, with the war in Europe over, the Cold War had begun. America was no place for people of their political faith. She and Bill were under investigation by Hoover's FBI. They had heard that the heroine of Stead's latest novel was a young communist. Evidently they didn't stop to read too many pages.

It was hard now to find either work or publishers. Sliding into poverty the couple moved back and forth between Belgium, Switzerland, England and France. They were outcasts. Afflicted as ever by erotic yearnings, Stead sought to seduce Bill's friends, largely without result. She was humiliated. Critical acclaim had brought little cash. *Letty* was banned in Australia. Bill wrote some historical novels which sold well in East Germany. It was impossible to get the money out. When, twenty-six years after they had become lovers, the couple were finally able to marry, they were living in slum conditions and Stead was advertising for work in the local papers. She did not mention the ceremony in letters to friends.

Stead, Rowley tells us in her biography, 'had a knack of arousing hostility'. Even in the days of first love when Blech did everything for her, she was uneasy with the situation. She was too used to the battle of life. She needed to make the brutal gesture, to assume the extremist position. Certainly, when Blech lay dying she was not kind to him. She was scathing of his suffering. He wasn't really sick. Afterwards she regretted it. Living exclusively on steak and alcohol, she defended his political opinions, now far beyond the pale, with renewed vigour. But she couldn't work, she considered her life over: 'my life was for that, wasn't it? To live with Bill. I didn't know that was it, but it was.' Needless to say, all this complicated her eventual admission to the literary canon. Novels as fine as those published by any contemporary Nobel – *Cotter's England, Miss Herbert* and *A Little Tea, A Little Chat* – were admired but not celebrated.

It is no surprise that Stead was a very poor essayist and even poorer public speaker, unless, that is, we are to take her novels themselves as vast inconclusive essays, *Letty Fox* as the speech of someone endlessly changing her mind. The problem was that Stead could never isolate any particular message she had to get across. She wanted to seduce, but also to provoke, or rather, to seduce through provocation, the provocation that any single message was unconvincing. The best writing, she claimed, was driven by an 'intelligent ferocity' that would be able to speak all the contradictions that could not be spoken in any essay, friendship, or political movement, all the experience that risked driving a person mad if it was left unsaid, and risked driving a reader mad when it was. We must love her, in short, for telling us things we do not want to hear.

In none of Stead's novels does this formula work quite as splendidly as in *Letty Fox*, if only because Letty herself is the incarnation of this drive. Never are her men, or the reader for that matter, more enamoured of Letty than when she is unfaithful and bitchy. After her failed honeymoon with the ideal Wicklow, after her refusing even to talk to him on the return train to New York, he nevertheless comes back to her: 'I scolded Wicklow when he came to see me,' she says. 'He grinned, sat down on a stool, took off his hat, and remarked, "You're more fascinating as a termagant, Letty, than a sweet little wife."'

As a writer, Stead is a termagant to whom one is always happy to return. I would advise a more comfortable seat than a stool. The gesture of removing the hat, do please note, is obligatory.

Writerly Rancour

That artists are often animated by an intense and even rancorous spirit of rivalry is a commonplace. That the nature of writing, as opposed to painting or music, makes it possible for that rivalry to emerge explicitly in the work itself is no more than a logical consequence of certain givens. But what do we actually think about writerly rivalry and rancour? Is it merely a foible, the stuff of gossip columns – Lawrence versus Joyce, Amis versus Barnes, seconds away for round thirteen of Rushdie versus Le Carré? Can we take Pope's *Dunciad*, or Shelley's *Peter Bell the Third*, or even Paul Theroux's recent demolition of V.S. Naipaul, with an indulgent pinch of salt as no more than unhappy by-products of more instructive performances, the sort of caprices understandable in those of great talent and ambition? Or could it be, rather, that such rancour as these works exhibit is intimately bound up with the creative process itself, that there is fizz of contradiction, of aspiration and frustration, at the very heart of the writing endeavour that inevitably leads to the harbouring of resentment and bitterness? Seen as an occupational hazard rather than an unpleasant character trait, writerly rancour may have more to tell us than we imagined.

When Samuel Beckett's Molloy goes to the seaside he lays in a store of 'sucking stones'. 'They were pebbles,' he says, 'but I call them stones.' Sixteen to be precise. He wants to suck them in order, 'turn and turn about', as he puts it. For order gives him pleasure. It's a combination of physical and mental gratification that Beckett is describing here, as when Rousseau in *The Confessions* gives us his eulogy to the delicate and logistically demanding pleasures of reading while eating. But if he is to have this gratification – sucking the stones in order – Molloy has to keep track of them, distinguishing one from the other as he passes them from pocket to mouth, from mouth to pocket, the two pockets of his greatcoat, the two pockets of his filthy old trousers. It's a complicated proposition for a muddled vagrant and in the end he comes to the conclusion that in order to suck all sixteen stones one after the other, rather than finding himself sucking some twice or even three times and others never, he will have to 'sacrifice the principle of trim', have to keep all the unsucked stones on one side, shifting them over to the other one by one after sucking. This puts him off balance for considerable periods and he feels 'the weight of the stones dragging me now to one side, now to the other'. And this is uncomfortable. 'Here then,' concludes Molloy gloomily, 'were two incompatible bodily needs at loggerheads. Such things happen.'

Beckett's story offers a hilarious exposition of conflicting impulses: the search at once for complete control *and* complete comfort. As the project is repeatedly frustrated, the suspicion grows that ultimately the one can only be achieved by sacrificing the other, and above all by sacrificing symmetry, the which, we should remember – and perhaps this was inevitable for a man so fascinated by Dante – often serves in Beckett's work as a metaphor for a world that has meaning, or even a surrogate for such a world. Symmetry is the territory of the *Divina Commedia* where everything is in the place God put it and nothing out of line; hence its sacrifice is no small thing.

In any event, at the end of an immensely long rigmarole Molloy suddenly gives up the farce, the hubristic endeavour if we like, of trying to reconcile incompatibles, and does so in a typical display of rancour and disdain:

> But deep down, I didn't give a tinker's curse about being off my balance, dragged to the right hand and the left, backwards and forwards. And deep down it was all the same to me whether I sucked a different stone each time or always the same stone until the end of time . . . And the solution to which I rallied in the end was to throw away all the stones but one, which I kept now in one pocket, now in another, and which of course I soon lost, or threw away, or gave away, or swallowed.

Beckett's work is full of such scenes: somebody embarks on a delicate and improbable project involving the reconciliation of irreconcilables, then gives up in a flurry of anger. This in itself might be eloquent enough of the artistic endeavour, which has often been described as a process of reconciling opposites. But there is more to the passage than that.

Let us imagine the writer at work as being subject to two dominant impulses 'at loggerheads': the impulse for comfort, and the impulse for truth. All of us will recognise the impulse to comfort: as one sets out to establish a vision of the world – something inevitable in the writing of narrative – one trusts it will be of a variety one can feel comfortable with. I don't mean by that that one seeks to portray the world as a nice place to be – the opposite might be the case – but that our vision of 'how the world is' be something that enhances our own sense of self, that keeps us content, or at least not *unhappily unhappy:* in short, we hope it will be something we can live with. In this sense, Pope's vision in *The Dunciad* of a world stifled by the dullness of his contemporaries is a vision he no doubt feels, as the one beacon of consciousness revealing that gloom, not entirely uncomfortable with. Others will find self-esteem in exposing degradation and awfulness from a presumed moral high ground; it affords the delirium that one is being educational, even useful. Others again find that there is a certain consolatory pleasure to be had from insisting in one's writing on the fragility and perhaps even impossibility of happiness. Whatever. Psychology has plenty of words for describing the psyche's habit of interpreting events in such a way as to feel less uncomfortable with them. It is a process necessary for sanity, and we all do this, for the most part unconsciously.

But the writer more than others is elected, or condemned, to deal simultaneously with that other impulse, *the impulse for truth*. Indeed, the less journalistic a writer's work, the more he invents, so the more concerned he becomes with truthfulness. For a journalist to find and then tell a truth, in the sense of a demonstrable fact, may sometimes be difficult, but is not impossible, if only because limited to this or that event or statistic. The creative writer, on the other hand, is seeking to create verisimilitude, of one form or another, *across the board*, has to give *the whole truth*. Indeed, the claim to have understood, represented, demonstrated or even decided ('legislated' Shelley claimed) *how things truly are* is part of the writer's hubristic enterprise.

Precisely, however, as he aspires to such verisimilitude, the writer will simultaneously be aware of the urge to cheat – usually in response to the impulse for comfort. Witness Dickens as he considers the decision: does Little Nell die or not? It would be more comfortable if she lived. The book would also be more welcome to his public who have made it very clear they don't want her dead. Dickens had a very intimate relationship with his public. And Dickens likes Little Nell. So his sorrow as he prepares to dispatch her must be that he knows that for a full and truthful picture of how the world is within the frame he has set up, the girl must die. Fortunately, Dickens has the ultimate comfort of a Christian Paradise hovering in the wings to cover his back. Little Nell has flown to Paradise. How often, pre-twentieth century, the Christian solution has been wheeled in at the end to offset, indeed *to make possible*, a despairing vision of how things truly are. One thinks of Troilus's rancour and despair suddenly resolved as Chaucer has his eternal soul float up into the celestial spheres. Sadly, this particular shift is no longer available to many of us.

The compulsion to truth is present, of course, in all art forms: all of them one way or another have to generate recognition and conviction in their public. But the particular problem for those dealing with words is the way they bear, aspire to bear, defined meaning. Hence the challenge with any extended piece of writing is that meanings accumulate, and like it or not a world view, even a philosophical position, can be extrapolated, discussed and criticised within the very medium – language – in which the work was generated. The protagonist of Robert Walser's story 'The Painter' sets out to write a light-hearted, thoughtless diary to take his mind off his painting, but to his surprise the medium doesn't allow this: 'I don't know why,' he says, 'but the more I write things down, the more I am gripped by an irresistible sense of responsibility for what I write.' '*Irresistible*' would seem to be the key word. It is not what the protagonist wanted. It has to do with the medium. Some of the things he writes down are painful to him. Pleasure and honesty are at loggerheads. The writing process forces the writer to become aware of that in the same way that Molloy's struggles with his sucking stones bring him to the sad truth that fundamental needs may well prove incompatible.

Of course the collision between comfort and truth can occur in any sphere of life. One of the most famous examples might be

Darwin's immense unhappiness when his discovery of the principles of evolution destroyed his crudely fundamentalist Christian faith. How rancorously then he complained of religion not being true! How grimly he proceeded to elaborate the principle that had destroyed his spiritual comfort. Equally troubled, the hitherto successful naturalist, Phillip Henry Gosse, made a heroic attempt to reconcile comfort and truth by elaborating a theory that God had indeed created the world in seven days, but had done so in such a way that it appeared to have been the result of evolution over many millions of years. Here was creativity! The critic's objection – why would God wish to deceive us thus – was too much for Gosse. As a naturalist he was a discredited and broken man. But he kept his religion. Darwin lost his hope but kept his troubled fame and his sense of having been entirely logical.

But if others must occasionally suffer from such incompatibility, it is absolutely endemic to the writer's aspiration to create a world at once convincing *and* pleasurable. As he seeks to do that, and particularly as he grows older and is less easily subject to illusion, more conscious of his own motives, the impulse to truth, or simply this enhanced consciousness, makes him irritatingly aware of the inadequacy of his world, or creation of it, of the fact, in short, that he is not God (anybody who feels that I am being extravagant here has simply not understood the Promethean nature of the artist's aspirations).

But what further rankles is the reflection – reflection, as Hamlet once and for all demonstrated, has a way of rankling – that it is precisely this awareness of shortcomings, this seeing through one's own work, that confers on the writer a sense of superiority and encourages him to struggle to achieve more, to deepen his vision. That is, the writer would not actually have it any other way, but is not entirely happy with the way it is. He has thus attached his identity to a process which cannot bring serenity. Indeed, he fears serenity as something that would detract from his capacity for creativity. Walser's painter turned diarist acknowledges: 'What is happiness: to be always at ease, I think! But artists never, or only rarely, feel at ease.'

Necessarily, the conflict between impulse to comfort and impulse to truth goes beyond the confines of the work itself, to the way it is received. For not only does the author want to be happy with his vision, and have others recognise its appropriateness, but he does this chiefly because he also wishes to be recognised himself.

Here, the word 'recognition' requires some clarification, for I do not just mean praise. Praise is wonderful, but not the same as recognition. To be praised one might run a hundred metres faster than anyone else, or one might write a genre novel of the exact variety you suspect everybody wants. Or one might condemn multinationals. Or Zeus, to shift the context – for who is more obsessed with recognition than the gods – might simply help men by adjusting the weather in their favour. But that would mean stooping to *their* vision of things. It would mean pandering to their requirements. No it is recognition one is after, recognition of what one really is, what one really can do. There is an existential anxiety here that if it doesn't go beyond vanity – does anything? – certainly represents its acme.

Cioran writes: 'No one can renounce at least a shadow of immortality, and even less deny himself the right to seek it everywhere and in whatever form of reputation, beginning with the literary. Since death has come to be accepted by all as the absolute end, everybody writes.'

In short, this is the mind grappling with the fact of its own extinction.

The thirst for recognition adds a further complexity to the conflict between the impulse to comfort and the impulse to truth, and with it a further cause for rancour. Consider Giacomo Leopardi. Tiny, hunchbacked, ugly – in this, even worse off than the dwarf-like Pope – the man is indubitably great, because he is so terribly clear-sighted about the human condition, about human illusion and yet manages to present his unhappy intuitions so beautifully that, at least for the period of reading, there is great enjoyment.

But beautiful poetry or no, Leopardi's gloomy vision to a considerable extent denied him success in his own lifetime, at least outside a small and clear-sighted elite. Like the older Dickens, he was constantly being told his work was too depressing and pessimistic (what did Dickens go around reading to people late in life, but his *early* work). Leopardi thus had good reason to feel rancorous. Not only was his clear-sightedness, his heightened consciousness, as he frequently tells us in his diary, a burden to him, but it denied him the consolation of success in his lifetime.

All the same, and here we approach the core of the matter, Leopardi knew that it was precisely this clear-sightedness, his ability to turn it into poetry, that made his work great, *regardless of its immediate reception*. So that in a way he would not have wished to have seen things differently.

Or would he? In his diary he comments: 'If I could not take refuge in posterity, in the certainty that with time my work will find its rightful place, I would have sent literature to the devil a thousand times.' Yet – another turn of the screw – right in the middle of that sentence, his clear-sightedness, the impulse to truth, forces him to introduce the parenthesis '(an illusory refuge, I know, but it's the only one and absolutely necessary to the serious man of letters)'.

So one writes, raising consciousness of illusion to the highest and most uncomfortable levels, but can do so only in the thrall of another illusion: that posterity will recognise you for having so beautifully destroyed illusion – and that this will be a consolation. How infuriating.

When aged twenty-eight Leopardi is for the first time able to leave his tiny provincial village of Recanati and visit Rome, what does he gain from it? Only the further bitterness of confirming for himself, 'close up, the falsity, ineptitude and stupidity of literary judgements'. A stupidity which, like the 'dullness' Pope describes in *The Dunciad*, could only make his place in posterity *less* likely. He comments bitterly: 'everything in this world is done out of the simple and constant forgetfulness of that universal truth that all is nothing'. But this was precisely the universal truth he expended all his energies seeking to express in a beautiful way. It's worth noting how potency and impotency stand shoulder to shoulder here: the stronger the mind and its powers, the more trapped it becomes in its awareness of futility. 'No future here,' comments Beckett's narrator in *Worstward Ho*. Then continues: 'Alas, yes.' Thus, contaminated, or ennobled by its philosophical content, the writing project has a tendency to devour itself. How many times in his diaries Leopardi wishes he could forget the whole thing. Not for nothing he was the first poet to write an ode 'To a Winner with the Ball'.

The possible causes for rancour then, for one who undertakes both to represent the world and to create a work that will give pleasure *and* bring recognition, real recognition, are many, and mutually self-sustaining: rancour towards the world for being as it is, towards oneself for having adopted a particular position; rancour towards others for not recognising the truth of the matter, towards oneself again for seeking the recognition of people who are unworthy . . . (Perhaps the reason for the terrible retribution the gods wreaked on those who could not recognise them was simply their irritation with themselves for having sought such recognition.)

But the most easily vented rancour of all goes on those who, as the writer sees it, have cheated, and gained the world's acclaim on easy terms . . .

For the author's quarrel with other authors – which is usually different from a critic's or reader's quarrel – has intimately to do with how they have dealt with the struggle between comfort and truth. The other authors have taken an easy way out, they have lied, they have not persisted in exposing the truth of things. They have been lazily grandiloquent, over-optimistic. Here is Montale, brushing aside the pompous, immensely popular D'Annunzio at the height of Fascism:

> Don't ask us for the word that squares
> Our shapeless spirit on all sides
> To proclaim it in letters of fire that shine
> Like a lone crocus in a dusty meadow . . .
>
> Don't ask us for the phrase that can open worlds,
> Just a few gnarled syllables, dry like a branch.
> This, today, is all that we can tell you:
> What we are not, what we do not want.

At its most basic the other authors have committed the terrible crime of not having cultivated a sufficiently high level of consciousness. And thus they have won public affection. After all, as Schopenhauer tells us, 'most people have . . . as the supreme guide and maxim of their conduct the resolve to get by with the least possible expenditure of thought'. Why should they read writers who wake them up? What does Pope accuse his fellow writers of if not 'dullness', a lack of perception, a lack of *wakefulness*. Beckett picks up the theme beautifully in this charming swipe at the British literary establishment in *Molloy*. The old vagrant is speaking of his ditch-sleeping habits.

> In winter I wrapped myself in swathes of newspapers, and did not shed them until the earth awoke, for good, in April. *The Times Literary Supplement* was admirably adapted to this purpose, of a never failing toughness and impermeability. Even farts made no impression on it.

Tough and impermeable, insensitive to the most fundamental realities ('I can't help it, gas escapes from my fundament on the least pretext,' Molloy says), the *TLS* is something to be cast off when the world awakes 'for good'.

An author's attack on other authors then, however mistaken sometimes, however self-serving, is not *just* pettiness, it is also a spreading out from the struggle going on at the heart of his own work. Here I am, the writer tells himself, struggling to reconcile reality with some kind of acceptable form, to achieve Kierkegaard's and Nietzsche's dream of making – *if only for the duration of the work* – necessity loveable, of putting the mind and the world into some acceptable relationship, and this other person, whether by craft or obtusity, cheats by offering the world some candied vision, or by pretending the important problems are soluble, are merely a question of American imperialism, or British colonialism, or communism, or racism, or male chauvinism. If this continues, how will I ever be recognised after I am dead?

Don Quixote is an interesting case here. We all know that Cervantes began the book as a satire of immediately preceding authors. What are they lampooned for? Their ludicrously untrue presentation of reality. 'They are all fictions invented by idle brains . . . to pass the time.'

So far, then, the book's inspiration has much in common with *The Dunciad,* or indeed with all screams for elbow room. But as the work progresses another and subtler source of rancour is seen to be at work. Don Quixote, for all his foolishness, for all his outrageous violence, is an attractive person and his desire to see the world as an extension of his own idealistic mind, as obeying noble rules and regulations, as being full of beautiful damsels, etc., is a recognisable and, in the end, *attractive* desire. It has to do with the mind's ancient quarrel, its perennial struggle to come to terms, its own terms, please, with everything that is not itself. So that while on the one hand the silly books that nurtured Don

Quixote's mentality are despised, nevertheless we identify with the yearnings for glory and control, writerly yearnings if ever there were, and in Cervantes' ultimately kind treatment of Don Quixote we can't help suspecting the ancient rancour that the world refuses to be as we wish it, and, arising from that, the ancient envy of the mad, of those, that is, who despite all the evidence believe the world *is* as the mind wishes it to be. 'Everything is folly but folly itself,' says Leopardi.

Writers, then, frequently criticise authors on their telling of the truth. But more rarely there is the alternative charge that someone has just been brutally pessimistic, or brutally truthful and nothing else, without turning his work into art, without giving pleasure. This, it seems, is more acceptable when the content deals with the condemnation of social injustice, political tyranny and the like, for then there is the implied optimism: here we all are concerned about injustice, eager to have things changed. But when it comes to matters existential, what is the point of being merely pessimistic? Thomas Bernhard is sometimes accused of this. And in Italy, where I live, Beckett is likewise accused. The case is instructive because it suggests both the way a writer's rancour may be channelled and the pitfalls of translation. Here is a moment from the Italian version of *Watt* where Arsene gives the book's inexperienced protagonist a foretaste of how he will feel a few years hence:

> Personalmente, come'è ovvio, rimpiango tutto. Non una parola, non un'azione, non un pensiero, non un bisogno, non un dolore, non una gioa, non una ragazza, non un ragazzo, non un dubbio, non una certezza, non uno scherno, non una voglia, non una speranza, non un timore, non un sorriso, non una lacrima, non un nome, non un volto, nessun momento, nessun luogo, che io non rimpianga, esageratamente. Uno schifo, dal principio alla fine.

For those not familiar with Italian, here is my own translation of that translation back into English.

> Personally, as is obvious, I regret everything. Not a word, not an action, not a thought, not a need, not a pain, not a pleasure, not a girl, not a boy, not a doubt, not a certainty, not a scorn, not a desire, not a hope, not an anxiety, not a smile, not a tear, not a name, not a face, no moment, nowhere, that I do not regret excessively. Crap from beginning to end.

It is not surprising that Italian critics object that, while one may occasionally feel like this, it hardly makes for good reading, the only element of grim humour lying in the scandal of the excess. But here is Beckett's original.

> Personally of course I regret everything. Not a word, not a deed, not a thought, not a need, not a grief, not a joy, not a girl, not a boy, not a doubt, not a trust, not a scorn, not a lust, not a hope, not a fear, not a smile, not a tear, not a name, not a face, no time, no place, that I do not regret, exceedingly. An ordure from beginning to end.

Worth noting here is the way, while the translation retains the negative content, it entirely loses the fun of Beckett's demonstration that even the most miserable vision can be disguised by the mode of presentation, if you so choose. With the monosyllabic, nursery-rhyme anapaests, the symmetrical organisation of opposites, the lovely change of pace as the piece ends – 'no time, no place' – and the amusing shift of register in 'exceedingly' and 'ordure', the English reader hardly notices what a miserable statement this is.

The paragraph is in fact a parody of another and most important consequence of the artist's rancour about the impossible task he has set himself: his growing vocation for seduction, for inventing, that is, some artistic means that will allow him – at least for the space of his narrative – to present the truth, as he sees it – including Cordelia's death, and Little Nell's and the miserable destiny of Isabel Archer and Anna Karenina's suicide – in such a way that people will be charmed.

There is a curious moment in *The Odyssey*, when Helen and Menelaus are back in Greece and Telemachus visits them. They wish to speak of Troy, because Troy is the most important experience of their lives. But it is too painful. Menelaus must remember Helen's betrayal. Helen must remember the dead lovers. Telemachus must remember his father missing, believed dead. The truth is too depressing to be comfortable with. Helen gets up, goes into another room, finds a drug she was given in Egypt and slips it into the wine. This is a drug, Homer says, 'that robs grief and anger of their sting and banishes all painful memories'. And so it is. She and her husband, and Telemachus, have a wonderful evening recalling the unbearable truth of Troy, and then fall serenely asleep.

The artist's dream is to conjure that seductive drug from his way with words and narrative. Only by presenting us with those truths which are all-important to us, but usually too difficult to face, can he get us entirely in his thrall, rather than merely amuse us with a pastime. Only by getting us in his thrall can he present those truths and leave us mostly unscathed. Otherwise he must just amuse us with tales of gallant knights. So it is that the only really significant reading experiences are those where one sets out with scepticism, only to find oneself enchanted, overwhelmed by a vision that, with Promethean peremptoriness, fired with an ancient antagonism, demands our acquiescence.

Which allows me to come at last to Prospero. Since for recognition of the artistic mind's essential rancour and its intimate relation to his genius for seduction and self-affirmation, the greatest, the most explicit example remains *The Tempest*, a title that speaks worlds.

People like to forget what an angry, punitive fellow Prospero is. How quickly he dismisses his daughter's 'brave new world'! 'One more word/shall make me chide thee, if not hate thee,' he tells Miranda when she appeals for Ferdinand's life. And to Ariel: 'If thou more murmur'st, I will rend an oak./And peg thee in his knotty entrails, till/thou has howl'd away twelve winters.' His magician's spells, however beautiful, are designed to bind, not please, to regain through the enchantment of the mind the sovereignty he so foolishly relinquished at the political level. The whole play is steeped in the vocabulary of sovereignty and thralldom. One is either controlling or controlled, and the world is of such a nature that it must be brutally manipulated if the miracle of Miranda and Ferdinand's love is to have any chance at all. And if this rancorous, vengeful magician does in the end forgive, how grudgingly and sceptically it is done! And that only when every enemy is securely in Prospero's power, only when the gesture of relinquishing power provides the final claim to superiority, the ultimate demand for recognition.

Then the wonderful final irony: the Duke, the artist, reveals – how infuriating – all the while he appeared the sovereign, he was in fact in his audience's thrall, they had to be kept constantly in mind.

> Let me not,
> Since I have my dukedom got
> And pardon'd the deceiver, dwell
> In this bare island by your spell;
> But release me from my bands
> With the help of your good hands.

Like Leopardi two centuries later, Shakespeare alerts us to the contradiction at the heart of the writer's aspirations: his strength as magician and seducer, his weakness in needing recognition for this strength. Prospero seems to be trapped on the very stage that was the scene of his triumph, the world he watched over and made conscious for us. In the end the writer will ever be dogged by the reflection that once the work is over, he ceases to be god. And the work itself will ever be fuelled by the rancour consequent on that knowledge, and the rancorous determination that everybody else be aware they share the same limitations. Here is Beckett's Malone giving us a splendid combination of vindictiveness and awareness of the futility of seeking recognition at all:

> Let me say before I go any further that I forgive nobody. I wish them all an atrocious life and then the fires and ice of hell and in the execrable generations to come an honoured name.

The wonder is that in taking it to such extremes Beckett can actually seduce us with these negative emotions. The humanistic project of generating sympathy and a sense of shared destiny is most nearly achieved when the artist's essential rancour is most openly recognised.

References

The first number in the left column refers to the page, the second to the line on which the quotation ends.

Hell and Back

1, 7   Gospel According to St Luke, 18, 22

1, 26   Dante, *Inferno*, trans. Robert and Jean Hollander (New York, Doubleday, 2001), Canto I, ll. 1–3

2, 19   J.L. Borges, *Selected Non-Fictions*, trans. E. Weinberger (New York, Viking, 1999), p. 337

2, 21   D.H. Lawrence, *Apocalypse* (London, Penguin, 1995), p. 61

4, 24   Dante, *Inferno*, op. cit., Canto III, l. 9

4, 27   Ibid., Canto III, l. 36

4, 31   Ibid., Canto III, ll. 56–7

5, 4   Ibid., Canto IV, l. 42

5, 10   Ibid., Canto IV, ll. 44–5

5, 34   Ibid., p. xxxiii

6, 2   *Mundaka Upanisad*, 1, 1

6, 6   Loc. cit.

6, 33   Dante, *Inferno*, op. cit., Canto VII, l. 99

6, 34   Ibid., Canto XVII, l. 40

7, 5   Ibid., Canto XXIX, ll. 1–3

7, 10   Ibid., Canto XXIX, ll. 11–12 (trans. Hollander)

8, 15   Dante, *Hell*, trans. D.L. Sayers (London, Penguin, 1949), Canto XXVI, ll. 94–102

9, 3   Dante, *Inferno*, trans. H. Longfellow, Canto V, ll. 46–51

9, 21   Dante, *The Inferno of Dante*, trans. Robert Pinsky (New York, Farrar, Straus & Giroux, 1994), Canto XXVIII, ll. 22–8

10, 10 Dante, *Dante's Inferno*, trans. various (New Jersey, The Ecco Press, 1993), p. xii

10, 28   Ibid., Canto IV, ll. 25–31

11, 19   S. Mallarmé, *Sur L'évolution Littéraire*, in *Oeuvres Complètes*, ed. Mondor and Jean-Aubry, p. 867.

11, 28   Dante, *The Divine Comedy of Dante Alighieri, I Inferno*, trans. J. Sinclair (New York, Oxford University Press, 1939), p. 75

12, 6   Ibid., p. 77

12, 27   Dante, *Inferno*, op. cit., Canto V, ll. 28–36

13, 6   Ibid., Canto V, ll. 88–93

14, 6   Ibid., Canto XXVIII, l. 48

15, 9   Ibid., Canto XIX, ll. 10–12

16, 16   Ibid., Canto XXXIV, ll. 30–1

16, 24   Ibid., p. 619

17, 2   *L'Arena*, Verona, 9 October 2000

17, 18   Dante, *Inferno*, op. cit., Canto XVIII, ll. 134–5

18, 12   Ibid., p. xxix

18, 25   Ibid, p. 473

18, 28   Ibid, p. 103

18, 31   Ibid., Canto XX, l. 28

18, 33   Ibid., Canto XX, l. 28 (trans. Hollander)

19, 1   Ibid., Canto XX (trans. Sinclair, op. cit.), p. 251

19, 25   Ibid., Canto XX, l. 28 (trans. Sayers, op. cit.)

19, 32   Dante, *Inferno*, op. cit., Canto XII, ll. 29–30

20, 7   Ibid., Canto XII, ll. 41–5

20, 9   Ibid., Canto III, l. 6

21, 3   Ibid., Canto XVI, l. 44

21, 5   Ibid., pp. 288–9

22, 11   Samuel Beckett, *Watt* (London, Calder & Boyars, 1972), pp. 154–5

The Universal Gentleman

23, 2   J.L. Borges, *Selected Non-Fictions* (New York, Viking Penguin, 1999), p. 7

23, 5   Ibid., p. 8

23, 10   Ibid., p. 484

25, 1 Ibid., p. 3

25, 6 Loc. cit.

25, 16 Ibid., p. 250

25, 18 Ibid., p. 75

25, 19 Ibid., p. 282

25, 22 Ibid., p. 291

27, 4 J.L. Borges, *Collected Fictions*, trans. Andrew Hurley (New York, Viking Penguin, 1998), p. 88

27, 8 Ibid., p. 91

27, 9 Loc. cit.

27, 15 Ibid., p. 94

27, 21 Loc. cit.

27, 25 Ibid., p. 95

28, 19 Ibid., p. 101

28, 28 Ibid., p. 192

28, 28 Ibid., p. 191

29, 3 E. Cioran, *La chute dans le temps*, (Paris, Gallimard, 1964), p. 181

29, 11 J.L. Borges, *Collected Fictions*, op. cit., p. 193

31, 9 J.L. Borges, *Selected Non-Fictions*, op. cit., p. 210

31, 20 Loc. cit.

31, 31 Ibid., p. 211

32, 2 Loc. cit.

32, 12 Loc. cit.

32, 13 Loc. cit.

32, 17 Loc. cit.

33, 8 Ibid., p. 240

33, 17 Loc. cit.

34, 11 Ibid., p. 417

34, 25 Ibid., p. 425

35, 9 Ibid., p. 481

35, 9 Ibid., p. 195

35, 30 Ibid., p. 427

36, 8 Ibid., p. 68

36, 14 Ibid., p. 219

36, 16 Loc. cit.

36, 21 Ibid. p. 19

36, 23 Ibid., p. 84

37, 10 Ibid., p. 374

37, 16 Ibid., p. 313

37, 34 J.L. Borges, *Selected Poems*, trans. various (New York, Viking Penguin, 1999), p. 95

38, 2 J. Woodall, *Borges, A Life* (London, Hodder & Stoughton 1996), p. 177

38, 26 Ibid., p. 219

39, 3 *Selected Non-Fictions*, op. cit., p. 332

39, 10 Ibid., p. 344

39, 16 Ibid., p. 110

39, 21 Ibid., p. 346

39, 26 Ibid., p. 490

40, 3 Ibid., pp. 513–14

42, 25 Ibid., p. 311

42, 26 S. Beckett, *Malone Dies* (London, Calder & Boyars, 1975), p. 7

42, 29 H. Green, *Loving, Living, Party Going* (London, Penguin, 1993), p. 464

Here Comes Salman

45, 3 A. Schopenhauer, *Essays and Aphorisms*, trans. R.J. Hollingdale (London, Penguin, 1970), p. 165

46, 19 S. Rushdie, *Haroun and the Sea of Stories* (London, Granta Books, 1990), p. 109

47, 11 S. Rushdie, *The Ground Beneath Her Feet* (London, Viking, 1999), p. 299

47, 24 Ibid., p. 303

48, 8 S. Rushdie in interview with John Banville, *New York Review of Books*, 4 March 1993

48, 14 Loc. cit.

48, 24 H. Mantel in *New York Review of Books*, 16 February 1995

49, 15 P.B. Shelley, *A Defence of Poetry*, London, 1840

49, 19 S. Rushdie, *The Ground Beneath Her Feet*, op. cit., p. 123

50, 8 Ibid., p. 21

52, 32 Ibid., p. 75

52, 34 Ibid., p. 122

54, 13 Ibid., p. 23

54, 23 Ibid., p. 84

54, 27 Ibid., p. 90

55, 3 Ibid., p. 123

55, 26 Ibid., p. 215

56, 4 Ibid., p. 23

56, 14 Ibid., p. 99

56, 27 Ibid., p. 147

57, 5 Ibid., p. 148

57, 26 Ibid., p. 324

58, 11 R. Calasso, *Ka* (New York, Knopf, 1998), p. 102

58, 14 Ibid., pp. 102–3

58, 34 J. Kerouac, *On the Road* (London, Penguin, 1991), p. 38

59, 2 Loc. cit.

59, 5 S. Rushdie, *The Ground Beneath Her Feet*, op. cit., p. 287

59, 16 Ibid., p. 497

59, 31 Ibid., p. 498

60, 15 Ibid., p. 334

Surviving Giacomo

61, 5 R. Damiani, *All'apparir del vero, vita di Giacomo Leopardi* (Milan, Mondadori, 1992), p. 11

62, 15 Ibid., p. 22

62, 17 Loc. cit.

63, 15 G. Leopardi, *Zibaldone* (Milan, Mondadori, 1997), p. 85

63, 17 Ibid., 17 December 1819

64, 2 G. Leopardi, *Le operette morali* (Milan, Garzanti, 1998), p. xii

64, 3 Loc. cit.

64, 22 R. Damiani, *All'apparir del vero*, op. cit. p. 192

64, 28 Ibid., p. 191

64, 29   Ibid., p. 194

64, 32   Ibid., p. 195

65, 20   I. Origo, *Leopardi, A Study in Solitude* (New York, Books & Co., 1999), p. xvii

65, 25   D.S. Carne-Ross, 'The Strange Case of Leopardi', *New York Review of Books*, 29 January 1987

65, 29   Loc. cit.

66, 5   I. Origo, *Leopardi*, op. cit., p. 177

66, 10   Loc. cit.

66, 13   D.S. Carne-Ross, op. cit.

66, 18   G. Leopardi, *Le operetti morali*, op. cit., p. xxxiv

66, 21   I. Origo, *Leopardi*, op. cit., p. 222

66, 32   R. Damiani, *All'apparir del vero*, op. cit., p. 423, also G. Leopardi, *Zibaldone*, op. cit., 3085)

67, 3   Loc. cit.

67, 24   S.T. Coleridge, 'Dejection: an Ode'

67, 26   Loc. cit.

67, 27   G. Leopardi, *Le operette morali*, op. cit., p. 295

68, 21   I. Origo, *Images and Shadows*, (London, John Murray, 1970), p. 3

69, 3   R. Damiani, *All'apparir del vero*, op. cit., p. 421

69, 4   Loc. cit.

69, 14   I. Origo, *Images and Shadows*, op. cit., p. 173

69, 26   G. Leopardi, *Il sogno*

70, 25   E. Cioran, 'The Tree of Life', *The Fall into Time* (Chicago, Quadrangle Books, 1970)

71, 13   I. Origo, *Leopardi*, op. cit. p. 326 (also G. Leopardi, *Zibaldone* op. cit., 3085)

71, 16   Loc. cit (quoting G. Leopardi, *Amore e morte*)

72, 15   I. Origo, *Leopardi*, op. cit., p. 224

72, 19   I. Origo, *Images and Shadows*, op. cit., p. 259

72, 30   G. Leopardi, *Zibaldone*, op. cit, pp. 259–60

75, 3   G. Leopardi, 'A Silvia'

77, 2   G. Leopardi, 'To Silvia', trans. J. Galassi, T. Parks, *New York Review of Books*, 23 March 2000

77, 16   G. Leopardi, 'L'infinitò' (original Italian: 'E' il naufragar m'è dolce in questo mare')

77, 25   G. Leopardi, *Zibaldone*, op. cit., p. 60

79, 11   Ibid., pp. 259–60

79, 27   I. Origo, *Leopardi*, op. cit., p. 292

79, 28   Ibid., p. 283

80, 4   Ibid., p. 270

80, 8   Ibid., p. 35

The Hunter

81, 6   M. de Cervantes, *Don Quixote*, trans. J.M. Cohen (London, Penguin, 1950), p. 937

81, 10   Loc. cit.

81, 13   G. Leopardi, *Zibaldone*, Mondadori, 17 Dec 1823

81, 15   E. Cioran, *La chute dans le temps* (Paris, Gallimard, 1964), p. 166

81, 19   M. de Cervantes, *Don Quixote*, op. cit., p. 939

83, 6   G.W. Sebald, *Vertigo* (New York, New Directions, 2000), p. 3

83, 9   Ibid., p. 33

83, 13   Ibid., p. 141

83, 22   Ibid., p. 5

84, 1   I. Calvino, *The Road to San Giovanni* (London, Vintage, 1993), pp. 87–8

84, 4   G.W. Sebald, *Vertigo*, op. cit., p. 3

84, 10   G.W. Sebald, *The Emigrants*, (London, Harvill Press, 1996), quotation placed before first story.

84, 18   G.W. Sebald, *Vertigo*, op. cit., p. 6

84, 24   Ibid., p. 11

84, 33   Ibid., p. 13

85, 12   Ibid., p. 21

85, 15   Loc. cit.

85, 17   Ibid., p. 22

85, 18   Ibid., p. 28

85, 19   Loc. cit.

85, 21   Ibid., p. 29

86, 6   Ibid., p. 141

86, 11   Ibid., p. 171

86, 24   Ibid., p. 228

87, 6   Ibid., p. 52

87, 15   Ibid., p. 142

87, 26   Ibid., p. 59 (trans. from the Italian, T. Parks)

88, 15   Ibid., p. 62

88, 18   R.M. Rilke, *Letters to a Young Poet*, letter of 16 July

89, 18   G.W. Sebald, *Vertigo*, op. cit., p. 63

90, 5   Ibid., p. 79

90, 15   Ibid., p. 131

92, 4   Ibid., pp. 103–4

92, 13   Ibid., p. 252

92, 17   Ibid., p. 1

92, 30   Ibid., p. 205

92, 33   Ibid., p. 206

93, 16   Ibid., pp. 207–8

Different Worlds

95, 25   T. Parks, *Cara Massimina* (London, Vintage, 1999), p. 11

97, 9   These and other remarks in M. Kundera, *Testaments Betrayed*, trans. L. Asher (New York, Harper Collins, 1995). See in particular the essay on Kafka.

97, 14   D.H. Lawrence, Foreword to *Women in Love* (Thomas Seltzer, 1920)

97, 16   M. Proust, *Contre Sainte-Beuve* (Paris, Gallimard, 1978), p. 225

97, 24   M. Kundera, *Testaments Betrayed*, op. cit., p. 110

97, 26   Loc. cit.

98, 18   M. Kundera, *The Art of the Novel* (London, Faber & Faber, 1990), pp. 129–30

99, 13   D.H. Lawrence, *Women in Love* (London, Penguin, 1982), p. 53

99, 22   Ibid., pp. 113, 57, 430, 396, 397

100, 2   *Donne Innamorate*, trans. A. dell'Orto (Milan, Rizzoli, 1989), pp. 94, 24, 499, 455

101, 7   D.H. Lawrence, *Women in Love*, op. cit., p. 579

103, 31 S. Beckett, 'Dante . . . Bruno. Vico . . . Joyce'. In *I can't go on, I'll go on* (New York, Grove Weidenfeld, 1976), p. 117

104, 18 See *Fondi Alberto Mondadori, Arnaldo Mondadori, Autori, Fascicolo Vittorini*. Available for consultation at the Mondadori publishing house, Milan

106, 9   R. Calasso, *Le nozze di Cadmo e Armonia* (Milan, Adelphi, 1988), p. 67

108, 5   R. Calasso, *The Marriage of Cadmus and Harmony*, trans. T. Parks (New York, Knopf, 1993), p. 51

111, 9   R. Calasso, *Le nozze di Cadmo e Armonia*, op. cit., p. 67

112, 11 R. Calasso, *The Marriage of Cadmus and Harmony*, op. cit., p. 51

Sentimental Education

117, 28 V. Seth, *An Unequal Music* (London, Viking, 1999), p. 166

117, 30 Ibid., p. 82

118, 12 Ibid., p. 3

118, 29 Ibid., p. 83

119, 24 Ibid., p. 38

119, 34 Ibid., p. 40

120, 4   Loc. cit.

121, 3   Ibid., p. 71

121, 21 Ibid., p. 62

122, 4   Ibid., p. 71

123, 23 Ibid., pp. 79–80

124, 11 Ibid., p. 136

124, 24 Ibid., p. 125

125, 15 Ibid., p. 385

126, 10 *New York Review of Books*, 27 May 1993

126, 29 V. Seth, *An Unequal Music*, op. cit., p. 90

127, 1   Ibid., p. 43

127, 8   Ibid., p. 63

127, 11   Ibid., p. 125

128, 3   Ibid., p. 306

128, 8   J.M. Coetzee, *Disgrace* (London, Secker & Warburg, 1999), p. 181

128, 30   J. Donne, quoted from V. Seth, *An Unequal Music*, op. cit., unnumbered page before text.

129, 13   V. Seth, *An Unequal Music*, op. cit., p. 239

129, 19   Ibid., p. 380

129, 24   Ibid., p. 381

A Chorus of Cruelty

131, 5   E. Cioran, *La chute dans le temps* (Paris, Gallimard, 1964), pp. 142–3

131, 22   G. Verga, *Cavalleria rusticana and Other Stories* (London, Penguin, 1999), p. xxiv

133, 33   G. Verga, *Little Novels of Sicily* (Vermont, Steerforth Press, 2000), p. vii

134, 7   Verga quoted in *Encyclopaedia Britannica*

134, 8   G. Verga, *Little Novels of Sicily*, op. cit., p. viii

134, 17   G. Verga, *Tutte le novelle, Vol. I* (Milan, Mondadori, 1998), p. 99

136, 19   Ibid., p. v

136, 21   G. Verga, *I Malavoglia* (Milan, Mondadori, 1999), p. vii

137, 18   G. Verga, *Tutte le novelle, Vol. I*, op. cit., p. 29

137, 33   Ibid., p. 16

138, 12   Loc. cit.

138, 31   G. Verga, *Cavalleria rusticana*, op. cit., p. xii

139, 7   G. Verga, *Little Novels of Sicily*, op. cit., p. 81

139, 13   G. Verga, *Cavalleria rusticana*, op. cit., p. 173

140, 4   G. Verga, *Tutte le novelle, Vol. I*, op. cit., p. 282

140, 12   G. Verga, *Cavalleria rusticana*, op. cit., p. 173

140, 16   S. Beckett, *First Love*, quoted from *Collected Shorter Prose, 1945–80*, (London, Calder, 1984)

140, 20 G. Verga, *Little Novels of Sicily*, op. cit., p. 81

140, 27 G. Verga, *Cavalleria rusticana*, op. cit., p. 173

141, 2 G. Verga, *Little Novels of Sicily*, op. cit., p. 81

141, 8 G. Verga, *Cavalleria rusticana*, op. cit., p. 74

141, 9 G. Verga, *Little Novels of Sicily*, op. cit., p. 82

141, 9 G. Verga, *Tutte le novelle, Vol. I*, op. cit., p. 283

141, 12 G. Verga, *Cavalleria rusticana*, op. cit., p. 174

141, 16 G. Verga, *Little Novels of Sicily*, op. cit., p. 82

141, 26 G. Verga, *Cavalleria rusticana*, op. cit., p. 176

141, 30 Ibid., p. 75

142, 2 G. Verga, *Little Novels of Sicily*, op. cit., p. 86

142, 3 G. Verga, *Tutte le novelle*, op. cit., p. 286

142, 34 G. Verga, *I Malavoglia*, op. cit., p. 89

143, 4 Loc. cit.

143, 14 Ibid., p. 75

144, 30 G. Verga, *Cavalleria rusticana*, op. cit., p. 89

144, 32 G. Verga, *Tutte le novelle, Vol. I*, op. cit., p. 174

145, 7 Ibid., p. 168

145, 26 L. Dumont, 'La maladie totalitaraine' in *Essais sur l'individualisme*, (Paris, Editions du Seuil, 1983)

146, 3 G. Verga, *I Malavoglia*, op. cit., p. xv

147, 6 G. Verga, *Cavalleria rusticana*, op. cit., p. xi

147, 17 G. Verga, *Tutte le novelle, Vol. I*, op. cit., p. 174

Voltaire's Coconuts

151, 7 I. Buruma, *Voltaire's Coconuts* (London, Weidenfeld & Nicholson, 1999), p. 176

151, 18 Ibid., p. 208

153, 27 Ibid., p. 158

154, 10 Ibid., p. 164

154, 16 Ibid., p. 60

157, 22 Ibid., p. 53

157, 30 Ibid., p. 279

158, 16 D.H. Lawrence, *Women in Love* (London, Penguin, 1982), p. 430

158, 31 I. Buruma, *Voltaire's Coconuts*, op. cit., p. 54

159, 5   Ibid., p. 69

159, 18 Loc. cit.

159, 32 Ibid., p. 23

160, 1   Ibid., p. 98

160, 8   Ibid., p. 202

161, 3   F. Nietzsche, *Beyond Good and Evil* (London, Penguin, 1990), p. 183

161, 10 I. Buruma, *Voltaire's Coconuts*, op. cit., p. 98

162, 5   Ibid., p. 120

162, 16 Ibid., p. 122

162, 29 Ibid., p. 119

163, 22 G. Leopardi, *Discorso sopra lo stato presente dei costumi degl'italiani* (Milan, Feltrinelli, 1991), p. 47

163, 32 Ibid., p. 51

Literary Trieste

167, 19 J. Cary, *A Ghost in Trieste* (University of Chicago Press, 1993), pp. 242–3

168, 6   Ibid., p. 137

168, 12 Ibid., p. 138

169, 29 Ibid., pp. 4–5

170, 19 Ibid., p. 9

170, 26 Loc. cit.

170, 29 Loc. cit.

172, 12 Ibid., pp. 140–1

172, 19 Ibid., p. 87

172, 25 Ibid., p. 89

173, 24 Ibid., p. 159

174, 2   Ibid., p. 133

174, 25 Ibid., p. 149

174, 30 J. Joyce, *Ulysses* (London, Penguin, 1973), p. 704

175, 27 J. Cary, *A Ghost in Trieste*, op. cit., p. 151

176, 13 P. Celan, _Gesammelte Werke_ (Frankfurt, Suhrkamp, 1983), vol. 3, p. 175

176, 33 J. Cary, _A Ghost in Trieste_, op. cit., p. 148

177, 14 I. Svevo, _La coscienza di Zeno_ (Milan, Mondadori, 1988), p. 382

Party Going

180, 10 H. Green, _Party Going_ (London, Vintage, 2001), pp. 6–7

182, 3   Ibid., p. 7

182, 14 H. Green, _Surviving, The Uncollected Writings of Henry Green_ (London, Harville, 1993), p. 245

183, 13 H. Green, _Party Going_, op. cit., p. 64

184, 19 H. Green, _Surviving_, op. cit., p. 193

184, 28 H. Green, _Party Going_, op. cit., p. 56

185, 18 Ibid., p. 59

186, 2   Ibid., p. 51

186, 4   Ibid., p. 103

186, 6   Ibid., p. 21

187, 6   Ibid., p. 1

187, 10 Ibid., p. 2

187, 23 Ibid., p. 1

187, 25 Ibid., p. 95

187, 33 Ibid., p. 83

188, 12 Ibid., p. 105

188, 31 Ibid., p. 1

189, 14 Ibid., p. 19

190, 7   H. Green, _Surviving_, op. cit., p. 237

191, 10 H. Green, _Party Going_, op. cit., p. 140

The Enchanted Fort

193, 3   D.H. Lawrence, _Apocalypse_ (London, Penguin, 1995), p. 60

193, 7   Ibid., p. 61

193, 22   D. Buzzati, *Il deserto dei Tartari* (Milan Mondadori, 1989 – see back cover)

194, 4   Ibid., p. 9

195, 2   D. Buzzati, *The Tartar Steppe* (London, Penguin, 2000), p. 1

195, 10   Loc. cit.

198, 6   D. Buzzati, *Il deserto dei Tartari*, op. cit., p. 57

199, 1   Ibid., p. 23

In the Locked Ward

201, 2   J. Neugeboren, *Imagining Robert* (New York, William Morrow), p. 227

201, 11   Ibid., p. 41

201, 20   Ibid., p. 18

201, 25   Ibid., p. 62

201, 26   Ibid., pp. 34, 51

202, 3   Ibid., p. 62

202, 15   Ibid., p. 215

203, 24   Ibid., p. 44

203, 28   Ibid., p. 91

203, 31   Ibid., p. 92

205, 21   Loc. cit.

206, 1   Ibid., p. 132

206, 6   J. Neugeboren, *Transforming Madness* (New York, William Morrow, 1999), p. 118

206, 31   Ibid., p. 273

206, 33   Ibid., p. 274

207, 11   Ibid., p. 275

207, 16   Loc. cit.

207, 31   Loc. cit.

208, 18   G. Gabbard, 'The Ungrateful Patient', Congress for Psychodynamic Psychiatry, Venice, Italy, 9 April 1999

208, 21   Loc. cit.

209, 2   J. Neugeboren, *Transforming Madness*, op. cit., p. 347

Fascist Work

211, 5   S. Mallarmé, *Les dieux antiques* (Paris, Gallimard, 1925), p. 54

212, 14   P.B. Shelley, *A Defence of Poetry*, London, 1840

213, 4   E. Braun, *Mario Sironi and Italian Modernism, Art and Politics under Fascism* (Cambridge University Press, 2000), p. 32

213, 13   Ibid., p. 24

213, 30   Ibid., p. 32

214, 13   Ibid., p. 39

216, 5   Ibid., p. 26

216, 11   G. Leopardi, *Discorso sopra lo stato presente dei costumi degl'italiani* (Milan, Feltrinelli, 1991), p. 45

216, 17   Ibid., p. 47

216, 21   Ibid., p. 60

216, 22   Ibid., p. 61

217, 9   Ibid., p. 51

217, 21   Ibid., p. 72

218, 26   E. Braun, *Mario Sironi*, op. cit., p. 193

218, 32   Ibid., p. 12

219, 31   Ibid., p. 236

220, 31   Ibid., p. 177

221, 7   M. Sironi, *Scritti editi e inediti* (Milan, Feltrinelli, 1980), p. xii

221, 15   E. Braun, *Mario Sironi*, op. cit., p. 99

221, 33   Ibid., p. 158

223, 19   Ibid., p. 98

223, 26   Loc. cit.

223, 31   Ibid., p. 174

224, 1   Ibid., p. 1

224, 3   Ibid., pp. 174–5

224, 20   Loc. cit.

224, 31   M. Sironi, *Scritti*, op. cit., p. xix

226, 13   E. Braun, *Mario Sironi*, op. cit., p. 194

226, 27   M. Sironi, *Scritti*, op. cit., p. 294

226, 29   Ibid., p. 328

228, 15   E. Braun, *Mario Sironi*, p. 209

Sightgeist

229, 12 J. Saramago, *Blindness*, trans. G. Pontiero (New York, Harcourt Brace, 1997), p. 218

232, 3 Quoted by James Wood in *The New Republic*, 30 November 1998.

232, 5 E. Cioran, *The Fall into Time*, trans. R. Howard (Chicago, Quadrangle Books, 1970), p. 57

232, 7 E. Cioran, *History and Utopia*, trans. R. Howard (London, Quartet, 1996), p. 96

232, 32 J. Saramago, *Blindness*, op. cit., p. 226

233, 5 T. Bernhard, *Concrete*, trans. D. McLintock (London, Quartet, 1989), p. 39

233, 10 J. Saramago, *The History of the Siege of Lisbon*, trans. G. Pontiero (New York, Harcourt Brace, 1996), p. 142

233, 11 J. Saramago, *The Gospel According to Jesus Christ*, trans. G. Pontiero (New York, Harcourt Brace, 1994), p. 127

233, 25 J. Saramago, *The History of the Siege of Lisbon*, op. cit., afterword, p. 314

236, 11 J. Saramago, *The Gospel According to Jesus Christ*, op. cit., p. 279

238, 13 Ibid., p. 262

239, 21 Ibid., p. 188

240, 23 Ibid., p. 251

240, 25 Loc. cit.

241, 23 Ibid., pp. 251–2

A Prisoner's Dream

243, 8 G. Leopardi, 'A Silvia'

245, 5 E. Montale, *Ossi di seppia* (Milan, Mondadori, 1991), p. 5 (trans. for essay, T. Parks)

245, 10 Loc. cit. (trans. for essay, T. Parks)

245, 15 E. Montale, *Collected Poems, 1920–1954*, trans. J. Galassi (New York, Farrar, Straus & Giroux, 1999), p. 39

246, 8   E. Montale, *Ossi di seppia*, op. cit., p. 40 (trans. for essay, T. Parks)

246, 20 Ibid., p. 5 (trans. for essay, T. Parks)

246, 29 Ibid., p. 121 (trans. for essay, T. Parks)

247, 11 Ibid., pp. 15–16 (trans. for essay, T. Parks)

247, 15 Ibid., p. 128 (trans. for essay, T. Parks)

247, 18 J. Keats, 'Ode to a Nightingale'

247, 29 E. Montale, *Ossi di seppia*, op. cit., p. 42 (trans. for essay, T. Parks)

248, 1   Ibid., p. 45 (trans. for essay, T. Parks)

248, 8   Loc. cit. (trans. for essay, T. Parks)

248, 17 Ibid., p. 39

248, 19 Ibid., p. 50

248, 21 'Intenzioni (Intervista immaginaria)', *La Rassegna d'Italia*, vol. 1, no. 1 (January 1946), p. 84–9. Also available in E. Montale, *The Second Life of Art*, trans. J. Galassi (New York, Ecco Press, 1982)

248, 26 Loc. cit.

249, 16 E. Montale, *Collected Poems, 1920–1954*, op. cit., p. 61

250, 7   E. Montale, *Cuttlefish Bones*, trans. W. Arrowsmith (New York, Norton, 1993), p. 79

251, 8   E. Montale, *Ossi di seppia*, op. cit., p. 60

255, 13 'Intenzioni (Intervista immaginaria)', op. cit.

255, 15 Loc. cit.

256, 12 E. Montale, *Collected Poems, 1920–1954*, op. cit., p. 502

256, 27 E. Montale, 'A Dialogue with E. Montale on Poetry' in *The Second Life of Art*, op. cit.

257, 11 E. Montale, *Collected Poems, 1920–1954*, op. cit., p. 287

257, 21 Ibid., p. 546

257, 31 P. Celan, *Gesammelte Werke* (Frankfurt, Suhrkamp, 1983), vol. 3 p. 175

258, 34 R. Calasso, *Ka*, trans. T. Parks (London, Cape, 1998), p. 28

260, 6   E. Montale, *Collected Poems, 1920–1954*, op. cit., p. 409–11

260, 13 E. Montale, *The Storm and Other Things*, trans. W. Arrowsmith (New York, Norton, 1988)

260, 17 E. Montale, *The Storm and Other Poems*, trans. C. Wright

(Oberlin College Press, 1978)

260, 20 E. Montale, *Provinsial Conclusions; a selection of the poetry of Eugenio Montale*, various translators, (Chicago, H. Regnery Co., 1970)

Unlocking the Mind's Manacles

261, 24 D. Lipset, *Gregory Bateson, The Legacy of a Scientist* (New York, Prentice Hall, 1980), p. 115

262, 2 Ibid., p 97

263, 2 G. Bateson, *Naven*, (Stanford, Leland Stanford Junior University, 1958), pp. 1–2

263, 21 D. Lipset, *Gregory Bateson*, op. cit., p. 157

263, 29 Ibid., p. 125

266, 10 V. Ugazio, *Storie permesse, storie proibite, polarità semantiche familiari e psicopatologie* (Turin, Bollati Boringhieri, 1999), pp. 28, 137

267, 30 D. Lipset, *Gregory Bateson*, op. cit., p. 237

268, 28 Ibid., p. 210

269, 10 Ibid., p. 211

269, 19 G. Bateson, 'Toward a Theory of Schizophrenia', *Steps to an Ecology of Mind* (New York, Chandler, 1972)

270, 21 E. First, 'The New Wave in Psychiatry', *New York Review of Books*, 20 February 1975

272, 17 M. Selvini, *Self-Starvation, From the Intra-pyschic to the Transpersonal Approach to Anorexia Nervosa* (New York, Jason Aronson, 1978), p. 230

276, 7 C. Anderson, *Journal of Marital and Family Therapy*, 1986, vol. 12, no. 4, p. 351

277, 3 M. Selvini, *Journal of Marital and Family Therapy*, 1986, vol. 12, no. 4, p. 356

277, 18 V. Ugazio, *Storie permesse*, op. cit., p. 111

279, 32 Ibid., p. 175

280, 6 Ibid., p. 145

281, 22 Ibid., p. 206

282, 34   W. Blake, 'London', *Songs of Innocence and Experience*
283, 5   V. Ugazio, *Storie permesse*, op. cit., p. 287

Christina Stead: Our Luck

285, 22   C. Stead, *Letty Fox: Her Luck* (London, Virago, 1978), p. 42
286, 28   Hazel Rowley, *Christina Stead, a biography* (Melbourne, Minerva, 1993), p. 15
286, 31   C. Stead, *Letty Fox*, op. cit., p. 330
287, 14   H. Rowley, *Christina Stead*, op. cit., p. 20
288, 28   Ibid., p. 52
288, 30   C. Stead, *Letty Fox*, op. cit., p. 278
288, 32   H. Rowley, *Christina Stead*, op. cit., p. 58
289, 30   Ibid., p. 55
290, 12   Ibid., p. 102
290, 34   Ibid., p. 95
293, 33   Ibid., p. 473
293, 34   Ibid., p. 488
294, 5   C. Stead, *Letty Fox*, op. cit., p. 386
294, 16   Ibid., p. 410
294, 26   Ibid., p. 3
295, 6   Loc. cit.
295, 20   Ibid., p. 7
296, 5   Ibid., p. 5
296, 8   Ibid., p. 404
296, 13   H. Rowley, *Christina Stead*, op. cit., p. 26
297, 24   Ibid., p. 316
299, 4   C. Stead, *Letty Fox*, op. cit., p. 330
299, 10   Ibid., p. 260
299, 13   Ibid., p. 409
299, 20   Ibid., p. 343
299, 31   Ibid., back jacket
300, 13   Ibid., p. 402
300, 24   Ibid., p. 483
301, 23   Ibid., p. 455

301, 34 Ibid., p. 502

302, 34 H. Rowley, *Christina Stead*, op. cit., p. 42

303, 8   Ibid., p. 476

303, 22 H. Rowley, *Christina Stead*, op. cit., p. 316

304, 3   C. Stead, *Letty Fox*, op. cit., p. 467

Writerly Rancour

305, 4   E. Cioran 'Odyssey of Rancour', *History and Utopia* (London, Quartet Books, 1996), p. 67

305, 6   J.J. Rousseau, *The Confessions* (London, Penguin, 1953), p. 432

306, 5   S. Beckett, *Molloy* (London, Jupiter Books [Calder], 1966), p. 73

306, 20 Ibid., p. 75

306, 24 Ibid., p. 79

306, 26 Loc. cit.

307, 16 Loc. cit.

309, 26 R. Walser, 'Un pittore', *I temi di Fritz Kocher*, trans. V. Rubelli Ruberl (Milan, Adelphi), p. 97 (unable to find an English edition and unable to read the original German, I have translated this from the Italian edition)

311, 3   Ibid., p. 128

311, 27 E. Cioran, 'Désir et horreur de la gloire', *La chute dans le temps* (Paris, Gallimard, 1964), p. 112

312, 23 G. Leopardi, quoted in R. Damiani, *All'apparir del vero* (Milan, Mondadori, 1998), p. 200

313, 3   Ibid., p. 213

313, 7   Ibid., p. 147

313, 13 S. Beckett, *Worstward Ho* (London, Calder, 1983), p. 10

314, 13 E. Montale, *Ossi di seppia* (Milan, Mondadori, 1991), p. 39

314, 19 A. Schopenhauer, *Essays and Aphorisms*, trans. R.J. Hollingdale (London, Penguin, 1970), p. 127

314, 29 S. Beckett, *Molloy*, op. cit., pp. 31–2

316, 8   G. Leopardi, *Zibaldone*, Mondadori, 17 Dec 1823

316, 33   S. Beckett, *Watt*, trans. Cesare Cristofolini (Milan, Sugarco, 1994), p. 49

317, 18   S. Beckett, *Watt* (London, Jupiter Books [Calder], 1963), p. 44

318, 16   Homer, *The Odyssey*, trans. E.V. Rieu (London, Penguin, 1946), p. 70 (Book 4, 11. 212–84)

319, 2   W. Shakespeare, *The Tempest*, Act V, sc. i, 11. 183–4

319, 3   Ibid. Act I, sc. ii, 11. 476–7

319, 6   Ibid. Act I, sc. ii, 11. 294–6

319, 28   Ibid., Epilogue, 11. 5–10

320, 11   S. Beckett, *Malone Dies* (London, Calder & Boyars, 1975), p. 8